KW-377-326

90 0936357 6

Silence and Confessions

Silence and Confessions

The Suspect as the Source of Evidence

Susan Easton
Reader in Law, Brunel Law School, UK

© Susan Easton 2014

All rights reserved. No reproduction, copy or transmission of this publication may be made without written permission.

No portion of this publication may be reproduced, copied or transmitted save with written permission or in accordance with the provisions of the Copyright, Designs and Patents Act 1988, or under the terms of any licence permitting limited copying issued by the Copyright Licensing Agency, Saffron House, 6–10 Kirby Street, London EC1N 8TS.

Any person who does any unauthorized act in relation to this publication may be liable to criminal prosecution and civil claims for damages.

The author has asserted her right to be identified as the author of this work in accordance with the Copyright, Designs and Patents Act 1988.

First published 2014 by
PALGRAVE MACMILLAN

Palgrave Macmillan in the UK is an imprint of Macmillan Publishers Limited, registered in England, company number 785998, of Houndmills, Basingstoke, Hampshire RG21 6XS.

Palgrave Macmillan in the US is a division of St Martin's Press LLC, 175 Fifth Avenue, New York, NY 10010.

Palgrave Macmillan is the global academic imprint of the above companies and has companies and representatives throughout the world.

Palgrave® and Macmillan® are registered trademarks in the United States, the United Kingdom, Europe and other countries

ISBN: 978–1–137–33381–0

This book is printed on paper suitable for recycling and made from fully managed and sustained forest sources. Logging, pulping and manufacturing processes are expected to conform to the environmental regulations of the country of origin.

A catalogue record for this book is available from the British Library.

A catalog record for this book is available from the Library of Congress.

PLYMOUTH UNIVERSITY
9009363576

For Blake, Holly, Teddy and Brio

WITHDRAWN
FROM
UNIVERSITY OF PLYMOUTH
LIBRARY

Contents

Acknowledgements

I would like to thank Julia Willan and Harriet Barker at Palgrave Macmillan for their editorial assistance. I am also very grateful to the production staff for their assistance. I have also benefited from discussions of the ideas in this book with staff and students at Brunel Law School.

Table of Statutes

Table of Cases

1
Introduction

Over the past two decades the relationship between the suspect and the state has been subject to considerable change. The impact of European Convention jurisprudence both before and after the Human Rights Act has highlighted the importance of due process rights for suspects and has strengthened protection at all stages of the criminal justice process from arrest to trial, sentencing and imprisonment. There has also been greater awareness of the problems facing vulnerable suspects and witnesses. At the same time there have been measures that have weakened protection for suspects. These include limits on the right to silence, the persistence of emergency legislation and the strengthening of the state's powers in the context of the war on terror and continuing cuts to legal aid and other services. There have also been advances in the collection of forensic evidence but this has raised a new problem of retention of biometric data. These issues have divided commentators on the criminal justice system, as well as politicians and the public.

New systems of disclosure and new sources of forensic evidence have also affected the relationship between the suspect and the state. The interrogation of suspects raises key principles regarding the treatment of the suspect, including the presumption of innocence and the right to a fair trial, as well as questions relating to privacy and non-degrading treatment. To understand the processes of interrogation and confession it is essential to consider the social context of interrogation, as well as the political context, as the issues of law and order and security have dominated the political landscape and successive governments have stressed their commitment to fighting the threat to the social order from antisocial behaviour and incivility and from terrorism and violent crime.

This book will examine the treatment of suspects in interrogation and at trial and consider the problems of reconciling the individual's right to be presumed innocent and the right to a fair trial with the need to convict the guilty to protect the public and for the efficient organisation of the criminal justice system. It employs a socio-legal approach, making use of empirical research drawn from the social sciences, including social psychology, to understand the challenges in maintaining the integrity of the interrogation process. This research has been valuable in letting in the light to illuminate the process of interrogation and the experiences of the suspect during interview. The problems with confession evidence will be discussed to highlight the dangers facing vulnerable suspects and the problems of identifying and preventing false confessions. The book explores the relationship between the state and the suspect and the equality of arms principle and the problem of reconciling competing interests and principles in the criminal justice process.

Chapter 2 considers the origins of the privilege against self-incrimination in English law and its historical development since the demise of the Star Chamber in the seventeenth century. Key landmarks in its evolution will be discussed, including the 1898 Criminal Evidence Act, the changes in Northern Ireland and the Reports of the Royal Commissions in 1981 and 1993. The progress of the law governing the right to silence is considered up to 1994, when radical changes were introduced. The reasons why the accused's right to silence aroused such intense criticism will be discussed and the views of a range of critics, including Bentham and the Criminal Law Revision Committee, are examined. Relevant empirical investigations are also considered, as a recurring theme in the debates has been the 'abuse' of the right by professional criminals seeking to evade conviction. Why were there demands for changes in the law and were these demands justified? Have changes in the system of advance disclosure addressed these problems? Reference will also be made to the statutory duty to answer questions under road traffic and financial services law and to the construction of silence in response to accusations at common law.

Chapter 3 will discuss in detail ss 34–38 of the 1994 Criminal Justice and Public Order Act, which permitted adverse inferences from the accused's silence in specified circumstances. The discussion includes the question of reliance on legal advice and the submission of a prepared statement in the context of no-comment interviews. Since 1994 there has been an extensive body of case law on the issues raised by these provisions, particularly on s 34, which has highlighted these problems. The impact of the change on the numbers of defendants speaking or remaining silent will also be examined.

The influence of international human rights law on the treatment of suspects, including the right not to be subjected to torture, inhuman or degrading treatment, and the privilege against self-incrimination is reviewed in Chapter 4. These rights are enshrined in international human rights law and have been deployed in the context of international criminal trials. However, the principal focus will be on European Convention jurisprudence which has become even more important since the enactment of the Human Rights Act 1998. Key cases, including *Murray v UK* App. No. 18731/91 (8 February 1996), *Funke v France* App. No. 10828/84 (25 February 1993), *Salabiaku v France* (1998) 13 EHRR 379 and *O'Halloran and Francis v UK* App. Nos. 15809/02 and 26524/02 (29 June 2007), will be considered, as well as tensions between Strasbourg and the domestic courts. Conditions in detention, extended detention and the privilege against self-incrimination will be discussed. Although the privilege has been seen as an essential element of the right to a fair trial, that right has not been treated by the Court as absolute and the situations in which the Court has been willing to accept limitations will be examined. The chapter will also refer to the broader issue of the internationalisation of criminal evidence and consider whether the impact of Convention jurisprudence and increased pressures to speak have moved the United Kingdom's criminal justice system closer to an inquisitorial system.

The legal framework governing interrogation in the Police and Criminal Evidence Act and its accompanying Codes is considered in Chapter 5. Reference is made to the improvements in the recording of interviews and access to legal advice and the weight attached to voluntary confessions. The exercise of exclusionary discretion in dealing with breaches of the Codes is also discussed. Despite the substantial improvements in the protections afforded by PACE, we will see that problems still remain in terms of access to legal advice. We will examine the particular problems faced by defendants who may be vulnerable because of learning disabilities, psychological problems and immaturity. The protection of the suspect in interrogation in the United States and Canada and recent developments in those jurisdictions will also be discussed.

Chapter 6 highlights the problem of false confessions in light of the available empirical research on this issue. False confessions have been a significant element of many miscarriages of justice. The reasons why suspects waive their right to silence and right to counsel will be explored. Reference will be made to the problem of tunnel vision and to the models of interrogation used in the United Kingdom, the United

States and Canada, including the Inbau–Reid technique and the alternative PEACE interviewing model. The impact of these techniques on the production of true and false confessions will be examined, as well as new techniques for testing the reliability of statements made under interrogation.

The relationship between the police and particular communities is considered in Chapter 7, to see whether there are particular issues in those communities which may affect their willingness to cooperate with the police and whether certain communities have been treated as suspect communities. Specific problems relating to sectarian groups in Northern Ireland will be discussed, as well as the detention and questioning of suspects and the use of emergency powers during the conflict. Contemporary counter-terrorism measures will also be examined, including restrictions on the movement of suspects, the use of stop and search powers under counter-terrorism law and the disparate impact of these measures on particular groups. The chapter will conclude with a discussion of the policing of black and minority ethnic communities.

Chapter 8 examines the implications of scientific and technological advances, including DNA profiling, as tools for both prosecution and defence, but which have arguably rendered the suspect's own testimony less significant. Has the construction of the DNA database and the routine use of bodily samples in criminal investigations changed the relationship between the suspect and the state? Should the refusal to comply with requests for samples be included within the privilege against self-incrimination? This has been a contentious issue, raised in Canada and the United States as well as the United Kingdom, but, as we shall see, with differing responses. The retention of DNA samples and profiles will also be discussed with reference to Article 8 of the European Convention on Human Rights.

In conclusion, Chapter 9 considers possible reforms in the light of the problems highlighted in the preceding discussion. While recognising the substantial improvements that have been made in the treatment of suspects in interrogation and at trial, it notes the persistence of miscarriages of justice and continuing problems with the production of false confessions, and argues for a corroboration requirement for confessions.

2
The Debate on the Right to Silence

Introduction

While the modern law of evidence has focused on the suspect as the key source of evidence, in fact this is a relatively recent development. Until the early 1990s the privilege against self-incrimination was firmly enshrined in the law of evidence. The privilege is used in a broad sense to cover immunity from being compelled to answer questions put by the police or other bodies, or in court, that may incriminate the speaker. It has also in the past included protection from adverse comment by judges on the failure to give evidence at trial or to answer questions in interrogation.

The privilege developed over centuries in response to the violence of forced interrogation and torture used throughout Europe in the sixteenth century as part of the Inquisition and in England in the seventeenth century in the court of James I and Charles I, in the Star Chamber and in the ecclesiastical court of the High Commission. In this period the church and the state united to stifle opposition, to detect both political and religious heresy and to censor political works. Their methods included torture, detention for long periods and arbitrary, degrading and humiliating treatment and punishments such as the pillory and mutilation. Interrogation was frequently used as a fishing expedition to elicit incriminating statements from suspects confronted with an often spurious charge on flimsy or no evidence. Both these courts were abolished in 1641 and in their place the common law courts established their supremacy. The privilege was extended to the common law courts and to courts using proper procedures. The privilege reflects the general abhorrence of the practices of the Stuart period which culminated in the English revolution. So the privilege developed in the late-sixteenth and seventeenth centuries in response to the use of oppressive and improper procedures. The privilege embodied the view that no citizen should be forced to incriminate himself on oath in the witness box.

The long shadow cast by the Star Chamber shaped the subsequent development of English law in the eighteenth and nineteenth centuries, including the development of the exclusionary rules of evidence denying witnesses competence on the grounds of interest.

From the abolition of the Star Chamber, in 1641, to 1898, the defendant himself was deemed incompetent to testify on oath in his own defence in criminal proceedings. However, in the nineteenth century he was allowed to make an unsworn statement from the dock. Yet, as we shall see, pressures on the defendant to speak during interrogation and at trial have survived the demise of these iniquitous tribunals. The vigorous questioning of the accused did not decline until the early eighteenth century. The privilege was not referred to in the petitions and parliamentary declarations precipitating the expulsion of the Stuarts. Wigmore (1961) has argued that the privilege slowly 'crept' into the English system, but in the United States it was a major constitutional landmark in the late 1780s, in the Constitution and the Bill of Rights. This may be why the privilege has been more strongly protected than in the UK. The privilege has been vigorously defended in the United States and was seen as essential to political freedom, as illustrated by the McCarthy hearings of the 1950s. Its importance was reasserted by the Warren Court in the 1960s, principally in *Miranda v Arizona* 384 US 436 (1966). *Miranda* has been under attack in recent cases, for instance in *Salinas v Texas* 570 U.S. (2013), where the majority of the court held that the accused's Fifth Amendment right against compelled self-incrimination was not violated when the prosecutor at his trial commented on his failure to respond to a police officer's question during a voluntary noncustodial interview prior to his arrest, and said that an innocent man would have spoken. Notwithstanding subsequent inroads into the protections of *Miranda*, which will be discussed in Chapter 5, *Miranda* still provides the key safeguard for the treatment of the suspect in custody.

In the United States the Fifth Amendment to the Constitution gives the defendant in a criminal trial the right not to incriminate himself and the right not to be forced to give evidence at trial: 'no person … shall be compelled in any criminal case to be a witness against himself.' There the privilege has been widely used in both civil and criminal trials, and in the context of grand juries, legislative committees and administrative tribunals. The Fifth Amendment applies outside criminal court proceedings to any context in which a person's freedom of action is compelled in any significant way to incriminate themselves. The privilege affirms a boundary beyond which the state's scrutiny of the individual's thoughts and beliefs is prohibited.

It reflects the view that it is inherently wrong and unfair to expect a man to accuse himself. It also reflects the concern to obtain reliable testimony and the risk of perjury if the accused is under pressure to speak (see Amar and Lettow, 1995; Stuntz, 1988; Seidmann and Stein 2000). Because of the constitutional foundation, the United States has to some extent resisted encroachments more vigorously than the UK. The privilege against self-incrimination expresses the aversion to coercive interrogation, of forcing a person to speak against his own interest and has a key role to play in protecting the individual from overzealous interrogators. It also protects the dignity of the suspect and his right to privacy.

As the Supreme Court said in *Murphy v Waterfront Commission of New York Harbor* 378 US 552 (1964), the privilege

> reflects many of our fundamental values and most noble aspirations: our unwillingness to subject those suspected of crime to the cruel trilemma of self-accusation, perjury or contempt … our fear that self-incriminating statements will be elicited by inhumane treatment and abuses; our sense of fair play which dictates 'a fair state–individual balance by requiring the government … in its contest with the individual to shoulder the entire load' … our distrust of self-deprecatory statements; and our realization that the privilege, while sometimes 'a shelter to the guilty', is often 'a protection to the innocent'.
>
> (at 55)

However, judicial concern with the strong protection of the rights of the accused has fluctuated, reflecting in part the composition of the Supreme Court and the political context of the fight against crime and the increasing punitiveness of politicians and the public.

The privilege is found in both federal and state constitutions but the wording of the privilege gives few insights into its meaning. A substantial jurisprudence has developed on its meaning, scope and application as well as its rationale, whether it is privacy, in protecting an area of individual sovereignty where the state cannot intrude, or autonomy, and the right to dignity. These may be balanced against the state's interest in law enforcement and public protection. The Supreme Court's jurisprudence has focused on the degree of compulsion which has also been a key issue for the Strasbourg Court.

The privilege against self-incrimination, in both the United States and the UK includes both the right of the accused not to testify at his trial but also to the rights of third-party witnesses not to disclose self-incriminating knowledge. Modern debates on the compellability of the accused as witness have focused on the right to silence, which can be viewed as both a right and a privilege. Efforts have also been made here and in the United States and Canada, as we shall see in Chapter 8, to extend the privilege to the refusal to supply bodily samples, with mixed results.

In *Miranda v Arizona* 384 US 436 the Supreme Court said that affirming the privilege (against self-incrimination) is the respect a government – state or federal – must accord to the dignity and integrity of its citizens. Although, as we shall see, the accused's right to silence in interrogation has been weakened by inroads into *Miranda*, at trial the right to silence remains and no adverse comment can be made on the accused's decision not to testify. In *Griffin v California* 380 US 606 (1965) it was noted by the court that while it was difficult to prevent a jury speculating on the accused's failure to testify, the judge should direct the jury that the accused was entitled not to testify and this should not be held against him to reduce that speculation to a minimum. The court ruled that such comment by judge and prosecution was prohibited and state law that authorised such comments was unconstitutional. In that case the prosecution had commented on the failure to testify and the trial judge had directed the jury that it could interpret the defendant's failure to account for incriminating evidence as affirming the truth of that evidence. But the Supreme Court said that allowing adverse inferences from the failure to testify would amount to punishing the defendant's silence and would violate the self-incrimination clause. The accused should not have to choose between giving evidence or having his silence used against him. In a later case, *US v Robinson* 485 US 25 (1988), comment by the prosecution was permitted, but only in the context of a claim that the defendant had not been given the chance to answer the case against him.

The development of the privilege against self-incrimination also reflects a 'futility' argument. It is impossible to guarantee the suspect will speak the truth and, as we shall see, interrogators' confidence in their lie-detection skills may be misplaced. The danger of perjury in forced testimony has been emphasised in Fifth Amendment jurisprudence. Confronted with the difficult trilemma of choosing self-incrimination, contempt or perjury, the suspect may prefer to lie. This is why the right to silence has been seen by some commentators, including Wigmore (1961), as taking us closer to the truth. This was noted by the Royal Commission on Criminal Procedure; even if suspects are persuaded to speak, the information may be false: 'the rack and the thumbscrew...and other less awful, though not necessarily less potent, means of applying pressure to an accused person to speak do not necessarily produce speech or the truth' (RCCP, 1981, para 4.36). The right embodies the law's recognition that it cannot command the impossible, as the Protestant writer and leveller John Lilburne argued in the seventeenth century. He had refused to take the oath and remained silent when arrested for publishing unlicensed Protestant tracts in 1637. He refused to speak on the ground that he did not want to contribute to the case against him and was imprisoned for three years (Lilburne, 1638). Modern debates on the use of torture in the wake of 9/11 have focused on its futility and the problems for the legitimacy of states as well as the principled objections to torture as an absolute wrong (Sussman, 2005; Waldron, 2010), although others have raised the question of whether it should be used in the most extreme situations to prevent loss of life (Dershowitz, 2002, 2004).

In the UK the right not to be subjected to comment on the failure to speak has now been lost. The major landmarks in the development of the privilege since the seventeenth century were the Criminal Evidence Act 1898, the Criminal Justice and Public Order Act 1994 (CJPOA) 1994, the Human Rights Act 1998 (HRA) and the Criminal Procedure and Investigations Act 1996 (CPIA). The compulsion to answer questions is also found in financial services legislation, road traffic law and counter-terrorism provisions. The privilege should also be considered in the context of changes in the practice of policing and the provision of legal advice.

Silence in court

The 1898 Act made the accused a competent but not compellable witness in his own defence. Prior to this Act the defendant was not permitted to testify on oath at his own trial. However, judges allowed the accused to make an unsworn statement from the dock, but this carried relatively little weight as it was not on oath. Under the 1898 Act the accused was a competent witness for the defence but not the Crown. This remains the case in current law despite the changes to the right to silence in the 1994 Criminal Justice and Public Order Act. So the accused remains a privileged witness and cannot be compelled to give evidence or be held in contempt if he or she refuses, in contrast to the majority of witnesses.

Section 1 of the 1898 Act stated that:

> Every person charged with an offence shall be a competent witness for the defence at every stage of the proceedings, whether the person so charged is charged solely or jointly with any other person. Provided as follows:
>
> (a) A person so charged shall not be called as a witness in pursuance of the Act except upon his own application;
> (b) The failure of any person charged with an offence to give evidence shall not be made the subject of any comment by the prosecution.
> (c) Nothing in this Act shall affect the right of the person charged to make a statement without being sworn.

So the defendant could choose to speak, remain silent or give an unsworn statement from the dock. Section 1(b) was subsequently repealed by the Criminal Justice and Public Order Act which means that such comment is now permitted (Schedule X). Section 1(c) was abolished by s 72(1) of the Criminal Justice Act 1982.

The accused could wait until the prosecution had closed its case before deciding whether or not to testify. The jury obviously would be aware of the accused's silence in court and may well have taken account of that silence. The accused could still be convicted if silent. The proviso in s 1(b) was intended to prevent the Crown from exploiting the accused's silence although silence could be taken account of by the jury (see *R v Jackson* [1995] 1 WLR 591). Under the 1898 Act the prosecution could not comment on silence in court, but counsel for the co-accused could do so, as the court made clear in *R v Wickham, Ferrara and Bean* (1971) 55 Cr App Rep 199. The judge could comment, but only within clearly defined limits. These limits were not stipulated in the 1898 Act, but clarified in the subsequent jurisprudence. For example, in *R v Waugh* [1950] AC 203 a trial judge repeatedly referred to the defendant's failure to testify which was criticised by the Privy Council for giving the jury the impression that an innocent man would speak. The judge's direction to the jury was based on Lord Parker's direction in *R v Bathurst* [1968] 2 QB 107, where it was stressed that the jury should be informed that the accused is not bound to give evidence, but can sit back and see if the prosecution have proved their case, and while the jury have been deprived of hearing his story tested in cross-examination, they must not assume that he is guilty because he has not gone into the witness box. This was followed in *R v Sparrow* [1973] 1 WLR 488. The judge should make clear that the accused is not obliged to testify and the jury should not assume the defendant is guilty because he had not given evidence, as made clear in *R v Martinez-Tobon* [1994] 2 All ER 90:

> The defendant does not have to give evidence. He is entitled to sit in the dock and require the prosecution to prove its case. You must not assume that he is guilty because he has not given evidence. The fact that he has not given evidence proves nothing one way or another. It does nothing to establish his guilt.
>
> (at 96)

So it was clear that the judges could not imply that silence indicated guilt, but trial judges' comments sometimes did stretch the limits of acceptable comment and appeals often succeeded on these grounds.

Silence during police interrogation

Questioning in detention is governed by PACE and the accompanying Codes of Practice. The Codes have been regularly updated since they were first issued in 1985 to take account of the changes to the right to silence and other developments and were most recently updated in 2012. Before the 1994 Criminal Justice and Public Order Act, the suspect would be cautioned prior to questioning and following any breaks in questioning and would be told that 'You do not have to say anything unless you wish to do so but what you say may be given in evidence' (Code C.10.4). So the caution reminded him of the right to silence. This was used until the revised Codes were implemented in April 1995, following the changes to the right to silence in the 1994 CJPOA. Under the pre-1994 law it was clear that the suspect was not obliged to answer any questions or to offer any information that could incriminate him and that no adverse inferences could be drawn. A failure to warn the accused of his right to silence could be used to ground an appeal.

It is well established in English law that the duty of a citizen to help the police with their inquiries is a moral obligation, but not a legal duty. As Lord Parker stressed in *Rice v Connolly* [1966] 2 QB 414, a citizen has every right to refuse to answer a question or to maintain silence throughout the interview. The suspect before the CJPOA was also free to be selective in answering questions, without entitling the jury to draw adverse inferences. But of course the jury would have been aware of the failure to answer questions in interrogation and may well have drawn adverse conclusions from this failure, despite judicial reminders of the right to silence and warnings against drawing such inferences.

While the judge was not allowed to comment in terms that encouraged the jury to equate silence with guilt, or to draw any adverse inferences or to treat silence as corroborating other evidence against the accused, appeals were often brought and sometimes succeeded on the grounds that judicial comment had exceeded the boundaries of acceptable comment. A statement by a trial judge that an innocent man might be expected to deny the charge was deemed unacceptable by the Court of Appeal in *R v Leckey* [1944] KB 80. The suggestion that 'you might well think that if a man is innocent he would be anxious to answer questions' was also held to be a misdirection by the Court of Appeal in *R v Sullivan* (1966) 51 Cr App R 102, although the court said this might well be what the jury were saying to themselves using their common sense.

It also meant that defences could be put forward at trial for the first time, thereby giving the defence an unfair advantage as the prosecution did not have sufficient time in some cases to combat that defence. In *R v Gilbert* (1977) 66 Cr App Rep 237, where a defence of self-defence was submitted for the first time at trial, the trial judge said the jury should ask itself whether or not it was remarkable that nothing had been said earlier. The Court of Appeal ruled that while it was possible to remind the jury that the defence was put forward for the first time at trial, the judge could not comment adversely on the accused's failure to make a statement earlier and 'to invite a jury to form an adverse opinion against an accused on account of his exercise of his right to silence is a misdirection' (at 244). However, the court noted that the law in some cases seems to conflict with common sense. The tactical use of alibis introduced at trial for the first time had already been limited by s 11 of the Criminal Justice Act 1967, which required the defence to give notice to the prosecution of an alibi within seven days of the end of committal proceedings.

The debate on the right to silence

Concern over the right to silence had been evident for some time before the 1994 changes. Indeed the attack on the right to silence had begun much earlier with Bentham's critique in the nineteenth century of the right to silence as the weapon of the guilty, but found new support in the 1970s and 1980s. In his discussions of criminal evidence Bentham had claimed that the rule then prevailing which prohibited defendants from testifying was one criminals might have devised for themselves. Bentham saw this rule as serving the interest of evil-doers: 'shutting the door against an article of true and unfallacious evidence necessary to conviction, operates as a licence for the commission of a crime' (Bentham, 1843: 338). It was one of a number of artificial rules of evidence that limit the evidence that should be available to the court, and once the prosecutor is denied access to the accused's testimony, argued Bentham, he is forced to search for inferior forms of evidence. It may also mean that the state will resort to more oppressive methods of evidence-gathering, including illegal searches.

Bentham's argument that silence inhibits the search for the truth is part of his general attack on exclusionary rules which obscure the truth, the ultimate goal of the criminal trial. Bentham advocated admitting as much evidence as possible: 'Let in the light of evidence. The end it leads to, is the direct end of justice, rectitude of decision' (Bentham, 1843, 336). He favoured a system of free proof as the best means of pursuing the truth. The only constraints on admissibility should be those internal to the process of proof, namely the principles of relevance and materiality. Relevant evidence should be excluded only when 'the letting in of such light is attended with preponderant collateral inconvenience, in the shape of vexation, expense and delay' and where no harm should result from its exclusion (ibid.). Excluding evidence on external grounds, he argues, is contrary to reason. Discovery of the truth is the prime purpose of the criminal trial and this supersedes other goals, including those we would now see as essential elements of the criminal justice process, including procedural fairness and respect for rights such as privacy.

But his remarks should be seen in the context of his time, when the resources of the state were clearly less developed than today where the prosecution may have access to independent evidence and other resources to assist in crime control that were unavailable in the nineteenth century. There were also far more constraints on the admissibility of evidence when Bentham was writing, including wide-ranging limits on competence. Bentham's model of the 'open trial' in which the jury assesses the evidence is in practice the exception as the majority of cases are dealt with by summary trial. Moreover, in many cases guilty pleas are entered, which may result in part from plea-bargaining prior to trial and sentence discounts, but it means the court's concern is with sentencing rather than truth-finding. Even where the trial is open, the notion of verisimilitude, of a single truth to be determined at trial by a thorough examination, may be problematic as there could be a plurality of truth-claims and the truth may be constructed as the trial progresses (Jackson and Doran, 1995). Bentham's model is closer to an inquisitorial than an adversarial model. In practice juries may also be influenced by emotions and biases or overestimate the probative value of evidence because of the emotional impact of the case, for example, in relation to evidence of bad character. Furthermore, the search for reliable evidence in the modern trial will exist alongside the aim of protecting the dignity of the accused and ensuring fairness to all parties in the trial. This is not to deny the importance of the rationalist goal, to convict the guilty and acquit the innocent, and failure to meet this is precisely what we mean by miscarriages of justice. But in practice other goals, including the protection of the suspect from improper conduct by the police, the importance of procedural fairness and the moral authority of the verdict, also need to be considered.

For Bentham the suspect is the key source of evidence as he is able to furnish the most information regarding his activities. 'The most satisfactory species of evidence,' he argued, is that given by the accused (Bentham, 1843, 451). It was also the safest form of evidence as the accused, he says, would be the very last person to willingly speak falsely to his own prejudice. His evidence is the most trustworthy and should be available to the jury. The assumption is problematic as we now know from research on false confessions that individuals may and do speak falsely to their own prejudice; this issue will be considered further in Chapter 6. There are relatively few contexts in which the individual's account is the only or the best source of evidence. One example would be cases where the person's beliefs, whether political or religious, are at issue, but here the criminal law has the least justification for intervention. In the past those suspected of crimes such as heresy were subjected to torture and persecution, while in modern contexts individuals have been subjected to show trials and close scrutiny of political beliefs by totalitarian regimes. Beliefs may only be dangerous if translated into practice and used to incite violence or other participation in criminal activities which can be addressed by the criminal law. It was precisely to protect political and religious beliefs from judicial interrogation that the privilege against self-incrimination developed in English law.

The rationalist model presupposes the superiority of the accused's evidence. Yet the quality of this evidence is by no means guaranteed. Confusion, fear or distress because of the pressures of interrogation or cross-examination or the accused's mental or physical state may taint that evidence. It is feared that pressures on the accused to speak may lead to unreliable evidence, although this view is stronger in Fifth Amendment jurisprudence than in Strasbourg. When silence is given evidential significance and becomes part of the armoury of the prosecution, the risk of wrongful conviction to vulnerable defendants increases. For this reason the Royal Commission on Criminal Justice and groups involved in campaigns for those involved in miscarriages of justice were critical of attacks on the right to silence in the 1980s and 1990s. The problem for juries is to reliably distinguish the suspicious from the innocent silence to prevent innocent defendants from being prejudiced. Silence may be a rational response in certain circumstances where the suspect is embarrassed or fearful, rather than an indication of guilt, and of course it may well be chosen on the basis of legal advice, but this may not be obvious to the jury.

Nonetheless, Bentham's observations on the exploitation of the right to silence by offenders were applied to ambush defences by the Criminal Law Revision Committee (CLRC) in its Eleventh Report on Evidence published in 1972. It was very critical of the right to silence, arguing that it was contrary to common sense to deny the jury permission to draw adverse inferences in the case of ambush defences, and that the guilty would wish to withhold an explanation while the innocent would wish to account for their position. The Committee noted that there was a large and increasingly sophisticated class of criminals 'who are aware of their legal rights and use every possible means to avoid conviction if caught' (CLRC 1972: para 21). The Committee thought that changes in the rules of evidence, including removals of restrictions on admissibility, were necessary to strengthen crime control. The limits on judicial and prosecutorial comment on silence were, it claimed, too favourable to the defence and should be removed, and the refusal to testify should be able to corroborate other evidence against the accused. It rejected the view that requiring a man to accuse himself is inherently unfair and could find no principled grounds for opposing change and allowing silence evidential status. Its recommendation that juries be permitted to draw adverse inferences from silence at both pre-trial and trial stages and its Draft Bill were subsequently enacted, with some minor modifications, in the 1994 Act, 22 years later.

The CLRC thought the jury should be able to draw an adverse inference from the initial failure to mention a fact later relied on in court and to treat that silence as corroboration of evidence against the defendant. A failure to testify also should be capable of corroborating evidence against him. However, it proposed that where the accused's mental or physical state made it undesirable for him to give evidence this should not apply. The CLRC took the view that while measures such as the right to silence may have been appropriate in the past, where the accused was in a weaker position, now the balance had swung in favour of the defendant and this resulting imbalance should be redressed in favour of the prosecution. The fact that juries were not able to draw inferences from silence gave an 'unnecessary advantage to the guilty' (ibid.: para 30). An argument often cited in the debate was that precluding adverse inferences from silence conflicted with common sense. This was also reflected in the jurisprudence on the right to silence. The Northern Ireland Court of Appeal had invoked common sense in cases on the Criminal Evidence (Northern Ireland) Order, such as *R v Martin* [1992] 5 NIJB 40 and common sense was also referred to in the House of Lords in *Murray v DPP* [1994] 1 WLR 1. But common sense may not be reliable if the common sense assumption is that silence signifies guilt, when there may be other reasons, such as fear, embarrassment, shielding a third party or a reluctance to be seen talking to the police, and these reasons may not be clear to the jury. Often cited is the situation where, following the death of child in which both parents are implicated, it is unclear which one is guilty and if neither speaks it will be harder to convict either of them, as the police will need their cooperation. However, the Royal Commission on Criminal Justice considered this and thought this situation might be addressed by extending the idea of absolute liability for a child (RCCJ 1993: para 4.25).

The CLRC's proposals met with considerable criticism and were not implemented in England and Wales until 1994. Changes modeled on the CLRC Report were, however, introduced in Singapore in 1976 in the Criminal Procedure Code (Amendment) Act 1976. Yeo (1983) says the changes in Singapore had little impact as the majority of suspects were already speaking in interrogation or at trial, but a later study by Tan (1997) found that the courts were relying more on inferences from silence after similar changes. Provisions reflecting the CLRC proposals were also introduced in the Republic of Ireland in 1984 and in Northern Ireland in 1988.

But the CLRC's views did not find favour with the Royal Commission on Criminal Procedure in 1981 whose recommendations were enacted in PACE (RCCP 1981). The Commission was established because of concerns over miscarriages of justice, including the *Confait* case. It reviewed the criminal process from investigation to trial in the light of concerns over the misuse of police powers. Its Report sought to achieve a balance between the positions of the prosecution and defence and to reconcile the rights of the suspect and the need to protect vulnerable groups during interrogation with the need to convict the guilty. Its starting point was that a balance must be struck between the conflicting interests in crime control and convicting the guilty and the right of the individual to be presumed innocent. As part of its inquiry, it commissioned several research studies, including on police interrogation, and considered the problems that might arise if the right to silence was curtailed as recommended by the CLRC. It took numerous submissions and visited other jurisdictions. It concluded that allowing adverse inferences from silence would be problematic and that the right to silence should be retained at both pre-trial and trial stages. Increasing pressure on the accused to speak would undermine the burden of proof by making the suspect the source of prosecution evidence.

Changes closely following the CLRC's proposals were introduced in the Republic of Ireland by the Criminal Justice Act 1984. It covered failure to account for substances or marks on one's person, clothing or possessions (s 18), or one's presence at a particular place or time (s 19), and created a new offence of failing or refusing without reasonable excuse to give the Gardai information or giving false information in relation to how one came by firearms or ammunition (s 15). Proposed provisions on ambush defences were withdrawn when the 1984 Act was enacted because of strong opposition, but a later amendment introduced a provision whereby an inference may be drawn from the failure to mention a fact relied on in the accused's defence which, in the circumstances existing at the time, called for an explanation (s 19A, inserted by Criminal Justice Act 2007). No inference under 19A can be drawn unless the accused has had an opportunity to consult a solicitor and the interview is electronically recorded, and the person cannot be convicted mainly or solely on an inference, although the inference may amount to corroboration of any evidence in relation to which it is material. A further provision, s 72A, inserted by the 2009 Criminal Justice (Amendment) Act, allows inferences to be drawn from the failure to answer a question material to the investigation of an offence, and concerns participation in any activity of a criminal organisation. While these provisions include the above safeguards, as Daly (2013) notes, there is no duty solicitor scheme in the Republic or the right to have a lawyer present during the interview itself.

A constitutional challenge to the provisions in the 1984 Act was brought in *Rock v Ireland* [1997] 3 IR 484 but the Irish Supreme Court deemed them a proportionate interference with the right to silence. There was already a provision introduced by s 52 of the Offences Against the State Act 1939 that if a person was arrested and detained in custody any member of the Gardai could demand a full account of the person's actions during any specified period and information in relation to the commission of an offence. A refusal to provide information or give false information would mean the person was guilty of an offence under this section and could be imprisoned for up to six months. In *The People (DPP) v Doyle* [1977] IR 336 the domestic court had said that s 52 limits what would otherwise be the right of a person to remain silent in certain circumstances and not to incriminate himself. The Irish Supreme Court upheld the constitutionality of s 52 but the Strasbourg Court in *Heaney and McGuinness v Ireland* App. No. 34720/97 (21 December 2000) ruled that it did breach the right to a fair trial under Article 6 as the degree of compulsion on the suspect destroyed 'the essence of their privilege against self-incrimination and their right to remain silent' (at para 55). The court found that the safeguards referred to by the government could not effectively and sufficiently reduce the degree of compulsion imposed by s 52, to the extent that the essence of the rights at issue would not be impaired, as the choice between providing the information or facing imprisonment remained. The security and public order concerns invoked by the government could not justify a provision with this effect and there had therefore been a violation of the applicants' right to silence and their right not to incriminate themselves guaranteed by Article 6(1). The presumption of innocence guaranteed by Article 6(2) had also been violated.

By the late 1980s the focus in the UK was more on how change might be implemented, rather than on matters of principle, and human rights issues were given less prominence. So many of the criticisms of the right to silence from the 1970s were revived by the advances in PACE. Advocates of change argued that the improved safeguards for the suspect in PACE, including the recording of interviews and access to legal advice, had improved the position of suspects considerably since the 1970s, when the CLRC Report was published, so that the fears of civil libertarians were no longer viable. It was thought that the duty solicitor scheme and enhanced provision of legal aid would offer further protection of the suspect. The benefits of PACE, including a statutory right of access to legal advice and verification of interviews, diminished or removed the need for the right to silence. The then Lord Chief Justice Lord Lane, in *Alladice* (1988) 87 Cr App R 380, argued for the need to change the law on the right to silence, given the new protections afforded by PACE. He said that s 58 of PACE, which gives the suspect the right to access to legal advice, does redress the imbalance between the police and the parties and for this reason comment on silence should be permitted. Defenders, in contrast, argued that PACE rested on the right to silence and without it the protections of PACE would be less effective. Nonetheless, despite the lack of empirical evidence to support the case for abolition or diminution of the right to silence, changes were introduced in Northern Ireland in 1988 which offered a testing ground for change and these provisions were then used as a model for the 1994 CJPOA. Similar provisions have also been recently introduced in New South Wales by the Evidence (Amendment) Act 2013.

The Criminal Evidence (Northern Ireland) Order

In Northern Ireland the debate over the right to silence in the 1980s primarily focused on terrorists rather than the career criminals who had preoccupied critics in the 1970s, although there were also some concerns about racketeering that was used to raise money for paramilitary groups. These fears about terrorism intensified with the increase in violence beginning with the murder of Airey Neave in 1979, followed by a spate of bombing attacks on mainland targets in the 1980s, culminating in the bombing of the Grand Hotel in Brighton during the Conservative Party conference in 1984.

A review of the Prevention of Terrorism Act by Lord Colville (1987) highlighted the increased use of the right to silence by those detained on suspicion of terrorist offences which, it claimed, hampered the RUC in obtaining convictions and recommended changes to allow adverse inferences to be drawn from silence. Special training was given to members of paramilitary groups to withstand interrogation, to construct a 'wall of silence', and to resist the usual psychological pressures to speak that most suspects experience during interrogation. The Secretary of State for Northern Ireland referred in Parliament to the fact that the RUC had claimed over half of those detained for questioning on serious offences, including terrorist offences, in Northern Ireland refused to answer any questions in interrogation.

Questions were raised regarding the evidence for this claim, but even if the figures were reliable, it is fair to say that the horrendous punishments meted out to suspected informers, including 'kneecapping', may well have deterred suspects from speaking (see Chapter 7). But the 'abuse' of the right by sectarian paramilitary groups was highlighted by politicians and the police to justify limits on the right to silence. In the 1988 trial of the 'Winchester Three', accused of conspiring to murder Tom King, the Secretary of State for Northern Ireland, the defendants exercised their right to silence which added fuel to the debate.

The Criminal Evidence (Northern Ireland) Order 1988 was based on the CLRC Report and on ss 18–19 of the Republic of Ireland's Criminal Justice Act 1984. It later became the model for the Criminal Justice and

Public Order Act. The jurisprudence on s 34 of the CJPOA was also influenced by the Convention challenges brought in relation to the Northern Ireland Order and to police practice in the province, notably by the case of *Murray v UK* App. No. 18731/91 (8 February 1996).

The Order allowed the court to draw inferences where an explanation of conduct is offered for the first time at trial that the accused could reasonably have been expected to mention it earlier (Article 3), from the failure to testify at trial (Article 4), from the failure to account for an object, substance or mark (Article 5), and the failure to account for his presence at a particular place (Article 6). The accused could not be convicted solely on an inference drawn from a failure under Articles 3–6 (Article 2(2)). The Order was later amended by the 1994 CJPOA to harmonise the provisions on corroboration, as initially the failure to speak under Articles 3–6 could be seen as amounting to corroboration of any evidence against the accused to which the failure is material. This differed from the CJPOA where silence does not constitute corroboration.

At the time the Order was passed interviews with terrorist suspects were not normally tape-recorded, and under the Emergency Provisions Act access to a solicitor could be deferred for up to 48 hours and extended for an additional 48 hours; a solicitor was not normally permitted to be present at interviews. However, by the mid-1990s, before the decision in *Murray v UK* App. No. 18731/91 (8 February 1996), the Chief Constable of Northern Ireland had permitted lawyers to sit in on interviews and this was formalised in the Terrorism Act 2000 which replaced the EPA and which was accompanied by a Code of Practice, including recording of interviews and the presence of a lawyer during interrogation.

The conditions in which many suspects were held at Castlereagh Holding Centre in Belfast had earlier been criticised by the UN Human Rights Committee and by Amnesty International because of the long periods of detention, the failure to record interviews, the use of solitary confinement and the poor physical conditions, and its closure was recommended (CCCPR/C/79, 1995, Amnesty International 1978). It finally closed in 1999. The Order was enacted swiftly by delegated legislation using an Order in Council which meant that there was no full Parliamentary debate on it, or scrutiny by the relevant Select Committee. The Order was announced in October 1988 and it had become law by 14 November of that year. The use of this procedure and the provisions themselves undermined confidence in the administration of justice in the province. It is also questionable whether the provisions were necessary even in the difficult conditions of the time, as the extensive emergency powers prevailing meant that the balance between state and suspect was already heavily weighted in the state's favour. The police already had additional powers to detain for a considerable period of time in the hope that the suspect would be encouraged to speak. Individuals suspected of terrorist activities could be and were excluded from the mainland by Exclusion Orders. Moreover, large numbers of people were arrested under antiterrorism legislation and were later released without charge. In any case, while intended to combat terrorism, the Order was an indiscriminate and disproportionate measure applied to all suspects, to all criminal proceedings, and was not confined to offences connected with terrorism.

The limits on silence imposed by the Order were soon subject to Convention challenges in the European Court of Human Rights (see Chapter 4). The Order was amended in 1999 to reflect changes after the European Court of Human Rights' decision in *Murray v UK* which also led to changes in England and Wales enacted in the Youth Justice and Criminal Evidence Act 1999. Articles 3, 5 and 6 do not now apply if the accused had not been allowed an opportunity to consult a solicitor before being questioned or charged, or refused to account for objects or marks or presence at a particular place (Criminal Evidence (Northern Ireland) Order 1999 SI 1999/2789). Research on the impact of the Order by JUSTICE and the Committee on the Administration of Justice (JUSTICE 1994) suggested that after the Order was passed clear-up and conviction rates fell between 1988 and 1992 and the number of guilty pleas declined. At first the Diplock judges seemed reluctant to draw adverse inferences, but by the 1990s they were more willing to draw adverse inferences from silence. However, Jackson notes that when changes were made to the right to silence there was 'little evidence to suggest judges were using it to fill a large evidential deficit in the prosecution's case' (Jackson, 2009: 220).

These changes in Northern Ireland received far less public debate than similar proposals for England and Wales. Instead attention was focused on extending the changes in the province to mainland Britain and a working group was established to consider this. Although civil libertarians within Northern Ireland raised concerns over the Order, the province was not included within the remit of the Royal Commission on Criminal Justice which reported in 1993, despite concerns over the treatment of suspects there. However, while many of the miscarriage of justice cases that precipitated the establishment of the Commission involved Irish suspects, including the Guildford Four, the Maguire Seven and the Birmingham Six, they had been convicted in mainland courts.

The Home Office Working Group on the Right to Silence

The Working Group on the Right to Silence was set up in 1988 and reported in 1989 (HOWG, 1989). It considered the changes necessary to combat ambush defences and to encourage early disclosure of defences. The Group noted that the CLRC 'had identified a legitimate problem which time has not lessened' and said that it was wrong 'that offenders – usually the more intelligent and serious offenders – should be able to manipulate the criminal justice system to their own advantage, either to escape conviction entirely or to delay and obstruct the judicial process' (HOWG 1989: para 7). It recommended that adverse inferences should be drawn from silence during questioning subject to certain safeguards. The changes proposed were not as radical as those enacted in Northern Ireland. It wanted statutory guidelines on factors to take into account. Both the prosecution and judge, it argued, should be able to comment on the failure to mention a fact later relied on at trial and the judge should guide the jury on factors set out in the guidelines and a new caution should be given. However, the Report made clear that the primary inference from the failure to answer questions or mention a fact later relied on at trial is that the subsequent defence is untrue and that it may have an adverse effect on the suspect's general credibility, but it should not amount to corroboration or constitute positive evidence of guilt, in contrast to the CLRC Bill and the Northern Ireland provisions. The Group recommended a requirement for advance disclosure where there is a risk of an ambush defence and proposed a pilot study to explore this. It also argued that the prosecution should be able to comment on the failure to testify within the same boundaries as judges and that judges should make more robust use of the existing right to comment.

   These proposals were criticised for adding to the length and complexity of trials and increasing the burdens on the defence. Initially the government deferred implementing these proposals to await the finding of the May inquiry into the Woolwich and Guildford bombings and to allow time for further reflection. But in the end the government decided to set up a Royal Commission on Criminal Justice to consider inter alia the removal of the right to silence. The Commission was established in the wake of revelations of miscarriages of justice including the Birmingham Six who had been released in 1991. But criticism of the right to silence did not abate. The former Metropolitan Police Commissioner Sir Peter Imbert had claimed in an interview with *The Guardian* in 1989 with echoes of Bentham that 'the right to silence might have been designed by criminals for their special benefit and that of their professional advisers. It has done more to obscure the truth and facilitate crime than anything else this century' (Imbert, 1989). Similar sentiments were expressed by his successor, Paul Condon, in 1993.

The attack on the right to silence in the 1990s

The changes introduced in Northern Ireland paved the way for similar changes on the mainland. They were cited approvingly by the then Home Secretary, Michael Howard, as an example of a successful limit on silence. At the 1993 Tory Party Conference he said 'The so-called right to silence is ruthlessly exploited by terrorists. What fools they must think we are. It's time to call a halt to this charade' and committed the government to its abolition. In the House of Commons he argued that the existing system was 'abused by hardened criminals' (Hansard 11.1.94, col 96). He referred to a study by ACPO (1993) which showed the frequent use of the right in interrogation.

By 1994 the right to silence had been subjected to a sustained attack on its 'misuse' from a range of groups, and with the Northern Ireland provisions by now well established, change in England and Wales seemed inevitable. These changes need to be understood in the political and social context of the time. Since the 1990s the debate has shifted further towards rebalancing the criminal justice system in favour of victims, witnesses and the public and improving conviction rates by a variety of means. This goal has co-existed uneasily with the increasing recognition of human rights. Of course even if a right is used by some guilty suspects, this does not invalidate its importance as it should be available to all suspects regardless of their motives, or the outcome of any subsequent trial.

One of the main elements of the attack on the right to silence in the late 1980s and early 1990s was the 'problem' of ambush defences, that is, defences where the suspect remained silent in interrogation but later gave an account which was 'sprung' on the prosecution, effectively ambushing them, as it was then too late to combat that defence. The courts had increasingly expressed their dissatisfaction with the limits on their ability to comment on silence and on the use of silence. These defences were the intended target of s 34 of the 1994 Criminal Justice and Public Order Act. But, as we have noted, the jury was always aware that the explanation had not been given so they could take account of this in considering the weight of the explanation before the 1994 changes.

The use of these defences was reviewed by the Royal Commission on Criminal Justice, chaired by Lord Runciman, which was set up to 'examine the effectiveness of the criminal justice system in England and Wales in securing the conviction of those guilty of criminal offences and the acquittal of those who are innocent, having regard to the efficient use of resources' (RCCJ 1993: i). It was explicitly asked to consider whether the courts might draw proper inferences from the failure of the accused to state his position. The Runciman Commission, however, took a similar approach to the RCCP and endorsed the right to silence based on the findings of the empirical studies undertaken for the Commission. The majority of the Commission recommended that the right to silence should be retained, adverse inferences should not be permitted from silence and the existing caution should be retained. It concluded that 'the possibility of an increase in the convictions of the guilty is outweighed by the risk that the extra pressure on suspects to talk in the police station and the adverse inferences invited if they do not may result in more convictions of the innocent' (RCCJ 1993, para 4.1.2). It also thought that it would undermine the presumption of innocence and the burden of proof if the failure to enter the witness box is deemed to corroborate the prosecution's case.

The Commission thought that vulnerable and less experienced suspects under the threat of adverse inferences were more likely to make false confessions, while professional criminals would either continue to say nothing or simply say that their lawyer had advised them to say nothing. The vulnerability of suspects had been a factor in the miscarriages of justice that led to the appointment of the Commission. At the time of the attack on the right to silence there was little evidence to support the claim that the guilty were abusing their right of silence and thereby being wrongfully acquitted. The Home Office Working Group had offered no evidence on this and it would be difficult to draw firm conclusions as so few suspects exercised their right. The Runciman Commission, however, found that silence was used in a minority of cases. Brown (1994) reviewed the research evidence available before the 1994 Act which indicated that the numbers answering no questions at all was 5 per cent outside the Metropolitan Police Area and between 7 and 9 per cent within it.

Empirical studies on various aspects of the criminal justice process, including the use of ambush defences, were conducted to provide evidence on which the Commission could reach conclusions. The Commission also found no evidence to support the disproportionate use of silence by the guilty or by professional criminals or to support the claim that silence in interrogation increased the chance of acquittal (RCCJ 1993, para 41.19). In fact, most of those who were silent in the police station either pleaded guilty or were found guilty.

The Commission's research also undermined the claim of an ambushing problem. Zander and Henderson's Crown Court study (1993) found that late defences sprung on the prosecution occurred in no more than 10 per cent of the Crown Court trials and that these cases were more likely to end in convictions than acquittal. This study examined 3,191 cases involving over 3,600 suspects. However, they did find that the use of the right to silence was higher in cases tried in the Crown Court. Research conducted by Leng (1993) for the Commission also showed that there were no evidence to support claims of an ambushing problem. Leng (1993) examined whether silence was a significant factor in cases where no further action was taken and in acquittals. He reviewed 1,080 cases from 1986–8 in six police stations. In only 4.5 per cent of the 848 cases in which interviews were conducted did suspects exercise their right to silence, about half of whom were convicted. Those who did exercise their right were more likely to have a solicitor present. He noted that for the cases that failed there was little evidence to suggest that the prospects for conviction would have been improved by attaching evidential significance to silence, or by increasing the pressure to speak. In some cases in which suspects were silent, the reason for silence was to protect others, although, as he notes, in most cases it is not possible to discover the motives for silence. In one half of the cases where suspects were silent, they were convicted, and only 10 per cent of those who were acquitted had declined to speak to the police. In most of the acquittals the reason was because the evidence was weak. In Leng's study only 1 case out of 59 contested cases was a potential ambush. Some late defences might have been based on legal argument which the suspect could not have reasonably been expected to be aware of at interview. Leng also examined 'no further action' cases and found that silence was used in only 4 per cent of such cases and estimates that in only 2 per cent of the NFA cases would compelling the suspect to speak have changed the outcome. In most of the 'silent' cases, however, inducing the suspect to speak would have had little impact. This was consistent with earlier research which suggested a link between waiver of the right, confession and conviction rather than between silence and convictions (Softley, 1980; Baldwin and McConville, 1980).

On the pre-1994 law even when individuals did offer a late defence, the judge was permitted to refer to the fact that the explanation given at trial had not been proffered earlier. So it may well have been that jurors did take account of this in their deliberations. Zander and Henderson (1993) found that juries were aware of the fact of silence in interrogation in 80 per cent of the cases they sampled. Moreover, the boundaries of judicial comment prior to 1994 allowed strong comment on the failure to testify and defendants ran the risk of negative conclusions by the jury even before the changes.

A study by Williamson and Moston (1990) also found that silent suspects in the sample were more likely to plead guilty than those who spoke. It also found that silence during interrogation did not affect whether a suspect was charged in cases where evidence was strong or weak, but silence made a charge more likely in cases where evidence was borderline. In Zander and Henderson's 1993 Crown Court study the acquittal rate in contested cases was lower for those who exercised their right to silence than for those who answered questions. This evidence led the Royal Commission to conclude that the right to silence should be retained. Professional criminals would still remain silent if they wished, even if adverse inferences were permitted, and would be better prepared to deal with this, but experienced and vulnerable suspects would be at greater risk. On balance the chance of wrongful convictions of the innocent would be increased by weakening the right to silence.

However, despite the lack of support for an ambushing problem evidenced by its research studies, the Commission acknowledged the frustrations felt by the police at no-comment interviews and their concerns over ambushing. It therefore proposed a new statutory framework of advance disclosure, covering defence and prosecution, which would speed up case preparation and resolution. Other suggestions made by the Commission included a new review body to deal with miscarriages of justice, the Criminal Cases Review Commission, which was established under the Criminal Appeal Act 1995 (see Chapter 6). The Commission also suggested better training of police officers in interrogation techniques, research on visual recording of interviews and pre-trial review of cases, recommendations which were implemented.

Advance disclosure

A new advance disclosure scheme was introduced by Part 1 of the Criminal Procedure and Investigations Act 1996 (CPIA); these changes were seen as part of the process of rebalancing the justice system and were intended to address the Commission's concerns. The CPIA and the Code of Practice issued under the Act govern the extent of the inquiries that need to be made, the material that should be discarded or retained and material that is considered relevant and which should be disclosed. The new scheme imposed duties on both prosecution and defence to disclose material with few exceptions. While the system of advance disclosure was intended to deal with purported problems arising from the right to silence, namely ambush defences, nonetheless the right was still restricted by the Criminal Justice and Public Order Act. Under the new scheme set up by the 1996 CPIA, defendants run the risk of adverse comment at trial if they then run a new defence or depart from a defence previously disclosed, or fail to give details of an alibi (s 11). In such cases the court or jury is entitled to draw such inferences as appear proper in deciding whether the defendant is guilty of the offence charged. It has been argued that advance disclosure does not undermine the privilege against self-incrimination as the defendant can still remain silent at trial. In *R v Essa* [2009] EWCA Crim 43, the Court of Appeal ruled that drawing inferences from the failure to disclose under s 11 is compatible with the Convention. A Code of Practice was issued under s 23 of the Act. There was already a provision requiring advance disclosure of alibi evidence in the 1967 Criminal Justice Act which was replaced by s 74 of the CPIA.

Section 23 of the CJIA requires the investigating police officer to reveal to the prosecutor all relevant material obtained in the course of an investigation. The CPS was obliged to pass a copy of the schedule to the defence and list any material that might undermine the prosecution's case. The defence was then under a duty to respond with a statement outlining its case and the investigator to look again at the unused material and advise the prosecutor of any material that might support the defence. The disclosure scheme was amended and streamlined by the Criminal Justice Act 2003 which imposes a continuing duty on the prosecution to disclose any unused material that might be relevant to the investigation that has been retained but does not form part of the case for the prosecution against the accused, but which will assist the defence case, or could be seen as capable of undermining the prosecution's case. So copies of or access to that material should be given to the defence. This disclosure test is objective, not subjective. A failure to disclose unused material to the defence that would exonerate them had featured in some miscarriages of justice. The CJA amendments also required the defence to give a more detailed statement and simplified the procedure for enabling the jury to draw an adverse inference from the defence's disclosure failure.

However, concerns have been raised by Leng (1995), Redmayne (2004) and Quirk (2006) that the scheme does not work satisfactorily because of lack of training of the police and lack of time of the CPS. Quirk (2006) has criticised the Act for wrongly treating the prosecution and defence as equal parties and for failing to take account of the quite different perspectives of the parties in an adversarial system. The increased burdens on practitioners, she argues, means that in practice tasks may be delegated to non-lawyers. It also fails to take account of the occupational culture of the police and tensions between the police and prosecution. While the CJA regime is an improvement on the CPIA, the disclosure regime relies on accurate scheduling and classification of material by inexperienced staff. Her research indicated that important material was being left out of the schedules and lack of appropriate training for police or prosecutors for the task. The impact of this change on the conviction rate is also doubtful, given that there was not convincing evidence to support an ambushing problem before the Act.

The statutory duty to answer questions

It should also be noted that despite the stronger right to silence prevailing before 1994, citizens have been for many years under a statutory duty to answer questions under threat of penalty imposed by a range of statutes. For example, under the Road Traffic Act 1988, there is a duty to give information regarding the identity of the driver in certain circumstances. This applies to offences under the Act as well as to offences under any other statutes relating to the use of vehicles on the road or manslaughter committed by the driver of a car. Section 172 (2) states that:

(2) Where the driver of a vehicle is alleged to be guilty of an offence to which this section applies –

(a) the person keeping the vehicle shall give such information as to the identity of the driver as he may be required to give by or on behalf of a chief officer of police, and

(b) any other person shall if required as stated above give any information which it is in his power to give and may lead to identification of the driver.

(3) Subject to the following provisions, a person who fails to comply with a requirement under subsection (2) above shall be guilty of an offence.

(4) A person shall not be guilty of an offence by virtue of paragraph (a) of subsection (2) above if he shows that he did not know and

could not with reasonable diligence have ascertained who the driver of the vehicle was.

As we shall see in Chapter 4, attempts to invoke the privilege against self-incrimination in withholding this information demanded under these provisions have failed in both the domestic courts and in Strasbourg, in *O'Halloran and Francis v UK* App. Nos. 15809/02 and 26524/02 (29 June 2007).

There has also been a statutory obligation for some time to answer questions posed by investigatory bodies, including Revenue and Customs, DTI inspections under the Companies Act 1985, and the Serious Fraud Office under the 1987 Criminal Justice Act, and the Financial Services Authority (formerly the Securities and Investment Board) under the Financial Services Act 1986. For example, responses in relation to DTI inquiries may be used in relation to proceedings regarding insider trading. Moreover, information may be pooled by investigatory bodies. Serious frauds may be investigated by both the SFO and DTI. A suspect can be summoned to the SFO and compelled to answer questions if he is suspected of having information relevant to an investigation and can be imprisoned for contempt if he refuses to cooperate with an inquiry. So these powers are more punitive than those under s 34 of the CJPOA.

In *R v Director of SFO ex parte Smith* [1993] AC 1, the House of Lords upheld the right of the SFO to compel suspects to answer questions and said that the statements could be obtained even where criminal proceedings had already begun. Their lordships said that it would be illogical to allow the SFO to ask questions without any ability to compel answers and this applied whether or not the suspect had been charged. It also noted that a person questioned under s 2 receives advance notice and is advised to have a lawyer present. A notice served by the SFO under s 2 CJA 1987 requires those being investigated to answer questions or produce documents. The powers of investigators in serious fraud cases under s 2 were approved by the RCCJ who also recommended more detailed advance disclosure by the defence in serious fraud cases. So for those suspected of economic crime, inroads had been made into the right to silence before the CJPOA; these had received little critical attention even at the height of the debate on the right to silence, as Raphael notes (1990), perhaps reflecting a lack of public concern over the fate of white-collar 'City' criminals.

The question of whether the use of information obtained in these inquiries could be used in subsequent criminal proceedings was considered in the *Saunders* case which highlighted the differences between the domestic courts and the Strasbourg Courts. In *R v Saunders, R v Parnes, R v Lyons* [1986] Crim LR 420 the defendants were convicted of theft, false accounting and offences under the Companies Act 1985, in relation to the takeover by Guinness of Distillers PLC. This case raised the issue of whether evidence obtained in interviews with DTI Inspectors under powers given by the Companies Act to compel the suspect to answer under threat of a fine or imprisonment for contempt could be used in subsequent criminal proceedings. The Court of Appeal decided that the inspectors were allowed to continue their inquiries into a company's affairs under the provisions of the Companies Act where it is clear that criminal offences have been committed, provided that their interviews are conducted independently of the prosecuting authorities and in a fair and objective way. The Companies Act allows the Secretary of State to disclose any information obtained under the procedures to the DPP with a view to bringing criminal proceedings.

However, the Strasbourg Court in *Saunders v UK* App. No. 19187/91 (17 December 1996) ruled that the right to a fair trial under Article 6(1) had been breached because statements made under compulsion had later been admitted in evidence against him at trial. The court stressed that the privilege against self-incrimination and the right to silence should apply equally to those accused of company fraud as others. Following this case the law was amended by s 59 of the Youth Justice and Criminal Evidence Act 1999 which 'amends enactments providing for the use of answers and statements given under compulsion so as to restrict in criminal proceedings their use in evidence against the persons giving them'. Schedule 3 amends the relevant statutes, including the Companies Act 1985, the Insolvency Act 1966, the Criminal Justice Act 1987 and the Financial Services Act 1986, to limit the use made of evidence obtained under those statutes. For example, in relation to the 1985 Companies Act s 434 (production of documents and evidence to inspectors conducting investigations into companies), after subsection (5) (use of answers given to inspectors) is inserted:

(5A) However, in criminal proceedings in which that person is charged with an offence to which this subsection applies –

(a) no evidence relating to the answer may be adduced, and

(b) no question relating to it may be asked, by or on behalf of the prosecution, unless evidence relating to it is adduced, or a question relating to it is asked, in the proceedings by or on behalf of that person.

The domestic courts and the Strasbourg Court have, however, distinguished between criminal proceedings and inquiries by an administrative body in considering whether the obligation to answer breaches the privilege, but the distinction may not always be clear cut. The Strasbourg Court has also distinguished compelled statements and the production of pre-existing documents and the production of bodily samples.

Other statutes imposed a duty of advance disclosure in criminal cases, for example advance notice must be given of the intention to adduce evidence in support of an alibi. This was originally in s 11 of the CJA 1967 and is now in the Criminal Procedure and Investigations Act 1996. Sections 9 and 10 of the 1967 Criminal Justice Act also allowed the judge to order the prosecution to supply a statement of its case and the defence to give to the court and prosecution a written statement setting out the general nature of the defence and the matters on which it takes issue. The judge or prosecution, with the leave of the judge, could then make 'appropriate comments on a departure from the defence or failure to disclose and the jury could draw such inferences as appear proper. These provisions were used as a basis for advance disclosure in the CPIA 1996 but show that there were pressures to disclose on the defence before the limits on the right to silence were imposed. Section 81 of PACE 1984 also requires advance disclosure of expert evidence in the Crown Court:

> s 81 Advance notice of expert evidence in Crown Court.
>
> (1) Criminal Procedure Rules may make provision for—
>
> (a)requiring any party to proceedings before the court to disclose to the other party or parties any expert evidence which he proposes to adduce in the proceedings; and
>
> (b) prohibiting a party who fails to comply in respect of any evidence with any requirement imposed by virtue of paragraph (a) above from adducing that evidence without the leave of the court.
>
> (2) Criminal Procedure Rules made by virtue of this section may specify the kinds of expert evidence to which they apply and may exempt facts or matters of any description specified in the rules.

The principles and procedures are now found in Part 33 of the Criminal Procedure Rules (2013).

There are also provisions under counter-terrorism law to answer questions, so under Schedule 7 of the Terrorism Act 2000, where an individual is questioned at a port or border area he must give the examining officer any information he requests. It is an offence to fail to comply punishable by fine or imprisonment (see Chapter 7).

Silence at common law

Silence may also be given weight in the situation where an accusation is made by a person other than the police. At common law if a person is accused by a party on equal terms then his silence is admissible to show his acceptance of the accusation being made. But the parties would have to be equal and the circumstances should be such that it was natural to reply (*R v Christie* [1914] AC 545). This was illustrated by cases of *R v Cramp* [1880] 14 CC 390, *R v Mitchell* [1892] 17 Cox CC 503 and *Parkes*. In *Parkes v R* [1976] 1 WLR 1251 the victim had been stabbed and he was accused by the victim's mother, the accused was silent and tried to stab her. The Privy Council said that the judge was 'entitled to instruct the jury that the defendant's reactions to the accusation including his silence were matters which they could take into account along with other evidence in deciding whether the defendant in fact committed the act with which he was charged' (at 1255).

A distinction has been drawn at common law between the questioning by the police or other persons in authority and accusations by those of equal status where the parties are on 'even terms'. So at common law adverse inferences cannot be drawn from silence unless the suspect and the questioner are on equal terms and the accusation is made in circumstances where it is reasonable to expect a response. This common law position on silence in response to third-party accusations is preserved by s 34(5) of the CJPOA:

5) This section does not –

(a) prejudice the admissibility in evidence of the silence or other reaction of the accused in the face of anything said in his presence relating to the conduct in respect of which he is charged, in so far as evidence thereof would be admissible apart from this section; or

(b) preclude the drawing of any inference from any such silence or other reaction of the accused which could properly be drawn apart from this section.

So inferences may be drawn from silence or from other reactions where a person is confronted by another on equal terms. In a more recent case, *R v Osborne* [2005] EWCA Crim 3082, the Court of Appeal stressed also that even where the evidence was relevant, it would still be open to the judge's discretion to exclude it. Three questions should be asked: could a jury conclude that the defendant adopted the statement in question, and, if so, is the matter sufficiently relevant to justify its admission in evidence, and, if so, would its admission have such an adverse effect on the fairness of the proceedings that the judge ought not to admit it. So the courts would now approach the question through the prism of s 78 of PACE. As we shall see, the effect of the CJPOA is to bring the position between equals closer to that between police and suspect despite the significant differences between them and in both cases to attach evidential significance to silence.

Conclusion

The debate on the right to silence, as we have seen, persisted for some time with critics claiming benefits from weakening the right. By 1994 the scene was set for significant change. The advocates of change had won the argument and the suspect's account was given new weight. The CJPOA can be seen as the result of a sustained attack on the right to silence over the previous decades. The provisions in the 1994 Act and the impact of change, including the implications for legal advice, will therefore be considered in Chapter 3. The effect of the provisions described above is to shift the focus on the suspect as the source of evidence and to shift the focus from the trial to the pre-trial stage, but without the safeguards of a public trial. Many of the problems in the miscarriage of justice cases occurred much earlier, in the process of interrogation. So in Chapters 5 and 6 we will consider further the related issues, including access to legal advice and awareness of the implications of speaking.

3
The Impact of the Criminal Justice and Public Order Act 1994

Introduction

The Criminal Justice and Public Order Act 1994 was based on the recommendations of the CLRC Report and on the provisions in the Criminal Evidence (Northern Ireland) Order. The effect of ss 34–37 of the Act is to allow the court or jury to draw adverse inferences from silence as appear proper in the circumstances specified in the Act. Section 38, however, makes it clear that the accused cannot be convicted on the basis of silence alone, that is, on the basis of an inference drawn under ss 34–37, but there must be other evidence against him. The provisions also stipulate that adverse inferences *may* be drawn so the jury may decide not to draw inferences regardless of the circumstances. The Act limited the right to silence both in court and during interrogation and these changes will be discussed before considering their implications and impact.

Silence in court

Under the 1994 Act the accused is still competent and non-compellable and cannot be committed for contempt if he or she fails to speak. However, the pressure to speak is clearly increased as the court or jury is now allowed to draw the proper inferences from the accused's silence without good cause. Both prosecution and judge may now comment on silence. Section 35 of the Act specifies the effect of the failure to testify:

35 Effect of accused's silence at trial.

(1) At the trial of any person for an offence, subsections (2) and (3) below apply unless—
　　(a) the accused's guilt is not in issue; or

(a) it appears to the court that the physical or mental condition of the accused makes it undesirable for him to give evidence;

but subsection (2) below does not apply if, at the conclusion of the evidence for the prosecution, his legal representative informs the court that the accused will give evidence or, where he is unrepresented, the court ascertains from him that he will give evidence.

(2) Where this subsection applies, the court shall, at the conclusion of the evidence for the prosecution, satisfy itself (in the case of proceedings on indictment with a jury, in the presence of the jury) that the accused is aware that the stage has been reached at which evidence can be given for the defence and that he can, if he wishes, give evidence and that, if he chooses not to give evidence, or having been sworn, without good cause refuses to answer any question, it will be permissible for the court or jury to draw such inferences as appear proper from his failure to give evidence or his refusal, without good cause, to answer any question.

(3) Where this subsection applies, the court or jury, in determining whether the accused is guilty of the offence charged, may draw such inferences as appear proper from the failure of the accused to give evidence or his refusal, without good cause, to answer any question.

(4) This section does not render the accused compellable to give evidence on his own behalf, and he shall accordingly not be guilty of contempt of court by reason of a failure to do so.

(5) For the purposes of this section a person who, having been sworn, refuses to answer any question shall be taken to do so without good cause unless –

(a) he is entitled to refuse to answer the question by virtue of any enactment, whenever passed or made, or on the ground of privilege; or

(b) the court in the exercise of its general discretion excuses him from answering it.

We can see from this that the court still has discretion to excuse the defendant from speaking and he may be exempted from the obligation where permitted under another statutory provision. Initially s 35 applied only to those over 14 but this was removed by s 35 of the Crime and Disorder Act 1998.

The mandatory exceptions include physical and mental conditions. The wording of s 35 makes clear that inferences *may* be drawn rather than *must*, so the jury is not obliged to draw inferences even without good cause and the judge should specifically direct them not to do so if appropriate. Of course, whether juries do draw adverse inferences from the failure to testify in a particular case and whether they are aware or not of innocent reasons for silence is difficult to discover, given the privacy and secrecy of the jury room. However, we know from recent research by Thomas (2010) that many jurors find it difficult to follow the judge's directions. Her study involved 797 jurors in three courts exposed to the same simulated trial and directions and she found that 'only a minority (31 per cent) understood the directions fully in the legal terms used by the judge' (Thomas, 2010: vi).

The appropriate procedures to be followed were set out in the 1995 Practice Direction and are now found in the *Criminal Practice Directions* [2013] EWCA Crim 163. The court should be satisfied that the defendant is aware of the opportunity to testify and the effects of choosing not to do so, under s 35, before drawing an adverse inference. If the defendant is represented and wishes to testify, his lawyer should inform the court. If the court is informed that the accused does not wish to speak, then the judge in the presence of the jury should ask the lawyer if he has advised his client of the implications of the failure to testify without good cause (CPD 39P.2, 39P.3). If the client has not been advised, then the case will be adjourned for the advice to be given. If the accused is unrepresented, then the judge will make clear to him the effect of s 35 (CPD 39P.5).

The Act did not include guidance on directing the jury or the appropriate boundaries of comment on silence, but it was discussed in *R v Cowan, Gayle and Ricciardi* [1995] 4 All ER 939 and a direction was formulated by the Judicial Studies Board. The Court of Appeal noted in *Cowan* that s 35 was generally applicable and not limited to exceptional cases. It stressed that the trial judge should tell the jury that the burden of proof remains on the prosecution and what the required standard is, that the defendant is entitled to remain silent and that an inference from the failure to give evidence cannot on its own prove guilt. The jury must be satisfied that the prosecution has established a case to answer before drawing any inferences from the defendant's silence; if, despite any evidence relied on to explain, or in the absence of any such evidence, the jury concludes that silence can only sensibly be attributed to the defendant's having no answer or none that would stand up to cross-examination, then they may draw an adverse inference. The court also stressed that the jury has a complete discretion as to whether inferences should be drawn, and, if so, their nature and extent. It made clear that it would not lightly interfere with a trial judge's discretion to direct or advise the jury regarding the drawing of inferences from silence. The court rejected the claim that s 35 shifts the burden of proof as the accused cannot be convicted on silence alone and the issue of the failure to speak can only be raised after the prosecution has established a prima facie case against the accused. However, it did allow Cowan's appeal because the judge's direction had not made sufficiently clear to the jury that they could not infer guilt solely from silence or the circumstances in which an adverse inference could be drawn.

The advice in *Cowan* in 1995 formed the basis of JSB Direction 39. It reminded the suspect of his right not to give evidence and said that:

> Failure to give evidence on its own cannot prove guilt but depending on the circumstances, you may hold his failure against him when deciding whether he is guilty ... If you conclude that there is a case for him to answer, you may think that the defendant would have gone into the witness box to give you an explanation for or an answer to the case against him. If the only sensible explanation for his decision not to give evidence is that he has no answer to the case against him, or none that could have stood up to cross-examination, then it would be open to you to hold against him his failure to give evidence. It is for you to decide whether it is fair to do so.

In *R v Becouarn* [2005] UKHL 55 the House of Lords said that the judge did not have to direct the jury that there might be reasons for not giving evidence, other than being unable to give an explanation or to address the prosecution's case against him, and approved the direction given by the Court of Appeal in *Cowan*. The jury should also be clear that they must not simply assume guilt from silence, as the Court of Appeal emphasised in *R v Whitehead* [2006] EWCA Crim 1486.

But while s 35 provides an exemption based on the person's mental or physical condition, this condition may not always be obvious to the court. If there is another 'good cause' or 'innocent' reason for silence, such as protecting others, this may also not come to the court's attention. For inarticulate or weaker defendants, there may be genuine fears of making themselves understood in court and they may prefer to take the risk of remaining silent. A nervous and unprepossessing individual who is intimidated by the atmosphere of the court may make an unfavorable impression on the tribunal and in interrogation. Lawyers in Northern Ireland interviewed in the JUSTICE study (1994) said that they felt pressured to advise clients to speak at trial following similar changes there, even if they were likely to make poor witnesses.

A distinction might be drawn between the pre-trial stage, where the defendant is more vulnerable because of his isolation, and the trial stage, where the defendant is in a stronger position in open court with judge and public in attendance and therefore protection may be seen as less important. But appearing in court is still intimidating to many defendants and witnesses, especially if they lack experience of the criminal justice system or are vulnerable. While the treatment of witnesses in court has been improved through the use of special measures, there has been more resistance to affording similar concessions to the accused. However, while some progress has been made, as we shall see later, in the treatment of vulnerable defendants, the trial experience may still be daunting.

Pre-trial silence

The current law on pre-trial silence is contained in ss 34, 36 and 37 of the Criminal Justice and Public Order Act. Section 34 deals with the effects of the failure to mention facts when questioned or charged:

(1) Where, in any proceedings against a person for an offence, evidence is given that the accused –
   (a) at any time before he was charged with the offence, on being questioned under caution by a constable trying to discover whether or by whom the offence had been committed, failed to mention any fact relied on in his defence in those proceedings; or
   (a) on being charged with the offence or officially informed that he might be prosecuted for it, failed to mention any such fact,

   being a fact which in the circumstances existing at the time the accused could reasonably have been expected to mention when so questioned, charged or informed, as the case may be, subsection (2) below applies.

(2) Where this subsection applies –
   (a) a magistrates' court inquiring into the offence as examining justices;
   (b) a judge, in deciding whether to grant an application made by the accused under paragraph 2 of Schedule 3 to the Crime and Disorder Act 1998

(c) the court, in determining whether there is a case to answer; and

(d) the court or jury, in determining whether the accused is guilty of the offence charged,

may draw such inferences from the failure as appear proper.

(2A) Where the accused was at an authorised place of detention at the time of the failure, subsections (1) and (2) above do not apply if he had not been allowed an opportunity to consult a solicitor prior to being questioned, charged or informed as mentioned in subsection (1) above.

(3) Subject to any directions by the court, evidence tending to establish the failure may be given before or after evidence tending to establish the fact which the accused is alleged to have failed to mention.

(4) This section applies in relation to questioning by persons (other than constables) charged with the duty of investigating offences or charging offenders as it applies in relation to questioning by constables; and in subsection (1) above 'officially informed' means informed by a constable or any such person.

(5) This section does not –

(a) prejudice the admissibility in evidence of the silence or other reaction of the accused in the face of anything said in his presence relating to the conduct in respect of which he is charged, in so far as evidence thereof would be admissible apart from this section; or

(b) preclude the drawing of any inference from any such silence or other reaction of the accused which could properly be drawn apart from this section.

(6) This section does not apply in relation to a failure to mention a fact if the failure occurred before the commencement of this section.

Following the enactment of s 34, the PACE Codes were amended. The new caution reminded the suspect of his right to silence but also warned him that silence may be subject to an adverse inference if he fails to mention a fact which he later relies on in court:

> You do not have to say anything. But it may harm your defence if you do not mention when questioned something which you later rely on in court. Anything you do say may be given in evidence.
>
> (Code C.10.5)

It should be given before a person is questioned regarding any offence and when a person is charged with or informed that they may be prosecuted for an offence (Code C.10(a) and C 16.(2)). Minor deviations are permitted provided the sense of the caution is retained (Code C.10.7). The caution should be explained to the suspect in a way which he is capable of understanding given his or her personal characteristics. They should be cautioned again after any breaks in questioning. Although the Codes have been updated and amended, most recently in July 2012, this caution has remained unchanged since the 1994 Act was passed. The caution is now more complex than the pre-1994 warning, which raises the question of whether the suspect has fully understood its meaning (see Chapter 6). The caution would not be given in the limited cases where adverse inferences do not apply, where the suspect has requested a solicitor but has not been allowed an opportunity to consult a solicitor and has not changed his mind about wanting to consult a solicitor (Code C 10.6 and Annex C: para 2). In this case the pre-1994 caution would be given.

Section 36 deals with the failure to account for objects, substances or marks on the suspect's person, clothing, footwear or in their possession or in a place where they are present at the time of arrest.

36 Effect of accused's failure or refusal to account for objects, substances or marks.

(1) Where –
  (a) a person is arrested by a constable, and there is—
     (i) on his person; or
     (ii) in or on his clothing or footwear; or
     (iii) otherwise in his possession; or
     (iv) in any place in which he is at the time of his arrest,

  any object, substance or mark, or there is any mark on any such object; and

  (b) that or another constable investigating the case reasonably believes that the presence of the object, substance or mark may be attributable to the participation of the person arrested in the commission of an offence specified by the constable; and
  (c) the constable informs the person arrested that he so believes, and requests him to account for the presence of the object, substance or mark; and

(d) the person fails or refuses to do so,

then if, in any proceedings against the person for the offence so specified, evidence of those matters is given, subsection (2) below applies.

(2) Where this subsection applies—
   (a) a magistrates' court inquiring into the offence as examining justices;
   (b) a judge, in deciding whether to grant an application made by the accused under paragraph 2 of Schedule 3 to the Crime and Disorder Act 1998
   (c) the court, in determining whether there is a case to answer; and
   (d) the court or jury, in determining whether the accused is guilty of the offence charged,

may draw such inferences from the failure or refusal as appear proper.

(3) Subsections (1) and (2) above apply to the condition of clothing or footwear as they apply to a substance or mark thereon.
(4) Subsections (1) and (2) above do not apply unless the accused was told in ordinary language by the constable when making the request mentioned in subsection (1)(c) above what the effect of this section would be if he failed or refused to comply with the request.
(4A) Where the accused was at an authorised place of detention at the time of the failure or refusal, subsections (1) and (2) above do not apply if he had not been allowed an opportunity to consult a solicitor prior to the request being made.
(5) This section applies in relation to officers of customs and excise as it applies in relation to constables.
(6) This section does not preclude the drawing of any inference from a failure or refusal of the accused to account for the presence of an object, substance or mark or from the condition of clothing or footwear which could properly be drawn apart from this section.
(7) This section does not apply in relation to a failure or refusal which occurred before the commencement of this section.

Section 37 refers to the effect of the failure of the accused to account for his or her presence at a particular place:

> 37 Effect of accused's failure or refusal to account for presence at a particular place.

(1) Where –
  (a) a person arrested by a constable was found by him at a place at or about the time the offence for which he was arrested is alleged to have been committed; and
  (b) that or another constable investigating the offence reasonably believes that the presence of the person at that place and at that time may be attributable to his participation in the commission of the offence; and
  (c) the constable informs the person that he so believes, and requests him to account for that presence; and
  (d) the person fails or refuses to do so,

then if, in any proceedings against the person for the offence, evidence of those matters is given, subsection (2) below applies.

(2) Where this subsection applies –
  (a) a magistrates' court inquiring into the offence as examining justices;
  (b) a judge, in deciding whether to grant an application made by the accused under paragraph 2 of Schedule 3 to the Crime and Disorder Act 1998
  (c) the court, in determining whether there is a case to answer; and
  (d) the court or jury, in determining whether the accused is guilty of the offence charged, may draw such inferences from the failure or refusal as appear proper.
(3) Subsections (1) and (2) do not apply unless the accused was told in ordinary language by the constable when making the request mentioned in subsection (1)(c) above what the effect of this section would be if he failed or refused to comply with the request.
(3A) Where the accused was at an authorised place of detention at the time of the failure or refusal, subsections (1) and (2) do not apply if he had not been allowed an opportunity to consult a solicitor prior to the request being made.

(4) This section applies in relation to officers of customs and excise as it applies in relation to constables.
(5) This section does not preclude the drawing of any inference from a failure or refusal of the accused to account for his presence at a place which could properly be drawn apart from this section.
(6) This section does not apply in relation to a failure or refusal which occurred before the commencement of this section.

Sections 36 and 37 were also modelled on the Criminal Evidence (Northern Ireland) Order. Section 37 was intended to deal with the situation of the kind in *Murray v UK* App. No. 18731/91 (8 February 1996) where the individual is found at a place where a crime has been committed or in which he might be implicated and may be relevant to involvement in terrorist offences. For an inference to be drawn under s 36 or 37 a special warning should be given (Code C.10.10) and a failure to give the warning would mean the court would not be able to draw the inferences that appear appropriate. Under both provisions, ss 36 and 37, the suspect must be advised of the failure to answer questions and the officer must make clear to him what specific fact he is being asked about and should be informed that the officer believes that this fact is due to the suspect's involvement in the offence and that a court may draw inferences from his silence. The suspect should also be under arrest at the time he is asked to give an account. It must be made clear to the suspect by the officer exactly what is being investigated, the specific fact the suspect is being asked to account for, namely whether the presence of the object, substance or mark, or the presence at the particular place is attributable to his participation in the commission of the offence. The officer should make clear that the court may draw such inferences from the failure to account for the fact, that a record is being made of the interview and that it may be given in evidence at trial (Code C.10.11).

Even where it does seem possible to draw inferences under ss 34–37, the court may exclude such inferences at its discretion under s 38(3). The judge may also direct the jury not to draw adverse inferences in certain cases, for example, if there are concerns regarding the behaviour of the police. The suspect must be in an authorised place of detention and cautioned before questioning. Although ss 36 and 37 raise issues regarding disclosure and access to legal advice, most of the post-1994 jurisprudence has focused on the issues raised by s 34. Before adverse inferences can be drawn under ss 34, 36 and 37 the suspect must be granted the opportunity to consult a solicitor.

Interpreting Section 34

The application of s 34 has raised a number of issues, including the problem of reasonableness and the effect of legal advice. There have been disputes regarding whether facts which did not seem material to the defendant in interrogation are now relevant. It may not always be clear which are the key facts that are relevant to the defence early on in the investigation. A fact that at the outset of the investigation did not seem significant may later become essential to the defence, following new information or testimony. Section 34 has generated numerous appeals on these issues, as well as on the appropriate direction to the jury.

The suspect is still not legally obliged to answer questions but does run the risk of adverse inferences if he fails to mention a fact that he later relies on in his defence. Section 34 allows inferences to be drawn when a person is questioned under caution before being charged (s 34(1)(a)) and when he is silent on being charged (s 43(1)(b)). So even if a no comment interview was deemed inadmissible, then it may still be possible to draw an adverse inference from silence on being charged, as made clear in *R v Dervish and Anori* [2001] EWCA Crim 2789. If at trial the accused does raise a fact on which he relies in his defence, he can be cross-examined on why it was not mentioned earlier. However, if all the evidence has been submitted, and the judge directs that no adverse inference can be drawn, then the jury will have to disregard the cross-examination on that issue.

The specific fact that the accused fails to mention has to be one that is relevant to the defence and that he could reasonably have been expected to mention, and there has to be reliance on it. The fact relied on obviously has to be known to the defendant at the time he was asked to disclose it (see *R v Nickolson* [1999] Crim LR 61). Reasonableness will be considered in light of all the circumstances, including the particular characteristics of the accused, his age, knowledge and his mental state. In *Argent* [1997] 2 Cr App R 27, one of the first cases on s 34, the Lord Chief Justice, Lord Bingham, said that there were several preconditions that must be met before adverse inferences may be drawn under s 34: namely there had to be proceedings against a person for an offence; the alleged failure to mention a fact later relied on had to occur before a defendant was charged or on being charged; and the alleged failure had to occur during questioning under caution by a constable or any other person within s 34(4). The questioning had to be directed to trying to discover whether or by whom the alleged offence had been committed and the alleged failure had to be the failure to mention any fact later relied on in his defence in those proceedings. This means that two factual questions need to be considered by the jury: first, was there some fact that he relied on in his defence; and, second, whether the defendant, when being questioned, failed to mention it. The fact he failed to mention must be a fact that, in the circumstances existing at the time, was one that he could reasonably have been expected to mention. The relevant time is the time of questioning and account should be taken of all the circumstances existing at that time. The Court of Appeal said that the circumstances could include legal advice, but also other matters such as the defendant's age and experience, his mental capacity and physical health, his personality, sobriety and tiredness. Attention should be focused on the actual accused with his qualities rather than a hypothetical person of ordinary fortitude. The court said these are issues for the jury to resolve in exercising their 'collective common sense, experience and understanding of human nature'. Drawing the appropriate inferences was clearly a matter for the jury, although there are circumstances where the judge should warn the jury against drawing adverse inferences.

In Argent's case, he had given two no comment interviews, acting on the advice of his solicitor, but at trial he gave an account of his movements on the night in question. He claimed that he had not encountered the victim on the night of the killing, was not carrying a knife and was accompanied by his wife, all facts to which he could have referred earlier. The court found the trial judge had directed the jury properly. However, the court did think evidence of a no comment interview before there had been a positive identification of the accused should have been excluded, but a later one after the identification should have been admitted.

Before adverse inferences may be drawn under s 34 it is essential that the accused is offered access to a solicitor, either in person, in writing or by telephone, although he may choose not to take advantage of this. The police must make clear to the suspect that he has the right to consult a lawyer before being questioned, charged or informed that he may be prosecuted and that he may receive free advice from the duty solicitor. The opportunity to receive legal advice was made a precondition of the activation of s 34 by s 58 of the Youth Justice and Criminal Evidence Act 1999, following the case of *Murray v UK* in the Strasbourg

Court. Access to a solicitor cannot be delayed because the solicitor might counsel silence.

Questioning should stop when the investigating officer takes the view that there is a realistic prospect of conviction (Code C 11.6, *R v Pointer* [1997] Crim LR 676) unless the officer still has an open mind regarding the suspect's involvement (*R v Gayle* [1999] Crim LR 502). If there is a second interview, where a fact is mentioned that was not mentioned at the initial interview, then adverse inferences may still be drawn (*R v McLernon* [1992] 3 NIJB 41. Adverse inferences may also be drawn if the fact relied on but withheld from the police had been given to a third party as the Court of Appeal made clear in *R v Taylor* [1999] Crim LR 77. However, reliance on the fact does not have to be through the defendant's own evidence, but can be construed through the evidence of other witnesses or through cross-examination of the defendant. This was made clear by the Court of Appeal in *R v Bowers* [1998] Crim LR 817 and the House of Lords in *R v Webber* [2004] UKHL 1.

While s 35(1)(b) of the CJPOA expressly stipulates that s 35 cannot be activated if the accused's physical or mental condition makes it undesirable for him to give evidence, there is no comparable provision in s 34. However, in *Argent*, the Court of Appeal noted that the reference to 'a fact which in the circumstances existing at the time the accused could reasonably have been expected to mention', suggested that the circumstances could include the suspect's age or mental capacity.

Whether the accused did refuse to answer particular questions will not be a matter for dispute given the routine recording of interviews now. But matters of reasonableness and the implications of legal advice may be more difficult to resolve. Even before the Act, juries found it difficult to interpret silence, but their task was made harder after the 1994 Act. The jury may draw inferences based on vague assumptions about what a person in that situation might do. As Jackson (1989) notes, the less responsive the accused is, the harder it becomes to make any inference on which the jury or court can be confident is the correct one. The Northern Ireland Court of Appeal in *R v Martin and others* [1992] 5 NIJB 40 commented that the word inference 'is part of everyday language frequently used and readily understood'. But it is questionable whether suspects or juries do appreciate its precise meaning or the type of inference that is appropriate. In *R v Cowan, Gayle and Ricciardi* [1995] 4 All ER 939 the Court of Appeal stressed that the jury has complete discretion whether to draw adverse inferences or not and to decide on the nature, extent and degree of adversity, following the approach in the Northern Ireland courts in *R v McLernon* [1992] 3 NIJB 41.

Section 38(3) makes clear that the accused cannot be convicted on silence alone, there must be some other evidence against him:

> A person shall not have the proceedings against him transferred to the Crown Court for trial, have a case to answer or be convicted of an offence solely on an inference drawn from such a failure or refusal as is mentioned in s 34(2), 35(3), 36(2) or 37(2).

However, in practice it may be difficult to prevent juries from placing considerable weight on silence during their deliberations.

No specific guidance on the inference was given in the Act. The Judicial Studies Board Specimen Direction initially said that the jury should be reminded that failure to give evidence on its own cannot prove guilt, but, depending on the circumstances, they may hold his failure against him when deciding whether he is guilty. But it may be difficult for the jury to understand this advice. The judge should make clear to the jury that the accused has the right to remain silent, but also that the defendant has a choice whether or not to rely on that right, to make clear what the facts are which the accused could reasonably have mentioned, and that there must be a case to answer, and the accused cannot be convicted only on an inference drawn from silence. The key issue to consider is whether he remained silent not because of legal advice, but because he had no satisfactory explanation to give. If the conclusion is that he is merely using legal advice as a shield to hide behind and has no satisfactory explanation to give, then the jury is entitled to draw inferences against him it deems appropriate. The judge may also observe to the jury that an explanation offered at trial after all the evidence has been heard may be less convincing than one offered at the time of interview (see *R v Bresa* [2005] EWCA Crim 1414).

There has been a shift away from using specimen directions. However, the JSB does still give guidance for crafting directions with reference to the relevant law. The 2004 Specimen Direction No. 40 is included in the Bench Book as this was approved by the Court of Appeal. The appropriate direction under s 34 should be discussed with counsel before closing speeches to see if such a direction should be given, the facts to which it should relate, and to identify permissible inferences and consider its terms. It may be decided that no such direction should be given; however, if a direction is appropriate the jury should be advised as follows:

> Before his interview(s) the defendant was cautioned. He was first told that he need not say anything. It was therefore his right to remain

silent. However, he was also told that it might harm his defence if he did not mention when questioned something which he later relied on in court; and that anything he did say might be given in evidence.

As part of his defence, the defendant has relied upon (here specify the facts to which this direction applies). But [the prosecution say] [he admits] that he failed to mention these facts when he was interviewed about the offence(s). [If you are sure that is so, this/This] failure may count against him. This is because you may draw the conclusion from his failure that he [had no answer then/had no answer that he then believed would stand up to scrutiny/has since invented his account/has since tailored his account to fit the prosecution's case/(here refer to any other reasonable inferences contended for)]. If you do draw that conclusion, you must not convict him wholly or mainly on the strength of it; but you may take it into account as some additional support for the prosecution's case and when deciding whether his [evidence/case] about these facts is true.

However, you may draw such a conclusion against him only if you think it is a fair and proper conclusion, and you are satisfied about three things: first, that when he was interviewed he could reasonably have been expected to mention the facts on which he now relies; second, that the only sensible explanation for his failure to do so is that he had no answer at the time or none that would stand up to scrutiny; third, that apart from his failure to mention those facts, the prosecution's case against him is so strong that it clearly calls for an answer by him.

(Add, if appropriate:) The defence invite you not to draw any conclusion from the defendant's silence, on the basis of the following evidence (here set out the evidence). If you [accept this evidence and] think this amounts to a reason why you should not draw any conclusion from his silence, do not do so. Otherwise, subject to what I have said, you may do so.

(JSB 2010: 394)

In *Murray v DPP* (1994) 1 WLR 1, the House of Lords emphasised that in interpreting silence:

it is not in every situation that an adverse inference can be drawn from silence, the more so because in all but the simplest cases the permissible inferences may have to be considered separately in relation to each individual issue. Everything depends on the nature of the issue, the weight of the evidence adduced by the prosecution upon it...and the extent to which the defendant should in the nature of things be able to give evidence may found no inference at all, or one which is for all practical purposes fatal

(at p 5).

There may be circumstances in which the jury should be directed not to draw an adverse inference, as indicated in *McGarry v R* (1998) EWCA Crim 2364.

The effect of legal advice

There has also been considerable debate on the implications of s 34 for the advice lawyers give their clients and whether advice to remain silent should prevent adverse inference from being drawn. When the law was changed the advice from the Law Society was that solicitors should state at the beginning of interview whether they are advising their clients to remain silent and if so the reasons why, so it would be clear at trial that silence was in response to this advice (Law Society 1994). If silence is advised then the solicitor should note his reasons for doing so in writing and on the police recording. Reasons for counseling silence might be concerns over safety of the client and possible reprisals, or over the quantity of evidence disclosed by the police, or because the client is distressed or confused at the time of the interview, or is suggestible.

When the law was changed it was thought that some lawyers would be more likely to advise silence and to then use the fact of reliance on legal advice to prevent the activation of s 34 at trial. This issue has exercised both the domestic courts and the Strasbourg Court since the CJPOA was enacted. The hope that legal advice would be protective was short-lived as it has now been firmly established in the domestic courts that acting on legal advice does not protect the accused from adverse inferences under s 34, although the Strasbourg Court is more sympathetic to treating reliance on legal advice as a reason not to draw adverse inferences from silence.

It might reasonably be argued that if the accused does genuinely rely on the solicitor's advice he should not be punished by adverse inferences. If the solicitor is reminding him of his right to silence, as the police also do when cautioning, then it seems unfair to penalise him for following that advice. But in *Argent* the Court of Appeal affirmed that the issue for the jury to consider is the reasonableness of the accused's conduct in all the circumstances, including, but not limited to, legal advice, rather than whether the lawyer's advice was correct or whether it complied with Law Society guidelines. Parliament has left the matter for the jury to decide, the court noted, and consideration of the issue cannot be precluded by the solicitor or the Law Society.

The issue was discussed in the domestic courts in *R v Condron and Condron* [1997] 1 Cr App R 185 where the defendants were convicted of possession of heroin with intent to supply, following discovery of wraps of heroin at their flat. They remained silent during interrogation, acting on legal advice as their advisor considered them unfit to be interviewed, because they were experiencing heroin withdrawal symptoms. However, a police doctor disagreed and the interview proceeded with the accused exercising the right to silence, and they were convicted. The Condrons admitted using heroin but denied supplying the drugs. At trial they gave exculpatory reasons to account for the presence of the drugs at their flat and the flat of a co-defendant. The trial judge had directed the jury that they could, if they wished, draw adverse inferences from the failure to mention facts later relied on at trial.

On appeal they argued that their no comment interviews should have been excluded as their silence was based on legal advice given in good faith, on the basis of ill health, rather than intended to 'ambush' the prosecution. The Appeal Court dismissed their appeal as the doctor had deemed them fit and it was up to the jury to consider whether they should have mentioned earlier facts they later relied on in court. It also said that the direction given in *Cowan* in relation to s 35 was also appropriate to s 34, namely the jury should be told that if they can sensibly attribute the defendant's silence only to having no answer, or one that would not withstand cross-examination, they may draw an adverse inference. The court stressed in *Condron* it is not the advice given by the solicitor that is important, but the reason why they were silent. Provided that the interview was properly conducted, it should be left to the jury to decide whether it was reasonable to fail to mention an innocent explanation for the drugs at the flat. The court also said that if the accused gives his reason for not speaking as legal advice this does not constitute a waiver of legal professional privilege. However, if evidence of the nature of advice is given that will be needed to persuade the court not to draw an adverse inference, this will be deemed to be a waiver of privilege and the trial judge should warn him of this. Once privilege has been waived, the defendant and the solicitor could be cross-examined on the reasons for and nature of the advice (see also *R v Bowden* [1999] 4 All ER 43). A similar approach was taken in *R v Roble* [1997] Crim LR 499, where the Court of Appeal noted that if the defendant just says he was advised by his lawyer not to speak this would not amount to a waiver, but if he gives the reasons for the lawyer's advice it would and usually it would be necessary to discuss those reasons to persuade the jury not to draw adverse inferences. In *Roble* the court again stressed that the fact of receiving legal advice was not as significant as the reason why the defendant followed the advice and whether it is reasonable does not depend on the correctness of lawyer's advice or whether it complies with the Law Society guidelines. The court also said in *Condron* that it would only be in exceptional cases that the judge should tell the jury not to draw an adverse inference.

However, the Condrons' case was considered in the Strasbourg Court. In *Condron v UK* App. No. 35718/97 (2 May 2000), the court said the trial judge's direction in the Condrons' case did amount to a breach of Article 6. Although the judge reminded the jury of the Condrons' explanation for silence, he did so in terms that left the jury free to draw an adverse inference even though it may have been satisfied regarding the plausibility of the explanation. The court acknowledged that where an explanation is demanded from the accused, silence can be relevant in assessing the prosecution's case against the accused. But the fact that the accused relied on his lawyer's advice to remain silent should be given appropriate weight by the domestic court. The presence of the solicitor is an important safeguard to protect the accused from compulsion to speak, and reliance on legal advice may be a proper reason for remaining silent. However, the fact that the construction of silence is a matter for the jury does not conflict with Article 6. Silence can be taken into account where the situation calls for an explanation and the 1994 provisions do seek to strike a balance between the accused's right to silence and the drawing of adverse inferences.

Similar concerns regarding the reliance on legal advice were raised in Northern Ireland in relation to Article 3 of the Northern Ireland Criminal Evidence Order, the counterpart of s 34. A study by JUSTICE and the Committee on the Administration of Justice found that solicitors were in a very difficult position following the imposition of the Order as it was difficult to advise the client, without full knowledge of the case against them at that stage (JUSTICE 1994). If they advised silence, they risked adverse inferences, and if they advised them to speak, they undermined their clients' right to silence. If they advised silence they could be called to give evidence that they felt undermined lawyer–client privilege. It was also not easy to predict the interpretation of Article 3 by a Diplock judge. While the inference drawn from silence might be guilt, there may also be innocent reasons for silence, including the fear of reprisals, or of implicating others, or a reluctance to appear in court or to undergo cross-examination.

Historically the presence of the lawyer has been seen as crucial in bringing the relationship between the state and the citizen into a more equal position. In cases such as *R v Chandler* [1976] 1 WLR 585 and *R v Horne* [1990] Crim LR 188, the lawyer's presence is seen as compensating to some extent the inequalities of power and resources between the police and the citizen. Before the 1994 Act, beneficial changes, including the access to a solicitor, were frequently cited as part of the case for limiting the right to silence. But not all suspects will benefit from access to a solicitor and there have also been concerns over the quality of legal advice in some cases, issues that we will consider further in Chapter 5.

The problem for the suspect is to know in advance of the trial whether the reliance on legal advice will be seen as reasonable. It is difficult for the solicitor to reach a decision on this, so it will be even harder for the suspect (see Easton, 1998, 2000). The suspect will need to assess whether or not the lawyer's advice should be followed, so, in effect, he or she will require as much or even greater knowledge than that of the adviser. As Cape (1997) has argued, the lawyer in effect is being 'side-lined'. It also means suspects must be cautioned that adverse inferences may be drawn even when they have remained silent on legal advice.

Since *Condron* the issue of the implications of reliance on legal advice has been reconsidered and the approach has not been consistent. We find a line of cases, including *R v Betts and Hall* [2001] EWCA Crim 244 and *R v Robinson* [2003] EWCA 2219 where reliance on legal advice has been given some weight. But in other cases, such as *R v Beckles and Montague* [1999] Crim LR 148, *R v Knight* [2003] EWCA 1977 and *R v Hoare and Pearce* [2004] EWCA Crim 784 it has been discounted in favour of reasonable reliance.

In *Betts and Hall* the Court of Appeal said that if a person is silent because he has no or no adequate explanation to offer, he is not protected by his lawyer's advice as simply using that advice to conceal his true reason for not mentioning the facts in question. But no adverse inference should be drawn unless the jury thinks that the accused had no innocent explanation to offer. The court could not draw an adverse inference if the jury accepted the claim of the defendant that silence was attributable to legal advice, so the jury should decide if the defendant's claim that he remain silent because he relied on legal advice was genuine. In *R v Robinson* [2003] EWCA 2219 the Court of Appeal said that if the reason for silence is that he acted on the advice of his solicitor, rather than because he had no answer, or no satisfactory answer, to give, then no inference can be drawn, although it did stress that this does not give a licence to the guilty to shield behind the lawyer's advice.

In *R v Beckles and Montague* [1999] Crim LR 148 the defendants were convicted of robbery, false imprisonment and attempted murder. The victim, having been robbed and held at Montague's flat, fell out of a window and was left paralysed. Montague gave a prepared statement in which he said he knew a man had fallen from the window, but he had nothing to do with it. Beckles gave a no-comment interview acting on legal advice. At trial the defendants admitted being at the flat for some of the time, but denied being in the room when the victim fell, and Beckles said he had not spoken initially acting on his lawyer's advice. The trial judge's direction followed the specimen direction with the addition made after *Argent* and reminded the jury that reliance on legal advice was not sufficient to stop the jury drawing adverse inferences under s 34, and it was up to Beckles to decide whether or not to follow that advice and a matter for the jury to decide what inferences to draw. The Court of Appeal approved the judge's direction and rejected the argument that inferences under s 34 should be limited to recent fabrication. It would undermine the purpose of s 34 to combat ambush defences if its scope were limited in this way. A similar view was taken in *R v Daniel* [1998] Crim LR 818.

In *Beckles* the Court of Appeal said that the jury should first ask whether the accused genuinely relied on and acted on the legal advice, and, second, whether it was reasonable to do so. The court said previous cases had affirmed that the jury should be free to draw the inferences it chooses from the failure to mention facts later relied on at trial. The mere fact of relying on legal advice will not protect the accused from adverse inferences, although it is now essential that the suspect has the opportunity to consult a lawyer before adverse inferences may be drawn. But the reliance must be reasonable reliance to protect the accused.

In *R v Howell* [2003] EWCA Crim 1, the Court of Appeal emphasised that there must be *objective* reasons for remaining silent sufficiently cogent to weigh in the balance against the public interest in the suspect giving an account to the police, and solicitors should bear this in mind when advising their clients. Just because silence was advised by the lawyer did not of itself prevent s 34 from applying, but the focus should be on why silence had been advised, so issues such as the person's mental or physical condition, or shock, intoxication or confusion might be relevant circumstances which may justify silence. So genuine reliance on legal advice is insufficient to protect against adverse inferences. This decision was subject to criticism, not least because it conflicted with the Strasbourg Court's approach in *Beckles v UK* App. No. 44652/98 (8 October 2002).

The accused may not be in a position to evaluate the quality of legal advice if he lacks legal knowledge. Howell gave a no-comment interview on the advice of his solicitor and said on appeal that he would have given a full account if he had not been so advised. However, the Court of Appeal thought that reliance on legal advice did not preclude adverse inferences and whether it is reasonable to expect the accused to mention the facts in question depends on the circumstances. A bad reason does not become a good reason just because the solicitor advised it.

The apparent conflict between *Betts and Hall* and *Howell* on the issue of reliance on legal advice was also considered obiter by the Court of Appeal in *Knight*, which decided that the issue should be resolved in favour of *Howell*. Reliance on legal advice *per se* does not protect the defendant, but the court should consider whether there are issues in the case, such as vulnerability, that should prevent adverse inferences being drawn.

In *R v Hoare and Pearce* [2004] EWCA Crim 784 the Court of Appeal followed *Howell and Knight*. It argued that when the defendant is claiming he remained silent on legal advice, the jury should consider whether it was reasonable to rely on the lawyer's advice, so reliance of itself not prevent adverse inferences being drawn. Even if the lawyer's advice is based on good faith and genuinely relied on, it is still open to the jury to draw an adverse inference if the jury is sure that the real reason is he had no explanation or no satisfactory explanation (consistent with innocence) to give. Of course he is entitled to rely on his right to silence, but this should be distinguished from the reason for relying on it. So this approach is designed to deal with tactical reasons for silence.

Reasons for the solicitor advising silence might include insufficient disclosure of the case against the accused, or the case is so complex, or there may be specific issues relating to intimidation or fear of reprisal if the client is seen as an informer. This was an issue in Northern Ireland as we shall see in Chapter 7. The adviser should inform the police at the interview why he is advising silence. In *Roble* the court said good reasons might include the failure of the interrogating officer to disclose sufficient information on the case against the accused to enable the lawyer to advise his client, or where the nature of the offence or the material is so complex or relates to matters so long ago that an immediate response is not feasible.

The lawyer should make clear if he or she is not satisfied with the level of disclosure. If the police are sparing with details of the case against the suspect then it is difficult for the lawyer to advise his or her client. In *R v Imran and Hussain* [1997] Crim LR 754 and *R v Farrell* [2004] EWCA Crim 597, the Court of Appeal said the investigating officer is not required to give the solicitor a full briefing of the case against the accused, but he must give enough information for the suspect to understand the nature and circumstances of his arrest. A failure to provide sufficient information for the lawyer to advise his client during the pre-interview briefing could be a valid reason for remaining silent and the officer may be called to justify his failure to do so in court.

The judge should also give a special direction to the jury where the explanation for silence is that the defendant was advised by his lawyer, pointing out that the fact of advice is an important consideration but the reasons for silence should be considered, including whether the client is using the advice as an excuse for evading the truth.

On the question of reliance, the Strasbourg Court has given more weight to the lawyer's advice. The question was considered in *Beckles v UK* App. No. 44652/98 (8 October 2002) where the Court of Human Rights endorsed the approach in *Betts and Hall*. The court took the view that if the defendant genuinely relies on legal advice, this should prevent an adverse inference being drawn. In this case the trial judge had not given enough weight to the accused's explanation, but had left the jury able to draw an adverse inference even if they were satisfied the explanation was plausible. So in this respect the Strasbourg Court is more protective of the right to silence than the domestic courts. It also noted in *Condron v UK* (1996) 22 EHRR 29 and in *Averill v UK* App. No. 36408/97 (6 June 2000) that acting on the lawyer's advice may be a proper reason for declining to speak and it may be unfair to draw adverse inferences in such cases, or where there are other good reasons for remaining silent.

One way of negotiating the hazards of s 34 is to use a pre-prepared statement. The Law Society revised its guidelines in 1997 following the decisions in *Argent* and *Condron* and recommended that the lawyer submit a prepared statement of the key facts from the client (Law Society 1997). The statement is made by the suspect in consultation with the lawyer, signed, dated and given to the police before or during the interview. It is intended to prevent adverse inferences being drawn and to combat any accusations of fabrication of facts which the accused could reasonably have been expected to mention. The police, once given the statement, can adjourn to consider it and reconsider any questions to put to the suspect, but can still continue questioning on the contents of the statement or any other relevant matters. The solicitor may also draft a prepared statement of brief facts to give to the police to protect his client from adverse inferences at trial. The defendant or the lawyer may read out a prepared statement from the accused, who may then refuse to answer any further questions in the hope that adverse inferences may not be drawn at trial.

The status of this statement was initially unclear but was clarified in *R v Knight* [2003] EWCA 1977. Knight gave the police a pre-prepared statement at the beginning of the interview and refused to answer questions, but evidence at his trial was consistent with the statement. On appeal his conviction was quashed because the trial judge wrongly directed the jury that adverse inferences could be drawn from his silence during the interview. The Court of Appeal reviewed the previous cases and said that making a prepared statement in itself did not prevent the activation of s 34. The making of a pre-prepared statement will not give automatic immunity against adverse inferences under s 34. But as the statement here included all the facts that were given at trial, the court said that the purpose of s 34 had not been undermined. But the prepared statement can only protect the accused from adverse inferences if evidence given at trial is consistent with that statement, as also made clear in *R v Turner (Dwaine)* [2004] EWCA Crim 3108. Provided the silence covers the matters in the prepared statement, then it would be unfair to draw adverse inferences under s 34.

Exercising the right to silence

A key aim of the changes in the Criminal Justice and Public Order Act was to increase the numbers speaking in interrogation and thereby reduce the number of ambush defences. The 'abuse' of the right to silence, as we have seen, was a major element of the attack on the right to silence but whether the Act did have a substantial impact on the exercise of the right should be considered. Before doing so, however, we need to bear in mind the low number of suspects remaining silent before the Act as the available research suggests that the majority of suspects waived their right to silence. The Royal Commission on Criminal Procedure (1981) conducted research prior to PACE which found that 4 per cent of suspects in their large sample exercised their right to silence. This was supported by other studies conducted in the 1980s, for example, by Smith and Grey (1983) and Mitchell (1983). A study of contested cases in the Crown Court in London and Birmingham in 1980 by Baldwin and McConville found that 6.5 per cent of the London sample and 3.8 per cent of the Birmingham sample exercised their right to silence (Baldwin and McConville, 1980). Sanders *et al*.'s (1989) study found 2.4 per cent of their sample exercised their right to silence in interrogation. Similar results were found in the early 1990s. Moreover, the number of solicitors advising silence was low. In McConville and Hodgson's (1993) study only 2.5 per cent of suspects in their study were completely silent and advice to remain silent from lawyers was the exception rather than the norm, even among solicitors who had a reputation for being 'civil rights oriented'. At that time advisers included clerks and former police officers, who mostly advised cooperation with police or left it to the client to decide. Where legal advisers did advise silence, the reasons included the lack of information available about the case against the suspect and the fear that some suspects, particularly suggestible ones, would make an incriminating remark. Sometimes it was because the adviser was unqualified and lacked the knowledge to advise the client. This study also found no evidence of a link between offence serious-ness and the exercise of the right to silence. In some cases the suspect remained silent despite advice to speak.

Research on the exercise of the right to silence under the pre-1994 provisions suggested that silence did not increase the chance of acquittal and may even have increased the chance of conviction (Leng 1993). However, it is difficult to reach firm conclusions on this issue as the verdict may reflect a number of issues and the numbers exercising the right to silence were small. The majority of suspects also testified at trial. Zander and Henderson (1993) found 70–74 per cent of defendants testi-fied in the Crown Court in their study. Even before the 1994 changes counsel would have considered whether the risks from speaking would be outweighed by the risk of remaining silent because the jury may well have taken a negative view of the failure to testify.

Prior to 1994 there was debate on the extent of the use of silence. Research conducted for the Home Office Working Group in London in the late 1980s found that 6 per cent of the sample answered no ques-tions during the whole interview (HOWG 1989 Appendix C). But if we add those who refused to answer some questions then the aggregated figure will be higher. Moston *et al.* (1992) sampled 1,067 cases and found that 16 per cent of the sample exercised their right to silence, but of this group only half were completely silent and half answered some ques-tions. They also found positive correlations between silence and legal advice, offence severity and previous convictions. Irving and McKenzie

(1989) conducted research on a small sample for the Police Foundation in 1989. They argued that there had been a sharp rise in the number of suspects refusing to answer questions after PACE came into force and that there was a positive correlation between the seriousness of the crime and the refusal to answer questions. A further study undertaken by ACPO (1993) in 1992 of 3,600 suspects found that 21.9 per cent of suspects refused to answer some questions, 10 per cent answered no questions at all, and those with past convictions were more likely to remain silent. Brown's (1994) review of studies conducted before the CJPOA found not more than 5 per cent refused to answer any questions outside the Metropolitan Police area. In London it was between 7 and 8 per cent. So the pre-CJPOA studies showed variations in the numbers found exercising the right to silence. It is difficult comparing studies before and after the Act as some may refuse to answer some questions while others refuse to answer any questions at all. We need to be clear that we are comparing like with like and when we refer to silence whether we are referring to a 'no-comment' interview where the suspect refuses to answer any questions, or to a refusal to answer some questions.

It is useful to compare the research undertaken by Phillips and Brown before the Act, but published in 1998, with Bucke, Street and Brown's research on the impact of the provisions published in 2000 as they included some of the same police stations in their research and framed similar questions (Phillips and Brown, 1998; Bucke *et al.*, 2000). Bucke, Street and Brown observed 13 police stations in 10 police forces, 8 of which had been used in the earlier study conducted by Phillips and Brown in 1998. The fieldwork conducted by Bucke, Street and Brown covered the period from the middle of August 1995 to the end of February 1996 and also included interviews with investigating officers, CPS staff, defence legal advisers and barristers.

In Phillips and Brown's study (1998), 10 per cent of suspects gave no-comment interviews while in Bucke, Street and Brown's study the number had fallen to 6 per cent. In Phillips and Brown's study, 13 per cent selectively answered questions, while this fell to 10 per cent in the Bucke, Street and Brown study. The authors found the fall was particularly marked in the groups previously identified as most likely to exercise the right to silence, namely suspects arrested in London, suspects receiving legal advice, black suspects and suspects arrested for serious offences. The fact that the exercise of the right to silence by suspects receiving legal advice fell suggests that advisers are more likely to encourage clients to speak. The authors found no significant rise in confessions with the number of suspects making confessions during police interrogation remaining at 55 per cent in both studies. One officer commented that suspects spoke more but this meant more untruthful accounts. The police officers interviewed on the impact of the CJPOA provisions thought that it had little impact on professional career criminals, as they were still likely to not answer questions, or to offer a prepared statement at the start of the interview and refuse to elaborate on it when questioned.

Bucke, Street and Brown conclude that the CJPOA provisions 'have had a marked impact on suspects' use of silence at the police station; police practices in relation to interviewing and disclosure; the advice given at police stations by legal advisers; the proportion of defendants testifying at trial; the way in which cases are prosecuted and defended at trial; and on judges' directions to the jury' (2000, p. xiii). This in turn has led to more productive interviews and more scope for investigating suspects' accounts. But they did not find any 'discernible increase in charges or convictions' (ibid. at xiii).

Some of the solicitors in their study reported that the CJPOA provisions on silence had made it harder to carry out their task of advising clients because of the complexity of the provisions and the implications of giving advice (2000, p. 24). However, they would still advise silence if the client was vulnerable because of his mental state or if there had been insufficient disclosure by the police. It was clear that they were more likely to advise clients to answer questions than to refrain from doing so. They also, in some cases, prepared statements that would be read out at the start of the interview following which the client refused to answer questions. They were now very cautious in advising clients on the issue of silence.

Bucke, Street and Brown therefore concluded that the CJPOA changes had affected pre-trial and trial practice with a reduction in the numbers remaining silent in interrogation. The police were making regular use of the special warning provisions in ss 36 and 37. They also found a consensus among respondents that more defendants were testifying at trial. Defence lawyers were more likely to advise clients to speak and their advice to clients at the pre-trial stage had also changed. But it was not clear that these changes had led to changes in either charging or conviction of defendants. As we saw earlier, changes in the disclosure regime in the CJIA 1996 had reduced the scope for ambush defences.

Research was also undertaken in Northern Ireland on the impact of the changes in the 1988 Criminal Evidence Order. Jackson *et al.* (2000) found that there was some evidence to suggest that the numbers speaking during interrogation and testifying at trial had increased after the changes. The proportion of scheduled defendants charged with terrorist offences refusing to testify fell from 64 per cent in 1987 to 46 per cent in 1991. For nonterrorist defendants it fell from 23 per cent to 15 per cent. By 1995, 25 per cent of scheduled defendants and 3 per cent of nonscheduled defendants refused to testify. However, they could not find any evidence to show that these changes had resulted in an increase in the conviction rates.

Conclusion

As we have seen, the changes imposed by the legislation were substantial and combined with the other statutory provisions have made inroads into the privilege against self-incrimination. Whether the increase in numbers of suspects speaking was sufficient to justify change is open to debate. It is also questionable whether the changes were necessary, given the new disclosure regime in the CJPOA. It has also generated a sizeable jurisprudence on the interpretation of s 34 and consumed a considerable amount of court time in debating these issues and has led to numerous appeals on misdirections to the jury, leading many commentators, including Birch (1999), to question whether the benefits outweigh the costs of the change. The increased focus on the suspect has also generated Convention challenges. When the 1994 Act was passed, there was speculation on whether it would be Convention compliant but, as we shall see in Chapter 4, it has survived Article 6 challenges. The Strasbourg Court has made clear in *Murray v UK* that the provisions in the Criminal Evidence (Northern Ireland) Order that are comparable to ss 34–38 of the CJPOA, are compatible with the right to a fair trial under Article 6 and that the right is not absolute, although access to a solicitor should be offered because adverse inferences may be drawn from silence. In *Heaney and McGuinness v Ireland* App. No. 34720/97 (21 December 2000) and *Saunders v UK* (App. No. 19187/91) 17 December 1996 the court has focused on the degree of compulsion exerted on the accused and whether the degree of compulsion destroys the essence of the right and renders it ineffective. These issues will be discussed further in Chapter 4.

4
The Influence of International Human Rights Standards on the Treatment of Suspects

Introduction

The contribution of international human rights law to the treatment of suspects, including the right not to be subjected to torture, inhuman or degrading treatment and the privilege against self-incrimination is assessed in this chapter. These rights are enshrined in international human rights law and have been deployed in the context of international criminal trials. The principal focus will be on European Convention jurisprudence which has become much more important since the enactment of the Human Rights Act 1998.

The privilege against self-incrimination and the right to silence have been treated by the Strasbourg Court as essential elements of a fair trial. However, the rights have not been treated as absolute and the situations in which the court has been willing to accept limitations will be discussed. The status of the privilege has been discussed in a wide range of contexts including detention, driving offences, obligations to provide information under financial services law and antiterrorist provisions. Key cases in Strasbourg and in the domestic courts that raise issues of Convention compliance will be considered.

The key sources of international human rights law

International human rights law is relevant to the treatment of suspects in a number of areas: during detention and interrogation by the police and by other state officials; at ports and airports; and in relation to a wide range of offences. The framework of international human rights law governing the treatment of suspects includes the International Covenant on Civil and Political Rights (ICCPR), the UN Universal Declaration of

Human Rights (UDHR) and the European Convention on Human Rights (ECHR). The key rights protected by the Universal Declaration on Human Rights are the right to non-degrading or inhuman treatment and punishment (Article 5) and the right to a fair trial and the presumption of innocence (Article 10). The UN Convention against Torture aims to prevent torture by states. It was adopted by the UN General Assembly in 1984 and came into force in 1987. The UN Committee against Torture (CAT) supervises states to ensure compliance with the Convention. States and individuals can bring complaints. A new Optional Protocol to UNCAT, adopted by the UN General Assembly in 2002, contained provisions for annual inspections and systems of monitoring of detention.

The ICCPR was adopted in 1966 and came into force in 1976. The UN Human Rights Committee established under Article 28 of the ICCPR oversees the implementation of the Covenant. A jurisprudence on treatment in detention has been developed in the Committee's own Reports. The Committee can also make recommendations to states. States can also complain to the Committee regarding the actions of other states and individuals can also approach the Committee when they have exhausted internal remedies. However, the Committee's decisions regarding individual claims and the recommendations in its Reports are not binding on states, although states are under an obligation to provide reports to the Committee, when requested, on measures taken to protect the rights specified in the Covenant. Some states, for example, the United States, have ratified the Convention, but with reservations. States, including New Zealand, have used the ICCPR as the model when drafting their own Bills of Rights.

Key rights in the ICCPR relevant to the treatment of suspects are the right to life, protected by Article 6, the prohibition on the use of torture, cruel, inhuman or degrading treatment or punishment in Article 7, the right to liberty protected by Article 9, so that the citizen should not be subject to unlawful or arbitrary arrest or detention, and the requirement that those deprived of their liberty should be treated 'with humanity and with respect for the inherent dignity of the human person' in Article 10. Article 14(1) protects the right to a fair and public hearing and Article 14(2) stipulates that everyone charged with a criminal offence shall have the right to be presumed innocent until proved guilty according to law. Article 14(3)(g) states that the individual may not be compelled to testify against himself or to confess guilt.

The rights of the accused are also protected at the International Criminal Court and at the tribunals which have investigated human rights abuses in the former Yugoslavia and Rwanda. A new jurisprudence of international criminal law has emerged from these new institutions. The UN's International Criminal Tribunal for the former Yugoslavia (ICTY) deals with war crimes that took place in the Balkans in the 1990s. It was established in 1993 and is the first war crimes tribunal created by the United Nations since the Nuremberg and Tokyo Tribunals. Its Rules of Procedure and Evidence give suspects the right to be assisted by counsel and for the cost to be paid by the tribunal if the suspect is unable to meet those costs, the right to remain silent, the right to be cautioned that any statements made shall be recorded and used in evidence, and the right to have the questioning audio or video recorded (IT/32/Rev.49). The suspect must be told of his right to legal assistance and for it to be provided without payment, of the right to remain silent, and cautioned that any statements may be used in evidence and that questioning shall not proceed without presence of counsel unless the suspect has voluntarily waived that right. If he changes his mind and decides he does wants counsel present, then the questioning should cease until that demand is met. If these safeguards are not followed, then the statements obtained from the suspect may be excluded at trial. Questioning of the suspect should not take place without counsel unless the suspect has waived his right. These provisions reflect the principle of equality of arms, that all parties should be equal before the tribunal, and are modelled on Article 14 of the ICCPR.

Similar due process rights are found in the *Rules of Procedure and Evidence*, adopted on 29 June 1995 by the International Criminal Tribunal for Rwanda (ICTR) established by UN Security Council Resolution 955 of 8 November 1994. The tribunal's aim is to prosecute persons responsible for genocide and other serious violations of international humanitarian law in Rwanda in 1994. The accused appearing at the tribunal, based in Arusha, has the right to examine witnesses and the right to an adversarial trial. The ICTY and ICTR were concerned with specific conflicts at specific times but they made clear the need for an independent permanent court, namely the International Criminal Court (ICC). The ICC, based in The Hague, is independent from the United Nations and is the first permanent treaty-based international criminal court. It was created by the Rome Statute to bring to justice perpetrators of serious crimes of concern to the international community, including genocide, crimes against humanity and war crimes. The Rome Statute, which is the legal basis for the establishment of the ICC, came into force in July 2002 and now has 139 signatories and 122 ratifications. Cases can be referred to the ICC by states parties or the UN Security Council. It affords the accused the highest standards of due process and principles including the presumption of innocence until the Prosecutor has proved guilt beyond reasonable doubt. It reflects both adversarial and inquisitorial principles, but has fewer constraints on evidence than adversarial systems, and the key principle governing investigation and trial in international human rights law is fairness.

The rights of the accused during an investigation are set out in Article 55 of the Rome Statute:

1. In respect of an investigation under this Statute, a person:
    (a) Shall not be compelled to incriminate himself or herself or to confess guilt;
    (b) Shall not be subjected to any form of coercion, duress or threat, to torture or to any other form of cruel, inhuman or degrading treatment or punishment;
    (c) Shall, if questioned in a language other than a language the person fully understands and speaks, have, free of any cost, the assistance of a competent interpreter and such translations as are necessary to meet the requirements of fairness; and
    (d) Shall not be subjected to arbitrary arrest or detention, and shall not be deprived of his or her liberty except on such grounds and in accordance with such procedures as are established in this Statute.
2. Where there are grounds to believe that a person has committed a crime within the jurisdiction of the Court and that person is about to be questioned either by the Prosecutor, or by national authorities pursuant to a request made under Part 9, that person shall also have the following rights of which he or she shall be informed prior to being questioned:
    (a) To be informed, prior to being questioned, that there are grounds to believe that he or she has committed a crime within the jurisdiction of the Court;
    (b) To remain silent, without such silence being a consideration in the determination of guilt or innocence;
    (c) To have legal assistance of the person's choosing, or, if the person does not have legal assistance, to have legal assistance assigned to him or her, in any case where the interests of justice so require, and without payment by the person in any such case if the person does not have sufficient means to pay for it; and
    (d) To be questioned in the presence of counsel unless the person has voluntarily waived his or her right to counsel.

The accused has the right to conduct his own defence or to use counsel. All questioning should be audio or video recorded (Rules of Procedure and Evidence 1CC-ASP/1/3 (Part II A 2002)). Article 55(2)(b) of the ICC Rome Statute also requires that the suspect is informed of his right to be questioned in the presence of counsel and goes further in advising the suspect that if he decides to remain silent this decision cannot be taken account of in determining guilt. These Rules should be applied by the court in its proceedings under Article 21 of the Rome Statute. The court's jurisdiction is limited to events since 1 July 2002 and so far 20 cases have been brought before it.

These new institutions have drawn on both civil law and common law traditions in developing their procedures. Statements obtained in breach of rights are not automatically excluded. Evidence obtained in breach of the ICC Statute or internationally recognised human rights is excluded if it is unreliable if admitting it would be antithetical to or seriously damage the integrity of the proceedings. There are similar provisions for the ICTY: 'no evidence shall be admissible if obtained by methods which cast substantial doubt on its reliability, or if its admission is antithetical to, or would seriously damage the integrity of the proceedings'. While this exclusion is discretionary rather than automatic, the tribunals, as Fairlie (2013) observes, have exercised their discretion robustly, for example in the *Karemera, Bagosora* and *Delalic* cases. Evidence has been excluded by the tribunals where they are not satisfied that statements have been made voluntarily or that the suspect has voluntarily waived his right to counsel.

In the UK, the principal source of protection for suspects and detainees in interrogation and at trial is the European Convention on Human Rights. The Convention came into force in 1953 and in recent years has been used extensively by detainees to challenge both their initial detention and their treatment at later stages of the criminal justice process. Rights closely follow those in the Universal Declaration of Human Rights. Article 3 protects the right not to be subjected to torture and inhuman or degrading treatment or punishment. Article 6, the right to a fair trial, includes 'the right to a fair and public hearing within a reasonable time by an independent and impartial tribunal established by law (Article 6(1)) and the right to be 'presumed innocent until proved guilty by a court of law' (Article 6(2)). In addition remand and sentenced prisoners' rights are protected by the European Prison Rules.

The European Committee for the Prevention of Torture (CPT) has also played an important role in protecting suspects in detention. It was established under the European Convention for the Prevention of Torture and Inhuman or Degrading Treatment of Punishment, which has been in force since 1989. The Committee conducts periodic visits to places of detention, including police stations, prisons, immigration centres and psychiatric hospitals. It aims to strengthen the protection of detainees from torture, inhuman or degrading treatment or punishment. It publishes General Reports as well as Reports on member states of the Council of Europe and its findings have generated standards covering a wide range of aspects of detention which are then used to assess states' standards on periodic visits. However, the Committee's findings are not binding on states and the Committee does not have a judicial function in contrast to the Strasbourg Court, but its reports have a significant impact and potentially affect large numbers of detainees. Although police detention is scrutinised by the CPT, recent reports on the UK have focused primarily on conditions in prison and young offenders.

International human rights law has improved the treatment of suspects, protecting their right to life, liberty and a fair trial in the UK. It has influenced the principles and practices of the treatment of suspects here and in many other jurisdictions and provided a framework for their humane treatment, both in interrogation and at trial. A jurisprudence of international human rights law has also developed and absorbed ideas from different jurisdictions and from the relevant case law arising from rights challenges under other international human rights Conventions. In drawing from these different sources, law has become more cosmopolitan and we find a cross-fertilisation of ideas in the various sources of law. So Convention jurisprudence has drawn from the findings of the CPT, for example, in criticising conditions of detention in *Peers v Greece* App. No. 28524/95 (19 April 2001) and the CPT in turn has referred to the court's findings. In addition, the Convention constitutes a guiding principle of European Union law.

Jackson and Summers (2012) argue that a common evidentiary framework is developing and 'key tenets of the rationalist tradition of evidence have been adapted across the common law and civil law traditions' (p. 29). Individual rights in the international human rights instruments adopted post-war have shaped evidentiary standards around the notions of equality of arms and adversarial rights, with reference to the privilege against self-incrimination, the right to a fair trial, the right to legal assistance and disclosure and the right to cross-examination. Although a sharp dichotomy is often drawn by evidence scholars between the adversarial system of exclusionary rules and the inquisitorial system of free proof, both systems have evolved with the key focus on the participation of the accused in the trial. They suggest that the Strasbourg Court has 'developed its own jurisprudence through the principles of the equality of arms and the right to an adversarial trial which is transforming rather than merely mixing together the two traditions' and see the court's model as participatory rather than adversarial or inquisitorial (ibid., p. 102).

The European Convention on Human Rights

The Convention has been the principal method by which international human rights law and standards have been applied to the treatment of suspects. With the passing of the Human Rights Act in 1998, Convention rights have become embedded in the domestic courts and a rights culture has developed. It is clear that the Strasbourg Court has played a key role in increasing the procedural rights of suspects in the UK. However, even before the HRA was passed the Convention had been used to challenge the treatment of the suspect in detention as well as in court. The court has treated the Convention as a living instrument which can respond to new conditions. The key rights for detainees are the right to life protected by Article 2, which has been invoked in relation to deaths in custody, and the procedures used to investigate them, as well as the use of lethal force on suspects. So the UK was found in breach of Article 2, the right to life, in *McCann and others v UK* App. No. 18948/91 (27 September 1995). The case concerned the killing by SAS officers in Gibraltar in 1988 of Daniel McCann, Sean Savage and Mairead Farrell, who were suspected of an impending terrorist attack on Gibraltar. No weapons were found on them or in their car, although a car rented by them in Spain contained Semtex and detonators. The court was critical of the automatic use of lethal force, the decision not to prevent them entering Gibraltar and the failure to allow for the possibility that the available intelligence was wrong. However, the court did not conclude that there was evidence of a premeditated execution plan but the operation as whole was not controlled in a way that respected Article 2. Within the context of detention and imprisonment Article 2 has also been used to improve the review procedures following deaths in custody, for example, in *Edwards v UK* App. No. 46477/99 (14 March 2002).

Other rights relevant to suspects are found in Article 3 which states that 'No one shall be subjected to torture or to inhuman or degrading treatment or punishment'; Article 5, which protects the right to liberty and security of person: everyone deprived of his liberty by arrest or detention is entitled to take proceedings to challenge the lawfulness of his detention and to do so speedily; and Article 6, the right to a fair trial. Article 6 is a wide-ranging right which has been used to assert the right to a fair and independent tribunal, the right to a hearing within a reasonable time, the right to legal representation and for a lawyer to be provided if the person cannot pay, the right to defend oneself in person or via a lawyer, the right to disclosure of material to the defence, the right to silence and the privilege against self-incrimination, the right to be given reasons for decisions as well as the principle of equality of arms. The accused should be able to defend himself without being at a disadvantage compared to the state or another party. Article 6(3) has been construed as entailing the right to disclosure of evidence on which the prosecution relies. What constitutes a fair trial may be open to argument and neither the presumption of innocence protected by Article 6(2), 'Everyone charged with a criminal offence shall be presumed innocent until proved guilty according to law', nor the right to legal representation referred to in Article 6(3), have been treated as absolute. The range of tribunals to which Article 6 applies has also been disputed. Nonetheless, while these principles of natural justice were well established in the common law, they have been further strengthened with the passing of the Human Rights Act. Further rights of importance to suspects and detainees are found in Article 8, the right to respect for the individual's private life, home and correspondence, which has been used to challenge the retention of DNA samples; Article 13, the right to an effective remedy when a Convention right is infringed by a national authority; and Article 14, the right not to be discriminated against in relation to other Convention rights, which has been used, for example, in relation to the discriminatory treatment of foreign nationals. Reference is often made to the 'rights revolution' in law and procedure and the impact of the Convention, strengthened by the Human Rights Act, has been substantial. All new legislation, primary and secondary, must be Convention compliant. Moreover, there have been numerous Convention challenges brought to Strasbourg and within the domestic courts on fair trial rights and other issues which, when successful, have improved the position of suspects and detainees in the UK. Before the Human Rights Act the procedures were lengthy and cumbersome in achieving a remedy. It could take many years to bring a case before the court and until 1998 all cases had to be assessed first by the European Commission on Human Rights to rule on their admissibility. Furthermore, in recent years the court has been more interventionist and has been more critical of prison conditions and less tolerant of reductions in the living conditions of detainees based on grounds of cost.

But when we look specifically at the jurisprudence on the treatment of suspects in interrogation, a more measured approach may be needed regarding the 'rights revolution' as the Strasbourg Court's commitment to procedural due process rights has wavered as it has tried to balance public interest issues with individuals' rights. In addition, many cases have failed in Strasbourg because more weight was given to other interests. On the one hand, the court has robustly defended the fair trial rights of the accused, including the privilege against self-incrimination, even in the face of strong public interest claims, but in some cases on preventive detention it has given more weight to states' claims of threats to the public and has been tolerant of the extension of 'temporary' measures. The court has been willing to defer to states' views on whether measures that limit rights should be temporary or imposed for longer periods in response to terrorist threats. In considering applicants' treatment the court has used the principle of proportionality to consider whether infringements of rights meet legitimate aims and whether they are necessary or could be achieved by less restrictive means. The principle of proportionality applied in evaluating limits on rights has proved to be very malleable. Moreover, in implementing rights under the Convention, states have been allowed a wide margin of appreciation, including in relation to the rules of evidence. While it is essential for states to ensure a fair trial, formulating specific rules on the admissibility of evidence has been seen largely as a matter for states. In addition, where there have been breaches of rights, derogations from Convention rights have also been made by the UK Government under Article 15(1) of the Convention, which allows states to derogate 'in times of war or other public emergency threatening the life of the nation'. The United Kingdom has also tried to avoid Article 6 and Article 7 claims by the creation of civil orders in a wide range of areas including controls on the movements of sex offenders and in dealing with antisocial behaviour, even though their breach may incur custodial penalties.

Furthermore, where rights claims have succeeded, this has, in some cases, led to considerable hostility to the Human Rights Act and to the Convention on the part of the UK Government, sections of the media and the public, fuelling demands for a withdrawal from the Convention. The UK Government is considering a British Bill of Rights and the Conservative Party has said that abolishing the HRA will be part of its manifesto for the next election. A Commission was set up by the government to examine a UK Bill of Rights in 2011 and it reported in

December 2012. The majority of the Commission were in favour of a UK Bill, with two members of the panel dissenting (Commission on a Bill of Rights, 2012). While currently remaining a party to the Convention, the UK Government has stressed the importance of reform and argued for a broader margin of appreciation for states on issues where questions have been fully considered by the courts in the context of UK domestic law and procedure. The debate has crystallized around the failure to deport foreign national offenders, because of their impact on the right to family life and the pressure from Strasbourg to grant sentenced prisoners' voting rights, and the compensation paid to offenders for violations of their human rights while in custody.

We also find increasing tension between the domestic courts and Strasbourg in recent years, as the domestic courts have started to challenge the authority of the Strasbourg Court in certain areas and to argue that many of the problems facing the court can be addressed more effectively within the domestic law context, for example in relation to the admissibility of hearsay evidence (Dennis, 2010; Jones, 2010; O'Brian, 2011). This issue was considered in a line of cases including *Al-Khawaja and Tahery v UK* (2009) 49 EHRR 1 where the Strasbourg Court had affirmed the right to confrontation and said that it would be wrong to base a conviction solely or mainly on an untested statement despite any counterbalancing factors. This issue was reconsidered after *Al-Khawaja* by the Court of Appeal in *R v Horncastle and others* [2009] 2 Cr App R 15, but the court remained of the view that Article 6 was not breached where a conviction was based solely or mainly on hearsay evidence and admitted under the Criminal Justice Act 2003, and this was upheld by the Supreme Court. It was not appropriate that there should be an absolute rule demanding automatic exclusion, so that counterbalancing measures could never be sufficient where the evidence was sole or decisive. The Law Commission and Parliament had considered this when they drafted the 2003 Criminal Justice Act. Some hearsay evidence is reliable and the jury may be trusted to assess the weight of the evidence. It is very rare that a case relies only on hearsay evidence as in most cases there is other available evidence. Moreover, there is the safeguard that the judge can stop the case if the hearsay evidence is unconvincing. The Supreme Court upheld the Appeal Court's decision in *R v Horncastle and others* [2010] 2 WLR 47. It noted that the European Court's jurisprudence on Article 6(3) had developed primarily in cases drawn from civil law jurisdictions and did not fully consider the safeguards present in common law systems.

The case of *Al-Khawaja and Tahery v UK* App. Nos. 26766/05 and 2228/05 (15 December 2011) then went to the Grand Chamber in 2011 which, to some extent, did take account of the view of the Supreme Court on the appropriate test and examined the available safeguards. In Al-Khawaja's case, the jury was able to assess the reliability of a second witness's allegation against the first witness. The admission of the statement was an important fact to be placed in the balance alongside procedural safeguards and those in the 2003 Criminal Justice Act were effective. The court concluded that where a hearsay statement was the sole or decisive evidence against the accused, its admission in evidence will not automatically result in a breach of Article 6(1). But if a conviction is based solely decisively on the evidence of absent witnesses it will subject the proceedings to the most searching scrutiny. So strong procedural safeguards and counterbalancing factors will be considered. The trial judge has the discretion to refuse to admit a hearsay statement if it is satisfied that the case for exclusion outweighs the case for admission. The court acknowledged the different systems and procedures but emphasised that it must apply the standard of review required by Article 6(3) irrespective of the system from which the case derives. The most recent conflict has been on the use of whole life sentences. In *Vinter and others v UK* App. Nos. 66069/09, 130/10 and 3896/10 (9 July 2013) the Strasbourg Court ruled that the whole life tariff where there is no prospect of release or review of the sentence breached Article 3. However, the Court of Appeal in *McLoughlin v R* [2014] EWCA Crim 188 argued that the Strasbourg Court was wrong in finding that the UK regime conflicts with Article 3 as there is a possibility of review as the offender can appeal to the Secretary of State for release on compassionate grounds in exceptional cases. Irrespective of the merits of the decision, these cases indicate a greater confidence of the domestic courts in challenging Strasbourg decisions and a willingness on the part of both courts to enter into a dialogue.

The interrogation of suspects

When the Criminal Justice and Public Order Act was passed in 1994 it was widely thought that it could come into conflict with the Convention and that the government would be forced to amend it because of Convention challenges. The UN Human Rights Committee in its Report in 1995 cited the changes to the right to silence as a particularly serious problem and a violation of Article 14 of the ICCPR (CCCPR/C/79, 1995). It thought that there was a danger that vulnerable suspects would be intimidated and that the provisions violated the UK's international treaty obligations. Convention challenges to the 1994 provisions and their predecessor, the Criminal Evidence (Northern Ireland) Order 1988, started to reach the Strasbourg Court by the mid-1990s. A key issue was the absence of a requirement for the opportunity of access to legal advice before permitting adverse inferences from silence.

The Criminal Evidence Order, as originally drafted, did not require the opportunity to consult a lawyer before the court was allowed to draw adverse inferences from silence. This issue was considered in the case of *R v Dermot Quinn* (23 December 1991) in Belfast Crown Court where the trial judge rejected the argument that inferences should not be drawn under Article 3, because the defendant had been interviewed by the police before his legal adviser arrived and that to do so would be unfair. The Northern Ireland Court of Appeal upheld the trial judge's ruling that the absence or denial of legal advice did not prevent the drawing of adverse inferences under Article 3 of the Order (*R v Dermot Quinn*, 17 September 1993). Quinn had been interviewed without a solicitor present, under the EPA, which did not give a right to legal advice and included powers to delay access.

However, the Strasbourg Court took a different approach when it considered the issue in *Murray v UK* App. No. 18731/91 (8 February 1996), where the court stressed the right of access to legal advice was crucial for fairness to be ensured under the Order. John Murray was charged with conspiracy to murder, aiding and abetting the false imprisonment of an informer and being a member of the IRA. He was arrested in a house in which a Provisional IRA informer had been held captive. His access to a solicitor was denied for 48 hours despite his expressly requesting a lawyer. He was interviewed at Castlereagh 12 times in two days, during which he remained silent. He saw a lawyer for the first time before the final two interviews, but the lawyer was not permitted to attend the interviews. The solicitor advised Murray to remain silent and he followed this advice in interrogation and at trial. He was convicted by a Diplock court which drew adverse inferences from his silence and this was upheld by the Court of Appeal. So the issues for the Strasbourg Court to consider were whether the provisions of the Criminal Evidence Order, allowing adverse inferences from silence and the delays in access to legal advice, breached his Article 6 rights to a fair trial and to the presumption of innocence. The case was considered first by the Commission who ruled that Murray had not been denied his right to silence, despite the use of the Order provisions, because he *had* remained silent and not given evidence against himself. The Commission noted that the adverse inference was drawn by a judge who was required to give a reasoned judgement, including the reasons why he was drawing an adverse inference and the weight given to them. This could be reviewed by the Appeal Court, so there were more safeguards than in jury trials. But denial of access to legal advice did breach Article 6. The Commission stressed that if inferences may be drawn from silence it is crucial that access to legal advice be granted as soon as possible. The rights of the defence in this case were adversely affected by limits on the right of access to a solicitor. The Commission's findings were upheld by the court. The court decided that, given the consequences of the Order, it was essential that the accused had access to a lawyer during police interrogation. When evidential significance is attached to silence it is crucial that legal advice is available and that detainees are fully aware of the case against them. However, the court said that drawing inferences from the refusal to account for one's presence at a place could not be regarded as unreasonable or unfair in the circumstances and the provisions in the Order allowing adverse inferences did not breach Article 6. But Article 6 was breached by the denial of access to a lawyer in the first 48 hours of detention. If the state permits adverse inferences to be drawn from silence then it is crucial that the suspect has access to legal advice in deciding whether or not to remain silent.

The court held that the right to remain silent and the privilege against self-incrimination, although not specifically mentioned in Article 6, were generally recognised international standards which lie at the heart of the notion of a fair procedure under the Convention and it would be incompatible with them to base a conviction solely on the accused's silence or a refusal to answer questions in interrogation or at trial. But at the same time, the accused's silence could be taken into account in assessing the persuasiveness of the prosecution's case in situations that clearly called for an explanation from him. Whether the drawing of adverse inferences breached Article 6 was a matter to be determined in the light of all the circumstances in the case, including the inferences that might be drawn, the weight attached to them by the national courts in their assessment of the evidence and the degree of compulsion inherent in the situation. In Murray's case, he had been able to remain silent in interrogation and in court despite the warnings and was a noncompellable witness and silence on its own could not be seen as indicating guilt. Although there was a level of indirect compulsion in the warnings received, he could not be compelled to speak or to testify. The proceedings were conducted by an experienced judge in a Diplock court and warnings were given before adverse inferences could be drawn. The prosecution had to establish a prima facie case against the accused and the trial judge retained a discretion not to use the silence provisions against the accused if appropriate. The question in each case was whether the evidence adduced by the prosecution was sufficiently strong to require an answer. If an explanation was called for, then a failure to respond could allow, as a matter of common sense, the drawing of an adverse inference that there is no explanation and the accused is guilty. The court rejected the claim that drawing inferences under the Order shifted the burden of proof or undermined the presumption of innocence.

Murray was significant in requiring access to legal advice before allowing adverse inferences to be drawn from silence, and subsequently the law was amended to take account of this requirement. Section 58 of the Youth Justice and Criminal Evidence Act 1999 gives effect to this decision and provides that ss 34–8 of the CJPOA do not apply if the accused had not been allowed an opportunity to consult a solicitor prior to being questioned or charged or before a request to account for his presence or objects, substances or marks. The Criminal Evidence Order in Northern Ireland was similarly amended. Section 58(4) also defines an authorised place of detention to include interrogation by Revenue and Customs officers. However, *Murray* also provided the stamp of approval to the new limits on the right to silence in both the Order and the CJPOA.

In *Averill v UK* App. No. 36408/97 (9 June 2000), the applicant was convicted by a Diplock court in connection with two murders. He had been detained in 1994 under the Prevention of Terrorism (Temporary Provisions) Act 1989. He argued that he had been denied his right to a fair trial under Article 6(1) because the judge drew adverse inferences from his silence and also denied his right to be presumed innocent under Article 6(2) and claimed that the denial of access to a solicitor for the first 24 hours breached Articles 6(1) and 6(3). By the time the case went to Strasbourg he had escaped from the Maze prison and was at large. The Strasbourg Court thought that the denial of the solicitor for 24 hours was incompatible with his rights under Article 6(1) in conjunction with Article 6(3). It was unfair to deny him access to a lawyer. However, it found no violation in relation to the adverse inferences drawn from silence. The court followed the approach in *Murray* and stressed that adequate safeguards were in place. The trial judge was under no obligation to draw adverse inferences and had to give reasons for his decision. There was strong incriminating forensic evidence in the case and the judge had been persuaded by that as well as drawing negative inferences from silence. Averill could reasonably have been expected to give an explanation in the circumstances, so neither Article 6(1) nor Article 6(2) had been breached in relation to the drawing of adverse inferences. In a later case, *Salduz v Turkey* App. No. 36391/02 (27 November 2008), the Strasbourg Court said that before a suspect is interviewed he should have the opportunity to consult a solicitor and this should apply whether or not adverse inferences may be drawn from silence. This was a fundamental safeguard for the suspect.

Conditions in detention and extended detention

Conditions in detention have also become subject to more scrutiny by the courts as prisons have become increasingly assessed against human rights standards (see, van Zyl Smit and Snacken, 2009; Easton, 2011). However, the review of conditions in detention has also included immigration removal centres, as well as police cells and the same principles have been applied to these different contexts. Section 76 of PACE, which regulates police interrogation in England and Wales, and which prohibits the use of torture and inhuman and degrading treatment and punishment, is modelled on Article 3 of the European Convention. Similar provisions are found in Article 5 of the UNDHR and Article 7 of the ICCPR. Article 3 of the ECHR is particularly valuable because it is non-derogable so it cannot be legitimately breached, even in times of public emergency or extreme civil unrest. Periodic visits by the European Committee for the Prevention of Torture have provided a further level of surveillance of detention. However, detainees in England and Wales are more likely to use the ECHR to pursue rights claims. As well as the treatment of suspects in detention, the Strasbourg Court has also considered whole life sentences for exceptionally grave crimes and extended detention under emergency provisions which also raise Article 5 issues.

In *Ireland v UK* App. No. 5310/71 (18 January 1978) the Strasbourg Court found that five of the 'in-depth' techniques of interrogation used at a Northern Ireland holding centre were inhuman and degrading, in breach of Article 3 of the Convention, from which no derogation is possible, but did not think they constituted torture, disagreeing with the Commission on this point. The detainees had been subjected to sensory deprivation, made to wear hoods over their heads, forced to stand against walls in a stress position, deprived of sleep, food and drink and subjected to continuous noise. The UN Human Rights Committee has also been critical of the infringement of civil liberties resulting from the use of emergency laws and of treatment in detention centres and the failure to comply with the ICCPR.

These issues have resurfaced in more recent decisions. The House of Lords in *A and others v Secretary of State for the Home Department* [2005] UKHL 71 ruled that statements obtained by torture overseas could not be used in proceedings in the UK. To do so would undermine the integrity of the judicial process. In *Jalloh v Germany* App. No. 54810 (11 July 2006) the Strasbourg Court stressed that even in the most difficult circumstances, such as the fight against terrorism and organised crime, the Convention prohibits in absolute terms torture and inhuman or degrading treatment or punishment irrespective of the victim's conduct (para 99). The use of evidence obtained by torture would breach Article 3 regardless of the weight of that evidence (para 105). In this case a suspected drug dealer was forced to vomit concealed drugs by having a tube put through his nose. The court did not think this amounted to torture, but it did constitute inhuman and degrading treatment and to admit the evidence of the drugs obtained in this way did breach Article 6. The court stressed that if evidence obtained in violation of Article 3 were introduced in criminal proceedings, it renders the trial as a whole unfair. However, the court seemed to leave open that ill treatment other than torture would not automatically lead to exclusion, but would be balanced against other safeguards and the public interest in prosecuting drug traffickers.

The issue of extended detention has also been frequently discussed by the courts. Until 1988 the powers of arrest under the Prevention of Terrorism Act allowed the police to arrest without a warrant a person whom the officer has reasonable grounds of suspecting to have a connection with terrorism. The suspect did not need to be suspected of a specific offence and could be held for seven days without charge. In *Brogan and others v UK* App. Nos. 11209/84, 11234/84 and 11266/84 (29 November 1988), the applicants, Brogan, Coyle, McFadden and Tracey, had been detained in Northern Ireland for periods from four to over six days, suspected of being involved in the commission, preparation or instigation of acts of terrorism under s 12 of the PTA 1984. The arrest was lawful under domestic law. However, the court held that detention for such a long period without being brought before a judicial authority, or being released promptly, did contravene Article 5(3) of the Convention, although it found no breaches of Articles 5(4) or 5(5). Article 5(3) provides that everyone arrested or detained in accordance with paragraph (1)(c) of Article 5 'shall be brought promptly before a judge or other officer authorized by law to exercise judicial power and shall be entitled to trial within a reasonable time or to release pending trial'. In *Brogan* the court said the particular circumstances of this case could not justify impairing the essence of the right guaranteed by Article 5(3).

Brogan is one of a long line of cases where the court was critical of the UK's treatment of suspects undergoing interrogation in Northern Ireland. The court acknowledged the problem of the increased terrorist threat to society but stressed the need for a proper balance between the defence of the institutions of democracy in the common interest and the protection of individual rights (para 48). The court said in *Brogan* that the fact that the arrest and detention was inspired by a legitimate aim to protect the community from terrorism was not, on its own, sufficient to ensure compliance with the specific requirements of Article 5(3) (at para 62). In response to the *Brogan* judgement the UK Government did not want to reduce the maximum period of detention and did not see judicial control as appropriate or feasible, and thought the existing powers to arrest and detain were necessary to control terrorism. It therefore decided to derogate using Article 15 of the Convention and Article 4 of the ICCPR, which allows for temporary deviations from provisions in times of public emergency threatening the life of the nation.

Most international treaties contain provisions for derogation at times of public emergency, including war and civil war. But even when states derogate, they still retain their other obligations under international law and should act in ways consistent with them. The UK has used Article 15 to derogate in response to concerns over terrorism in Northern Ireland and after 9/11. Article 15 jurisprudence makes clear that the state must be in actual and imminent danger, exposed to serious violence and political and social conflicts that threaten the life of the community. However, after *Brogan* suspects were held for shorter periods in the 1990s under the amended counter-terrorism provisions and access to a lawyer in interrogation was granted more readily (see Chapter 7).

The issue of extended detention under the PTA was reconsidered by the Strasbourg Court in *Brannigan and McBride v UK* App. Nos. 14553/89 and 14554/89 (25 May 1993). The court considered the UK's obligations under both the ECHR and the ICCPR. Brannigan had been detained for over six days with access to a solicitor delayed for 48 hours and McBride detained over four days. Brannigan and McBride challenged the lack of judicial control over the process of extended detention while the UK Government argued the need for extended detention to combat terrorism. The court noted the continuing threat of terrorism in Northern Ireland, and the fact that in the period 1972–1992 there had been over 3,000 deaths and many more injuries due to terrorism. While the death rate in the mid-1980s was lower than the early 1970s, the threat remained serious. The court was satisfied that there was an emergency at the relevant time of the applicants' detention in 1988 and that the UK Government had not exceeded its margin of appreciation. The majority of the court held that derogation from Article 5(3) in relation to detention in excess of four days was lawful as the threat of terrorist activity was sufficiently serious to justify the use of emergency measures under the PTA, including extended detention which prima facie breached Article 5. However, critics, including Liberty, questioned whether the measures were strictly required by the exigencies of the situation and whether the danger was sufficiently serious or exceptional. It is precisely at times of conflict and insecurity that human rights protection is crucial.

So although the court has become more interventionist in terms of conditions of detention inside prison, it has allowed considerable latitude to states to take account of the threat of terrorism, has widened the margin of appreciation to deal with suspects accordingly and has been willing to countenance the extension of temporary limits on rights to deal with that threat. After 9/11 the UK Government faced the problem of dealing with the threat from foreign nationals suspected of being involved in supporting and assisting al-Qaeda, who could not be deported to their states of origin because of fear of Article 3 breaches. The government therefore introduced extended powers of arrest and detention of foreign nationals in the Anti-Terrorism, Crime and Security Act 2001, initially intended as a temporary measure for 15 months and then to be reviewed annually by Parliament.

In *A and others v UK* App. No. 3455/05 (19 February 2009) the Strasbourg Court upheld the derogation notice filed in 2001 after 9/11 by the UK. It noted that the measures the UK Government had taken were reviewed annually by Parliament and the court would not disapprove them because they were not temporary. The applicants in *A* were 16 individuals detained under the Act, initially at Belmarsh, who challenged their detention as breaches of their rights under Articles 3, 5, 13 and 14. The Act included a power of appeal to the Special Immigration Appeal Commission so this case was first considered by the SIAC who thought there was a public emergency, but the measures adopted could not be objectively justified. The Court of Appeal disagreed and said there was objective justification and a rational connexion between the detention of non-nationals who could not be deported and the purpose of removing them, in *A and others v Secretary of State for the Home Department*

[2002] 20 EWCA Civ 1502. However, the House of Lords in *A and others v Secretary of State for the Home Department* [2004] UKHL 56 issued a declaration of incompatibility as in their Lordships' view it was a disproportionate response to the threat and discriminatory.

In Strasbourg the court found no breach of Articles 3 or 13 but did find breaches of Articles 5 (1), 5(4) and 5(5) in relation to some of the applicants. There was an emergency threatening the life of the nation, but the measures were disproportionate in discriminating between nationals and non-nationals in the system of preventive detention. The use of secret evidence by the SIAC violated the Article 5(4) rights of some of the applicants as they needed full details of allegations against them to instruct their advisers. There was no justification to support the distinction between nationals and non-nationals and immigration measures should not have been used to address security issues. But the court did not consider the derogation invalid even though it was not temporary. The applicants' treatment in detention was criticised by the CPT in its report published in 2005, but their findings were disputed by the UK Government. In January 2005 the government announced its intention to repeal part 4 of the Act and replace it with Control Orders restricting the movements of those suspected of involvement with terrorism. The applicants in *A* were released and subject to Control Orders instead under the Prevention of Terrorism Act 2005, but these orders were soon subject to further challenges and replaced by the less restrictive Terrorism Prevention and Investigation Measures (TPIMs).

The Strasbourg Court has also furthered the protection of the suspect in relation to access to legal advice. After *Murray* the court considered other issues relating to the CJPOA, including the implications of acting on legal advice. It has also placed more weight than the domestic courts on reliance on legal advice. In *Condron v UK* App. No. 35718/97 (2 May 2000), the applicants had remained silent on legal advice because they felt ill, suffering the effects of heroin withdrawal, although the police doctor deemed them fit to be interviewed, and were convicted of supplying heroin and possessing heroin with intent to supply. They argued that the trial judge's direction left the jury the option of drawing adverse inferences from the silence in interview even if they thought there was an adequate explanation for it and this breached Article 6(1). The Strasbourg Court thought that more weight should have been given to the reliance on legal advice and the jury had not been properly directed. They should have been directed that they could only draw adverse inferences if they were satisfied the applicants' silence could be sensibly attributed to their having no answer, or none that would stand up to cross-examination and their rights under Article 6(1) were therefore breached. In *Beckles v UK* App. No. 44652/98 (8 October 2002), the applicant argued that he had remained silent during interrogation on the advice of his solicitor. He claimed his right to a fair trial under Article 6(1) had been breached because the trial judge left the jury the option of drawing adverse inferences despite the circumstances of his silence. The Strasbourg Court agreed that the trial judge's direction was not given in a manner compatible with the exercise by the applicant of his right to silence protected by Article 6(1). The judge failed to give sufficient weight in his direction to the applicant's explanation for his silence in police interview. The direction did not contain reference to all matters that went to the plausibility of Beckles's explanation for a no-comment interview and therefore his rights under Article 6(1) had been infringed. Subsequently, the Court of Appeal quashed Beckles's conviction even though he had been convicted prior to the enactment of the Human Rights Act (*R v Beckles* [2004] EWCA Crim 2766).

The privilege against self-incrimination and the presumption of innocence

The importance of the privilege and the right to silence as established international standards has been emphasised in a line of cases in Strasbourg. However, the rationale and normative foundation of these rights has not always been fully expounded and the principles have not been applied consistently. Key rights relevant to the privilege against self-incrimination are the right to privacy and the presumption of innocence, which have figured frequently in Strasbourg's jurisprudence. The right to silence is predicated on the presumption of innocence and the principle that the burden of proof is on the prosecution to prove the guilt of the defendant. This *Woolmington* principle underpins English criminal law. However, inroads have been made into it. Although there is only one common law exception – insanity – there are numerous statutes that place the burden on the defendant expressly, for example, s 1 of the Prevention of Crime Act 1953 states that: 'Any person who without lawful authority or reasonable excuse, the proof whereof shall lie on him, has with him in any public place any offensive weapon shall be guilty of an offence'.

In addition, the burden may be placed on the accused by implication, where the defendant relies on any exception, exemption, proviso, excuse or qualification, as stipulated in s 101 of the Magistrates' Courts Act 1980 and applied in the Crown Court following *R v Hunt* [1987] AC 352.

Ashworth and Blake (1996) found that 40 per cent of offences triable in the Crown Court in 1995 departed from the *Woolmington* principle. Since then Parliament has continued to draft statutes with express exceptions and the courts have upheld express and implied exceptions before and after the Human Rights Act. In deciding whether Parliament intended to reverse the burden, the courts have considered issues including the seriousness of the offence and corresponding sentence length, the ease with which the accused can bear the burden, and the costs to the state of placing the burden on the prosecution, for example in licence and environmental protection cases. Where there are road safety issues, for instance, the domestic courts have been more willing to construe burdens on the defence as legal burdens, in contrast to cases involving very serious offences attracting long sentences, such as the membership of proscribed organisations, under the Terrorism Act 2000, where they have instead construed the burdens as evidential (see *Sheldrake v DPP; A-G's Reference (No. 4 of 2002)* [2004] UKHL 43, 3 WLR 976).

Reverse onuses and presumptions have been upheld by the Strasbourg Court in a number of cases and the court will apply the proportionality principle in considering whether a legal burden is justifiable. In *Salabiaku v France* (1998) 13 EHRR 379, the court said that it will consider whether the provisions strike the right balance between the public interest and the rights of the individual. Although Article 6 contains no explicit qualifications to limit the right on public interest grounds, the prevention of disorder or crime, or in the interests of public safety, in contrast to Articles 8 and 10 for example, the court has implied limits on Article 6, and has accepted reverse onuses and presumptions in some cases. The right to legal representation in Article 6(3) may also be restricted in limited circumstances. The notion of a fair trial has also been broadened to include the rights of witnesses and victims in *Doorsen v Netherlands* (1996) 22 EHHR 330. So the court has acknowledged that witnesses may, in some circumstances, be allowed to use screens and other measures, provided that the accused's lawyer is able to examine witnesses on his behalf.

The changes in the right to silence discussed in Chapter 3 have been subject to challenge under Article 6. A diminution of the right to silence raises issues in relation to the right to a fair hearing under Article 6(1) as well as under Article 6(2) of the Convention, the right to be presumed innocent. While under s 34 CJPOA, the burden of proof formally remains on the prosecution, in practice the suspect becomes the first port of call for the acquisition of incriminating evidence. With silence given evidential significance, the suspect is being asked to establish his own innocence, rather than requiring the prosecution to establish his guilt. The burden may weigh more heavily on the accused because of the inequality of arms between the suspect and the state. However, the Strasbourg Court has said that the drawing of adverse inferences *per se* does not breach Article 6, as it made clear in *Murray* and *Condron*.

Recent Strasbourg jurisprudence has acknowledged the need to strike a balance between the rights of the accused and the public interest in controlling crime and preventing disorder. The rival claims of the public interest in obtaining convictions of the guilty and in security have been assessed against the rights of the accused. The court has stressed that even where a society is facing serious threats from terrorism or crime, the suspect's rights should not be surrendered too easily.

In *Heaney and McGuinness v Ireland* App. No. 34720/97 (21 December 2000), the applicants were found in a house four miles from the scene of a bombing which caused deaths and injuries. Both suspects refused to answer questions and were convicted of failing to provide an account of their movements contrary to s 52 of the 1939 Offences Against the State Act. The court acknowledged that the privilege against self-incrimination and the right to silence are not absolute, as made clear in *Murray*, but they did find breaches of Articles 6(1) and 6(2) because the 'degree of compulsion imposed on the applicants by the application of s 52 of the 1939 Act with a view to compelling them to provide information relating to charges against them under that Act in effect destroyed the very essence of their privilege against self-incrimination and right to silence' (para 55). The need for security and good order could not justify a provision that extinguished the essence of their right to silence and privilege against self-incrimination (para 58).

However, in cases involving driving offences, the court has been less willing to find a breach of the privilege. In *O'Halloran and Francis v UK* App. Nos. 15809/02 and 26524/02 (29 June 2007), the applicants' cars were caught speeding by speed cameras. Both were asked to supply the name and address of the driver and told that failure to do so was a criminal offence under s 172 of the Road Traffic Act 1988. Mr O'Halloran admitted being the driver and was convicted for speeding. He failed at trial to have his confession excluded under ss 76 and 78 of PACE read in conjunction with Article 6. He complained that he had been convicted because of the statement he was compelled to give under the threat of a penalty comparable to that of the offence itself. Mr Francis did not supply the information, but he argued that being compelled to give the information had breached his right not to incriminate himself. Both applicants relied on Articles 6(1), the right to a fair trial, and 6(2), the presumption of innocence.

In this case the court treated the right to silence and the privilege as one right and rejected the applicants' arguments that the right was absolute and that to apply any form of direct compulsion to require an accused person to make incriminating statements against his or her will of itself destroyed the essence of the right. The court will instead focus on the nature and degree of compulsion used to obtain the evidence, the existence of any relevant safeguards and the use to which any material is put. The court noted that anyone who chooses to drive a car knows that they will subject themselves to a regulatory regime, including an obligation to inform the police regarding the identity of the driver. Moreover, the inquiry only applied under s 172 when the driver of the vehicle was alleged to have committed an offence and authorised the police to obtain information only relating to the identity of the driver. The offence was not a strict liability offence as s 172(4) allowed the driver to show that he did not know who the driver was or could not reasonably have known. Mr O'Halloran was not convicted just because of the information obtained under s 172. Mr Francis never made a statement and his refusal was not used in evidence regarding the speeding as he was convicted and fined for the refusal to supply the information. So the court found no breach of Article 6(1), given the special nature of the regime and the limited nature of the information sought, and no separate issue arose under Article 6(2). So here the court did not accept the privilege as absolute, but focused on the nature and extent of compulsion and whether the level of compulsion extinguished the right. A similar approach had been taken in the domestic courts in driver cases by the Privy Council in *Brown v Stott* [2003] 1 AC 681 where the court said the privilege could be limited where needed to achieve a legal aim to protect the public interest, as long as the limitation was proportionate.

A number of statutes also directly impose an obligation to answer questions or supply pre-existing documents to investigatory bodies as we saw in Chapter 3. The implications of these statutes for Article 6 were considered by the Strasbourg Court in a line of cases including *Funke v France* App. No. 10828/84 (25 February 1993), *Saunders v UK* App. No. 19187/91 (17 December 1996) and *JB v Switzerland* App. No. 31829/96 (3 May 2001). In *Funke* the accused was fined when he refused to supply his bank statements to customs officers when requested as part of an investigation into suspected tax evasion. Funke argued that his right not give evidence against himself, protected by Article 6(1), had been breached. While the Commission found no breach of Article 6(1), the court disagreed: there had been a breach of Article 6(1) as well as Article 8 in the search of his house and seizure of documents. The court stressed that the right to silence was embodied in the right to a fair hearing guaranteed by Article 6(1) of the Convention. Article 6 included the right of any person charged with a criminal offence to remain silent and not to contribute to his own incrimination. The right to inspect documents given under the French Customs Code could not supersede the privilege against self-incrimination said the court.

In *Saunders v UK*, the court developed its approach in *Funke* and affirmed the importance of the privilege notwithstanding the public interest in convicting fraudsters. Saunders was investigated by DTI Inspectors under powers given under the Companies Act 1985. Saunders argued that Article 6(1) had been breached because statements made under legal compulsion to DTI inspectors were admitted in evidence against him at a subsequent criminal trial, where he was convicted. The court said that although not specifically mentioned in Article 6, the right to silence and the privilege against self-incrimination are generally recognised international standards which lie at the heart of the notion of a fair procedure. They protect the accused against improper compulsion and contribute to the avoidance of miscarriages of justice, as made clear in *Murray* and *Funke*. The right not to incriminate oneself means that the prosecution should seek to prove their case without resort to evidence obtained through methods of oppression in defiance of the will of the accused to remain silent. The public interest in preventing fraud could not be used to justify the use of answers obtained by legal compulsion in a nonjudicial investigation to incriminate Saunders at his trial. His right had been infringed by reading out the transcripts of his responses to those questions to the jury to establish his involvement in an unlawful share-support operation. Moreover, fairness demands that the right not to incriminate oneself applies to all types of criminal offences, including company frauds. It would be wrong if differing degrees of fairness applied to different categories of accused and those accused of company frauds were treated differently from rapists or murderers. However, the court said the privilege does not extend to the use of material obtained from the defendant through the use of compulsory powers, but which has an existence independent of the will of the suspect, such as documents acquired pursuant to a warrant, blood, breath and urine samples, and bodily tissues for the purpose of DNA testing. Similarly, the domestic courts have said compelling the suspect to produce pre-existing documents which existed independent of the will of the suspect does not breach the privilege or the right to silence

(*R v S* [2008] EWCA Crim 2177). Following *Saunders v UK* the law was amended by s 59 of the Youth Justice and Criminal Evidence Act to limit the use of compelled statements.

In *JB v Switzerland* the Strasbourg Court found a breach of Article 6(1) when a retired ski instructor was fined when he refused to provide details of his sources of income when requested by the District Tax Office. The court noted that it was possible the information he had provided could have been used to ground a charge of tax evasion. The court distinguished this from the situation of a driver providing a blood or urine sample. It again stressed that the privilege against self-incrimination and the right to silence are generally recognised international standards and meant that the authorities should seek to prove their case without resorting to evidence obtained through methods of compulsion and oppression. By providing protection against improper compulsion, these immunities contribute to avoidance of miscarriages of justice.

The extraction and retention of bodily samples will be considered in more detail in Chapter 8 when we consider the body as evidence, but it should be noted that the court has acknowledged that the extraction of samples may constitute a breach of the Article 8 right to privacy, but it can be justified under Article 8(2) (*Peters v the Netherlands* App. No. 21132/93 (6 April 1994)). A claim under Article 3, the right not to be subjected to inhuman or degrading treatment is unlikely to succeed as current methods are mostly non-invasive (see *Ribitisch v Austria* (1995) 21 EHRR 573). Article 8 has also been used to challenge the retention of DNA samples. In addressing this issue the Strasbourg Court has applied the principle of proportionality and in the majority of cases has ruled that the extraction and retention of samples falls within Article 8(2), as it is necessary to prevent disorder or crime. However, in *S and Marper v UK* App Nos. 30562/04 and 30566/04 (4 December 2008), the court was critical of the UK system of retention of samples for those acquitted or where proceedings were halted, which could not be justified under Article 8(2), and fell outside the margin of appreciation. The court was critical of the blanket and indiscriminate nature of the system which took no account of the age of the suspect or the gravity of the offence and allowed indefinite retention. It also infringed on the presumption of innocence as the profiles of those acquitted were treated the same as those convicted. Volunteers could have their samples destroyed at their request but the acquitted could not. The UK law was subsequently amended to deal with the court's criticism in *Marper*.

So we can see that the court has considered a wide range of issues which affect the rights of the suspect in interrogation. However, its analysis of the privilege against self-incrimination has been criticised for its lack of depth and consistency by, for example, Choo (2012, 2013) and Redmayne (2007). Choo notes the reliance on the balancing of rights with competing interests without a full elucidation of its rationale, while Redmayne charts the problems with purported rationales in its jurisprudence. For example, the court's focus on the link between the privilege and the presumption of innocence and the prevention of miscarriages of justice is difficult, as Redmayne says, to apply to cases such as *Saunders* and *Heaney*. Corporate regulation and the prevention of terrorism were not seen as sufficient to justify the loss of the privilege in these cases. Nor can the witnesses in these cases be seen as vulnerable, but in any case there are other measures available to assist genuinely vulnerable witnesses. The court has also made clear that it does not see allowing adverse inferences from silence as breaching the privilege. The exclusion of bodily samples from the privilege is also problematic as we shall see in Chapter 8.

Conclusion

The privilege against self-incrimination, as we have seen, is strongly protected in international human rights law. By relieving the accused from pressure to speak we accord the suspect a level of human dignity which would otherwise be missing from interrogation and at trial. For Dworkin this right 'to be treated as a human being whose dignity fundamentally matters' is the most fundamental right underpinning due process rights (Dworkin, 2011, p. 335). So any limits on the privilege against self-incrimination, he says, would require a reason consistent with the original rationale for the right in question and marginal benefits to others would be insufficient. Even if one could secure an increase in convictions of the guilty by limiting the privilege, this would not justify the loss of human dignity of the accused in increasing the pressure to speak. The right to silence also plays a key role in redressing the unequal relationship between the state and the citizen. But in recent years the strong protection of rights claims has led to increasing tensions between the domestic courts and Strasbourg Courts, as we have seen, as well as increased governmental and public hostility to the court. However, within the framework of domestic law governing the process of interrogation, the concern to protect the rights of the suspect exists alongside the need to obtain reliable evidence and this will now be considered in more detail.

5
The Legal Framework of Interrogation

Introduction

The detention, treatment and questioning of suspects is governed by Code C of the Police and Criminal Evidence Act 1984 and the recording of interviews by Codes E and F. PACE came into force on 1 January 1986 and replaced the former Judges' Rules. Since then the Act and Codes have been revised several times and reviewed in 2002 by the Home Office and again in 2007. Originally there were four Codes; there are now eight. The PACE Codes were revised in 2012 in response to recommendations arising from IPCC investigations and these changes came into effect on 10 July 2012.

The law governing interrogation and any subsequent confession reflects a number of principles. The aim of the interrogation is to elicit information from the suspect, but any confession obtained should be made voluntarily. The principle of voluntariness is well established and was stated in *Warickshall* [1783] 1 Leach 263 where the court said that a voluntary confession was deserving of the highest credit and most likely to produce reliable evidence. The rules governing interrogation under the modern law in s 76 of PACE are broader and reflect the need to deter the potential use of coercive techniques as well as the need to obtain reliable evidence. There are other ways of pressuring suspects apart from bullying and harassment, including inducements and trickery. As well as reflecting the rationalist goal of obtaining reliable evidence, the law reflects the disciplinary or deterrent principle which seeks to deter police misbehaviour by excluding evidence resulting from impropriety, or where the police act in bad faith. Ashworth has also referred to the protective principle which recognises a right 'not to be subjected to certain forms of inducement and oppression' and aims to protect suspects 'from the disadvantages which result if evidence obtained through a violation of those rights were admitted at his trial' (Ashworth, 1977: 723). So the court performs a remedial role in raising and enforcing standards for the treatment and questioning of suspects and compensates those suspects whose treatment falls below that standard.

The suspect's treatment will also be assessed against the fairness principle under s 78 of PACE, which considers the adverse effect of admitting evidence on the fairness of the proceedings, and the right to a fair trial under Article 6, while s 82(3) also makes clear that the preceding sections do not undermine the court's power to exclude evidence at its discretion. Section 78 may be used to review the whole process of investigation and is not limited to interrogation. It has also been used to challenge the use of agents provocateurs and entrapment although with limited success. It has been used to exclude evidence regardless of its reliability.

A further principle, the legitimacy of the verdict, advanced by Dennis (1989), incorporates the factual accuracy of the verdict and the moral element of the integrity of the judgement. The moral authority of the verdict would be undermined if it were to be achieved by the violation of fundamental values of the criminal law, for example, the right of all citizens to be treated with dignity and respect, the recognition of autonomy and punishment based on desert. A factually inaccurate judgement would not possess legitimacy and the use of improper tactics would also violate the principle even if their use resulted in a factually accurate result as the moral authority of the verdict would be undermined. So the focus will be on whether the confession was made at all and as described and if it is authentic, whether the means used to obtain it are acceptable. The courts' construction of fairness under s 78 can be understood in terms of this principle.

Empirical research on the operation of Act and the courts' treatment of breaches of the Act and Codes have thrown light on its impact. Issues to be considered include access to legal advice, the recording of interviews, informal interviews, the courts' use of exclusionary discretion to deal with breaches of PACE Codes and the treatment of vulnerable suspects. Although the law of evidence may play an important role in disciplining the police and protecting the suspect, the first line of defence should be internal and external controls on the police, including an effective and independent complaints procedure.

The audio and visual recording of interviews

Interviews have been audio recorded at police stations since 1 January 1992. The procedures governing audio recording are set out in PACE

Code E, while visual recordings are dealt with in Code F. Audio recording should be used when interviewing a person cautioned of any indictable offence or triable either way offence (E.3.1.(a)), or when, exceptionally, the interviewer asks further questions about such an offence following charging the suspect or informing him that he may be prosecuted for that offence (E3.1.(b)), or where after the person has been charged or advised that they may be prosecuted for such an offence, the interviewer wants to tell them about any written statement or interview with another person (E.3.1.(c)).

Similar provisions for visual recording are found in Code F.3. The interviewing officer should visually record the interview in cases where it might be appropriate as above (F.3.1.(a–c)). In addition, visual recording might be appropriate with, or in the presence of, a deaf or deaf/blind or speech-impaired person who uses sign language to communicate (F.3.1.(d)) or with, or in the presence of, anyone who requires an appropriate adult (F.3.1.(e)), or in any case where the suspect or representative requests that the interview be visually recorded. Nothing in E.3.1 or F.3.1 precludes audio or visual recording at police discretion of interviews with people cautioned in respect of offences not covered in 3.1. The procedures for changing recording media, and taking breaks are set out in Code E of PACE. Reasons for taking breaks should be given on the audio recording. Following any breaks in audio or visual recording, the person should be reminded that he is under caution and should be cautioned again if necessary before resuming the interview.

There are exceptions under PACE Code E for not using audio recording, namely if it is not reasonably practicable to audio record because of equipment failure or the non-availability of a suitable interview room or recording equipment (E.3.3),in which case a written record should be made and the custody officer should record the reasons for not audio recording. The decision not to audio record may be made the subject of comment in court and the authorising officer should be prepared to defend that decision (E.3B). The custody officer may also authorise the interviewing officer not to visually record the interview if it is not reasonably practicable to do so and the authorising officer thinks the interview should not be delayed, or where it is clear that no prosecution will ensue or where the suspect refuses to be taken to a suitable interview room for visual recording (F.3.3). A Home Office review of visual recording suggested using it initially only in indictable and triable either way cases, but leaving it to officers' discretion in relation to other offences, and that the suspect should be able to refuse visual recording; both these recommendations are now given effect in Code F.

If, during the course of the interview, it becomes clear that the interview should be conducted under the Code of Practice for interviews of persons arrested under terrorism provisions, issued under the Terrorism Act 2000, then that Code should be complied with (E.3B). The Code applies to persons arrested under s 41 of and under Schedule 7 to the Terrorism Act 2000 and to post-charge questioning under s 22 of the Counter-Terrorism Act 2008. Visual recording of such interviews is now obligatory and the requirements are set out in Code H of PACE which deals with the detention and questioning of terrorist suspects under those provisions.

Audio and visual recording constituted significant advances for both interviewer and interviewee. From the police standpoint, it encouraged spontaneity and protected officers from allegations of impropriety as the court or jury could hear the precise questions, answers and any relevant silences. Audio recording resulted in fewer challenges to their evidence. Willis *et al.* (1987) conducted research on the impact of recording and found in two areas studied that there was an increase in the number of confessions obtained for recorded cases and in the amount of information obtained on other offences. Audio recording can also record nuances of speech.

Visual recording was also recommended by ACPO. It brings the closed world of the interview room closer to the public context of the trial. From the suspect's standpoint audio and visual recording make it much harder to fabricate confessions and easier to challenge the admissibility of improperly obtained confessions, and strengthens the suspect's protection in custody. Recording of interrogation is also seen as a basic due process right and is, as we saw in Chapter 4, an essential protection for defendants in the international criminal tribunals, the ICC, the ICTR and the ICTY, and is required in many states in the United States, as well as in Australia and Canada. Sullivan (2004) found that the police, prosecutors and judges in the United States prefer electronically recorded interrogations as they give an objective record, decrease false allegations of abuse and increase guilty pleas when a confession is made. It protects the police from false claims of coercion and gives the courts information on which to assess whether a confession is voluntary. In the United States reformers have argued that it should be mandatory and supported by federal and state law with consequences for non-compliance.

Visual recording is clearly better than audio recording or transcripts in capturing the demeanour of suspects. Baldwin (1992b) studied visually recorded interviews in four police stations in October 1990 and concluded that the presence of cameras provides the best way of protecting suspects and the police as any abuse will be revealed on camera. It also gives the court a full picture of the defendant's response, and by showing the demeanour of the suspect can increase confidence in the reliability of statements made in interview. However, it does not cover what happens pre-interview which may affect what is said in the interview. Moreover, symptoms of anxiety or nervousness by the suspect could be misread by juries as signs of guilt. The fact that it is recorded makes interview evidence more persuasive. With recording it is now easier to establish misconduct.

The recording of interviews is a necessary but not a sufficient protection for safeguarding suspects detained in custody. False confessions and impropriety during interview have persisted despite audio recording, notably in the case of the Cardiff Three, *Paris, Abdullahi and Miller* (1992) 97 Cr App R 99 where bullying and hectoring occurred during the interview, even though the interview was being recorded. However, that evidence will be crucial in challenging the validity of a confession and the safety of a conviction. McConville (1992) found that inducements and threats persisted despite recording as they were used when the recorder was switched off. Audio recording also allowed interviews to 'speed up', which may have increased pressure on suspects, and the suspect remains isolated. As we shall see in Chapter 6, recording *per se* does not necessarily prevent false confessions or impropriety but is an importance advance. It needs to be supplemented by competent and accessible legal advice, assistance from appropriate adults as necessary and scrutiny by the courts of the process of interrogation.

Access to legal advice

PACE also strengthened the suspect's access to legal advice while in detention. Confessions made in the absence of legal advice had featured in some of the miscarriage of justice cases, including Evans, Confait and the Guildford Four. Section 58(1) of PACE provides that a person held in custody in a police station or other premises shall be entitled, if he so requests, to consult a solicitor privately at any time. He should be permitted to do so as soon as is practicable and within 36 hours. Delay is only permitted under s 58(8) if there are reasonable grounds to believe that the exercise of the right will lead to interference with, or harm to, evidence connected with an indictable offence or interference with, or physical injury to, other persons, or lead to alerting of other persons suspected of having committed an offence but not yet arrested, or will hinder the recovery of any property obtained as a result of such offence, or where there are reasonable grounds to believe that the person detained for the indictable offence has benefited from his criminal conduct and recovery of the property constituting the benefit will be hindered by exercise of the right. Suspects should be informed that they may at any time consult and communicate privately with a solicitor, in person, in writing or by telephone, and that free independent legal advice is available from the duty solicitor (Code C.6.1). A solicitor may only be excluded from the interview 'if their conduct is such that the interviewer is unable properly to put questions to the suspect' (PACE Code C.6.9).

The duty solicitor scheme has improved access to legal advice, but, even with a solicitor present, the suspect may experience fear and disorientation from being in the interview room. Moreover, many suspects elect not to receive legal advice for a range of reasons; for example, they may not think a solicitor is necessary or may be worried about the cost. There may also be variations in access to legal advice between police stations and police areas which cannot be explained by differences in the offence profiles. When PACE was first introduced, there was an increase in requests for advice at the police station but the rate of request still remained relatively low, even though the advice was free and available. Variations have also been found in request rates between different groups, with men seeking advice more often than women, and black and minority ethnic groups and those with past convictions more likely to request advice (Bucke and Brown, 1997). Research conducted by Maguire (1988) soon after the introduction of PACE found that only a small proportion of suspects requested a solicitor or actually consulted a solicitor while in detention. Sanders *et al.*'s (1989) study of ten police stations found that the police discouraged access to a solicitor by suggesting it would mean spending more time at the police station. They also found that about 10 per cent of requests did not result in a consultation.

The PACE Codes were revised in 1991 and, as a result, more information was given to suspects on their right to legal advice, including the fact that it was free, but this did not lead to a substantial increase in the number of suspects requesting legal advice; for example, Brown *et al.* (1992) found an increase from 24 to 32 per cent. Considerable variation was found between police stations. In some cases advice was given by phone and advisers rarely attended. Without a solicitor present, the suspect will be more vulnerable, even if it is his choice not to consult a lawyer. Bucke and Brown (1997) studied 25 police stations in 10 force areas and found 40 per cent of detainees requested advice with 30 per cent consulting a solicitor. Even if a solicitor is present, this will still make it hard to determine the best course of action as far as the decision to speak is concerned. The solicitor should be able to advise on the client's right to silence and the implications regarding adverse inferences and also consider whether the suspect should offer a prepared statement, and then remain silent during questioning. As we saw earlier, a prepared statement may protect him from adverse inferences from silence under s 34 of the CJPOA, provided that he fully discloses the relevant facts on which he wishes to rely and does not deviate from them at trial. Silence on legal advice *per se* may not be sufficient to prevent s 34 being activated, unless the reliance on that advice is both genuine and reasonable rather than tactical. Section 58 of the YJCEA makes clear, following *Murray v UK,* that inferences from silence under ss 34–38 of CJPOA are not permissible if the accused has not been allowed an opportunity to consult a solicitor prior to being questioned or charged, or prior to requests to account for objects, substances or marks or his presence at a particular place, but does not require that the suspect avail himself of that opportunity.

There were no large-scale studies of access to legal advice between Bucke and Brown's (1997) study and Pleasence *et al.*'s study (2011) and no national data is systematically collected. In 2009 Skinns studied two police stations and found request rates of 68 and 51 per cent (Skinns, 2009a). However, Pleasence *et al.* (2011) think this finding is not indicative of general rates. Their research suggests that the numbers receiving advice at the police station has not increased as much as Skinns' study might indicate. Pleasence *et al.* examined over 30,000 custody records from four police force areas. They found considerable variation between police stations and a sharp drop in the request rate between the ages of 16 and 17. Although their research does suggest an increase in request rates since the 1990s, nonetheless it remains the case that a minority of detainees request advice, and we still find significant variations between police stations and police forces. In their study 44.9 per cent of suspects asked for legal advice and 81.3 per cent of these requests were granted, so this meant that 36.5 percent had consulted a solicitor. The figures for detainees were lower. They also found differences between force areas being studied and between police stations, even after controlling for other factors. There was even a difference between two custody suites which were recorded separately, but were in the same building. The major driver for a request was the seriousness of the offence. They also found women less likely to request advice than men and white British detainees less likely to request advice than most other detainees, and those aged 17–24 were less likely to request than other age groups. In the light of their findings, they recommend further monitoring of request and advice rates and of the way in which the PACE right to advice is operationalised, for example, whether the police dissuade detainees from requesting advice. The available material suggests variations in how the police interpret and apply PACE and how much information is given to detainees. Research by Kemp *et al.* (2012) also suggests that where detainees requested a solicitor 'this was associated with a highly significant increase in the length of time detainees spent in custody' (at 741). Their findings are based on the same custody records as the Pleasence *et al.* (2011) study. This is consistent with earlier studies by Phillips and Brown (1998) and Skinns (2009a) which also found increases in time spent in custody where legal advice was sought.

The quality of legal advice

Legal advice should be effective and informed. The solicitor's first duty is to his client and the adviser should protect the client's rights, including the privilege against self-incrimination. But he or she should also be able to assess the client's vulnerability and fitness for interview; so factors here would include age, disabilities, difficulties in understanding English, or whether the client is suffering from the ill effects of drugs or alcohol.

A major study of defence solicitors in the period 1988–91 was conducted by McConville et al. (1994) who also undertook research on access to legal advice for the Royal Commission on Criminal Justice (McConville and Hodgson, 1993). Their findings suggested that the advice was often poor quality, given by unqualified advisers, and advisers were confined to a passive role in the interview. The advisers themselves were often former police officers employed for police station advice work. They found that advisers rarely advised suspects to remain silent unless there were uncertainties over the law or insufficient information had been given by the police. They also, in some cases, failed to object to police bullying.

The passivity of defence lawyers was criticised by the Court of Appeal in *Glaves* [1993] Crim LR 685, where the court said the solicitor should interfere if the questioning by the police goes too far. In *Miller* [1990] Crim LR 36, the defence solicitor was criticised by the court for sitting passively through an improperly conducted interview. The failures of the defence lawyers were also criticised in the miscarriage of justice cases both before and after PACE. Any improper questioning or threatening behaviour should, of course, be challenged at the time. If the solicitor is passive and fails to intervene at the time, then this makes it more difficult to exclude the evidence later.

Sanders *et al.* (1989) found in their study that advice was often poor quality and in over half the cases surveyed given by non-qualified staff. In one quarter of the cases advice was given over the phone, which may not be sufficient unless the offences are very minor, and even where staff attended, they were often not solicitors but their representatives. The quality of legal advice was also questioned by the Royal Commission on Criminal Justice in 1993 (RCCJ, 1993). Baldwin's (1992a) research for the Commission found that in two-thirds of the cases in his sample the legal adviser did not speak; the police took charge of the interview and relegated advisers to a passive role. Baldwin was critical of the poor quality of recording of interviews and the passivity of legal advisers.

In response to these criticisms the training and monitoring of police station representatives were improved by a new system of accreditation. The Law Society introduced a new training kit, 'Becoming Skilled', and a new accreditation scheme for unqualified legal representatives giving advice at the police station. From February 1995 the Legal Aid Board would not pay for the advice given by police station advisers who are not accredited under the scheme. Probationary representatives and accredited representatives are assigned a supervising solicitor. Probationers must first pass assessment tests and a written examination if they have not passed relevant legal practice courses to acquire accreditation. Once qualified, Accredited Representatives have to undertake at least 25 police station attendances a year and engage in six hours Continuous Professional Development training. Since 2005 solicitors advising at a police station also need a police station qualification.

The majority of legal firms who conduct criminal defence work that is publicly funded do use accredited representatives, non-solicitor employees, to advise people at the police station who would otherwise have no legal representation. The register of police station representatives was regulated by the Legal Services Commission (LSC). Representatives will be called out to the station after the Duty Solicitor has spoken to the client on the phone. The Access to Justice Act 1999 provided that the Legal Services Commission should fund legal advice and assistance to individuals involved in criminal investigations, from initial questioning by the police to the point when the decision is made as to whether the individual is to be charged. The LSC would pay for advice given by the Duty Solicitor or the client's own solicitor and to accredited representatives in specified circumstances. The LSC was abolished by the Legal Aid, Sentencing and Punishment of Offenders Act 2012 (LASPO), and replaced by the Legal Aid Agency in 2013 who now carry out these functions. So the scheme is currently administered online by the Legal Aid Agency through the Defence Solicitor Call Centre.

The Solicitors Regulation Authority, in its standard of competence for the accreditation of solicitors and representatives advising at the police station, includes the ability to identify a client's vulnerability and how to identify inappropriate behaviour by the police and when and how to respond to it (SRA 2007, 1.1.6 and 1.1.7). The understanding of criminal law and procedures must also include an understanding of the implications of the Human Rights Act 1998 for advice and assistance at the police station (1.2.9), an ability to use language appropriate for the recipient (2.1.1), and to be able to identify whether an interpreter is needed (2.1.2). In the initial consultation with the client by telephone, he or she should advise the client to exercise the right to silence if questioned prior to the solicitor or representative's attendance (3.3.6). The adviser should also consult with the appropriate officers at the police station to determine the purpose of the interview and respond appropriately if refused permission to be present at the interview (3.6.5). In meeting the client, the adviser should assess the client's vulnerability and fitness for interview (3.7.3) and ascertain any complaints regarding maltreatment in custody and respond accordingly (3.7.4). This also applies to questioning by immigration officers. In assisting the client he or she should give 'reasoned and considered advice' regarding answering questions, the right to silence, the making of a written statement under caution, or the signing of a written record of any comment made to the police (3.8.3). The interview should be monitored by the adviser who should intervene where necessary. Any improper behaviour by, or questions from, the police should be responded to appropriately (3.9.3). Attempts to undermine the client's decision to exercise the right to silence should also be recognised and responded to appropriately (3.9.4). However, acting on a solicitor's advice will not prevent the activation of s 34 unless there is both genuine and reasonable reliance.

The legal representative should also ensure that appropriate provisions are in place for vulnerable clients to prevent them being disadvantaged (3.11.2), and the client is advised regarding the role of the appropriate adult or interpreter and the need to ensure that confidentiality is maintained (3.11.3). The appropriate adult should also be made aware of his or her role and the interpreter should be reminded of the duty to be impartial and to keep any information confidential (3.12.1;

3.12.2). Vulnerability may be an issue because of the client's age, mental disorder or disability, difficulty in understanding English, or a hearing or speech disability.

However, it is clear that the reforms in the criminal legal aid system and cuts in solicitors' and barristers' fees and new contracting arrangements announced in February 2014 will reduce the number of lawyers taking on legal aid work, which has fuelled fears regarding access to legal advice in the future.

Informal interviews

As interrogation at the police station became more tightly controlled, there were fears that the pressure on the suspect would be exerted outside the interview room and suspects would be asked questions at the crime scene. Initially when the PACE Codes were introduced the use of informal interviews increased (Wolchover and Heaton-Armstrong (1990)). Brown *et al.* (1992) found questioning outside the police station occurred in 10 per cent of the cases they studied. Moston and Stephenson (1993), in their research for the Royal Commission on Criminal Justice, noted that the arresting officers at the police station admitted interviewing suspects before arrival at the station in 8 per cent of cases while 31 per cent of the suspects in their sample said they had been questioned in the police car on their way to the station or at the crime scene, and many of these suspects had confessed. In many cases no records were kept of those informal interviews or the records were inadequate. Although Moston and Stephenson recommended recording of these interviews as well, they acknowledge that doing so legitimises them as interviews and obviously informal interviews are not conducted in the presence of a lawyer. In *Maguire* [1990] Cr App R 115, the admissions resulting from informal questioning were held to be admissible, even though made by a juvenile without an appropriate adult present.

Maguire and Norris (1993) in their research on criminal investigation argued that the police were under too much pressure to get results and that rules were breached routinely because the police were convinced they had the right suspect. Moreover, there was a lack of supervision by the CID and conversations occurred outside the police station. One officer said he regularly took 'the scenic route' back to the police station in order to question suspects although he was aware that he was breaching the PACE Code and would deny it if challenged. He would do this only with colleagues he could trust or when alone. The authors argued for a change in managerial culture with as much emphasis on procedural and legal compliance as on obtaining results. But later research by Choongh (1997) found that 20 per cent of the interviewees in his sample had also been asked questions informally, as had the suspects in Skinns's (2011a) study of police custody. So while there have been changes in interviewing techniques and the conduct of interviews at a formal level, these advances have been neutralised in some cases by the occupational culture of the police.

An aim of the PACE Codes was to reduce the number of informal interviews and limit their use to exceptional cases. Code C.11.1.1 stipulates that:

> Following a decision to arrest a suspect, they must not be interviewed about the relevant offence except at a police station or other authorised place of detention, unless the consequent delay would be likely to:

(a) lead to:
   • interference with, or harm to, evidence connected with an offence;
   • interference with, or physical harm to, other people; or
   • serious loss, or damage to, property;
(b) lead to alerting other people suspected of committing an offence but not yet arrested for it; or
(c) hinder the recovery of property obtained in consequence of the commission of any offence. ...

An interview is defined in Code C.11.1A as 'the questioning of a person regarding their involvement or suspected involvement in a criminal offence or offences which, under paragraph 10.1, must be carried out under caution'. Even a single question or answer amounts to an interview if it relates to the crime for which the suspect is arrested. In *R v Matthews* [1990] Crim LR 190, the Court of Appeal said that any discussion of the alleged offence between the police and the suspect constituted an interview, regardless of who initiated the discussion, and the suspect should be shown a copy of notes taken by the officer. The RCCJ also recommended that suspects should be able to comment on any alleged unrecorded admissions during the interview and this is now in PACE Code C 11.4. At the beginning of the interview, after cautioning the suspect, the interviewer should put to the suspect any significant statement or silence which occurred in the presence and hearing of a police officer or other police staff before the start of the interview and ask whether they confirm or deny that earlier statement or silence and if they want to add anything. A significant statement is defined as one that appears capable of being used in evidence against the suspect and a significant silence is a failure or refusal to answer a question or to answer satisfactorily when under caution, which might give rise to an inference under the CJPOA provisions. Nonetheless, whether informal interviews are excluded is a matter for the court's discretion, even though the suspect is in a more vulnerable position without a lawyer present and at greater risk of making a false confession. In *R v Joseph* [1993] Crim LR 206 an alleged admission made during a pre-police station interview was excluded because the suspect had not been told he was under arrest or that he could get police station advice and contemporaneous notes had not been taken.

Voluntary confessions

The current UK rules on admissibility of confession evidence that centre on oppression and unreliability, found in s 76 of PACE, reflect the courts' and Parliament's recognition of the vulnerability of the accused in police detention and the need for statements to be reliable. The law governing the use of confessions is designed to discourage inhuman and degrading treatment even when such treatment produces reliable evidence. The search for the truth has to be placed in the context of these fundamental legal values.

The use of torture in the context of police interrogation is clearly prohibited by s 76(2)(a) and 76(8) of PACE, as well as by international human rights instruments ratified by the UK. Methods used in Northern Ireland in the 1970s, approaching the threshold of torture, were criticised and prohibited in *Ireland v UK* App. No. 5310/71 (18 January 1978) as we saw in Chapter 4. Moreover, a confession obtained by torture by a third party abroad is inadmissible in the UK courts as the House of Lords made clear in *A and Others v Secretary of State for the Home Department* [2005] UKHL 71. However, pressures may be placed on suspects that fall short of torture, but constitute inhumane and degrading treatment and undermine the dignity of the accused and the legitimacy of the criminal justice system. Evidence of ill treatment has figured in some of the miscarriages of justice that we will consider in Chapter 6.

The fact that torture is prohibited on moral grounds affirms the principle that it is better for the guilty to be acquitted than to obtain convictions by unjust means which violate human rights and dignity. The development of the exclusionary rules on confession evidence reflects the recognition that testimony produced under pressure, whether through fear of sanctions or hope of benefits, may generate unreliable testimony. As we saw in Chapter 2, the aversion to forced testimony in the criminal justice process reflects the revulsion over the practices of the Star Chamber and High Commission. False confessions were a factor in some of the miscarriage of justice cases and, as well as constituting a failure to discover the truth, they undermine the legitimacy of the criminal justice system. However, confession evidence is accepted in English law as sufficient to obtain a conviction without corroborative evidence, provided that the confession is made voluntarily. As Lord Sumner said in *Ibrahim v R* [1914] AC 599:

> It has long been established...that no statement by an accused is admissible in evidence against him unless it is shown by the prosecution to have been a voluntary statement, in the sense that it has not been obtained from him either by fear or prejudice or hope of advantage exercised or held out by a person in authority.
>
> (at 609)

At common law the court would look at the circumstances and the particular suspect in examining whether their free will had been sapped to the point it crumbled. PACE focuses specifically on whether the treatment is oppressive or whether anything said or done by the police renders the confession unreliable. Oppression is covered by s 76(2)(a) of PACE. It is defined in s 76(8) as including torture, inhuman or degrading treatment, so it is modelled on Article 3 of the Convention, and covers the use or threat of violence. The Court of Appeal argued in *Fulling* (1987) 2 All ER 65 that oppression must be given its ordinary meaning of the exercise of authority or power in a burdensome, harsh or wrongful manner. The trial judge in this case had correctly admitted the confession. The police had told Fulling that her boyfriend was having an affair with the woman held in the adjacent cell and she said she confessed in the hope of being released earlier and thereby escaping the distress of being so close to the woman. But the court ruled that if the police had made such a remark, which they denied, it would not be sufficient to amount to oppression. In *Emmerson* (1991) 92 Cr App Rep 284 the Court of Appeal said that questioning that was rude or discourteous, involving bad language and a raised voice and which gave the impression of irritation and impatience, did not amount to oppression. The burden is on the prosecution to prove beyond reasonable doubt that the confession was not obtained by oppression, so the focus of the court will be on how the confession was obtained, not on whether it was true or false.

After *Fulling* a line of cases made clear that bullying, shouting, constant interruptions and falsely stating evidence in possession of the police did constitute oppression. In the Cardiff Three case, *R v Paris, Abdullahi and Miller* (1993) 97 Cr App R 99, Miller was interviewed over a period of five days and during that time was interviewed for 13 hours in a bullying and hectoring way which was clearly oppressive: 'The officers... were not so much questioning him as shouting at him what they wanted him to say. It is hard to conceive of a more hostile or intimidatory approach by officers to a suspect' (at 103). Miller denied involvement 300 times before making an admission. In *Beales* [1991] Crim LR 118 misstating the evidence against the accused and bullying the suspect were both seen as oppressive. While more extreme and oppressive behaviour is prohibited by s 76(2)(a) of PACE, more subtle pressures may be used, such as trickery or deception, which fall short of oppression.

Reliability is covered in s 76(2) of PACE, so the confession is inadmissible 'if it is made in consequence of anything said or done which was likely in the circumstances existing at the time to render unreliable any confession which might be made by him in consequence thereof'. The focus is on police behaviour and the causal connection between that behaviour and the unreliability of the confession. The reference to 'anything' here suggests that the potential scope is broader than inducements, threats or impropriety. However, at common law prior to PACE, the courts focused on whether the inducement or threat persuaded the suspect to confess, rather than whether the confession was unreliable. But s 76(2) of PACE refers explicitly to reliability. The court will consider all the circumstances, including the suspect's mental state, mental age and fitness to be interviewed, issues considered in *R v McGovern* (1991) 92 Cr App R 228 and *R v Sylvester* [2002] EWCA Crim 1327. In *McGovern* the Court of Appeal said that a confession made in breach of the PACE Codes by a 19-year-old woman with an IQ of 73, in the absence of a solicitor and when she was physically ill, should have been excluded. The breach also rendered a second interview inadmissible, although the solicitor was present on that occasion.

In *Weeks* [1995] Crim LR 52, the Court of Appeal said the fact that the interrogating officer threatened the suspect that if he did not tell the truth he would be kept in custody, was not sufficient to render his subsequent confession unreliable under s 76 of PACE, although the surrounding circumstances might do so. The thing said or done does not extend to anything said or done by the accused as made clear in *R v Goldenberg* (1989) 88 Cr App R 285.

Section 76(4) of PACE also stipulates that evidence obtained through a breach of s 76 will not necessarily be excluded, but will be a matter for the discretion of the court. There is no equivalent of the fruit of the forbidden tree doctrine found in the United States. However, s 76(5) of PACE makes clear that if the facts obtained as a result of the flawed confession are admitted, the prosecution will not be able to disclose in court the fact that that the information was acquired because of a statement made by the accused, unless evidence of this is given by the accused himself.

In the case of evidence obtained illegally or unfairly through means other than by a confession, such as evidence obtained from an agent provocateur or by entrapment, the court will consider the issue under s 78. At common law improperly obtained evidence was admissible as made clear in *R v Sang* [1980] AC 402. Although this common law discretion was preserved by s 82(3) of PACE, such cases are usually considered under s 78. The factors to consider were discussed in *R v Smurthwaite* [1994] 1 All ER 898. However, the court will consider a range of issues in deciding whether to exclude evidence under s 78, including whether the police could have obtained evidence without entrapment, whether the police had reasonable grounds for suspicion and the gravity of the crime, although as Redmayne (2012) has noted, the reasoning behind its decisions has not always been clear or consistent. In some cases of entrapment in the domestic courts the proceedings have been stayed as an abuse of process, as in *R v Latif* [1996] 1 WLR 104. The implications of covert recordings of suspects for Articles 6 and 8 were also considered by the Strasbourg Court in *Teixeira de Castro v Portugal* (1999) 28 EHRR 101 and *Ramanauskas v Lithuania* (2010) 51 EHRR 11.

Exclusionary discretion

As we have seen, the interview process and the conduct of the interrogators is firmly circumscribed and regulated by PACE and the Codes. Obviously issues of oppression and unreliability would render a subsequent confession inadmissible under s 76 of PACE. Evidence also may be excluded under s 78 if admitting it would have an adverse effect on the fairness of the proceedings. The case law reflects the disciplinary and reliability principles, seeking to discipline and deter the police from improper conduct, as well as ensuring the admission of reliable evidence. It also reflects the protective principle, that is, ensuring that the suspect is compensated for any failings by the police (see Ashworth, 1997) and the principle of the legitimacy of the verdict (Dennis, 1989), illustrated, for example, by the cases of *R v Absalom* [1988] Crim LR 748 and *R v Sanusi* [1992] Crim LR 43. But if the PACE Codes are breached this will not necessarily lead to exclusion of evidence as the breaches would need to be substantial and serious to be excluded under s 78. But the role of the courts has not always been forceful in relation to breaches of the PACE Codes so the problem of enforcement remains. In considering whether to exclude evidence under s 78 the court will consider if the breaches were substantial (see *R v Keenan* [1989] Crim LR 720) and who else was present at the time (*R v Dunn* [1990] Crim LR 572). In extreme cases of police misconduct or unlawful behaviour on the part of the state, the court may halt the proceedings as an abuse of process, as, for example, in the case of *R v Mullen* [1999] 2 Cr App 143, where the accused had been unlawfully removed from Zimbabwe to face trial in the UK.

When s 78 was enacted it was thought that the discretion would rarely be exercised in favour of the accused. But in fact the Court of Appeal did apply s 78 robustly in a line of cases in the late 1980s to enforce the Codes of Practice and to protect the suspect's rights. Although the exercise of exclusionary discretion developed in an ad hoc way, the application of the of the reliability, deterrent, protective, fairness and legitimacy principles was evident in a number of key cases dealing with significant and substantial breaches of PACE and the accompanying Codes. Breaches that have justified exclusion have included denial of access to legal advice in *R v Delaney,* [1988] 2 All ER 135, the failure to caution in *R v Hunt* [1992] Crim LR 582 and *R v Kirk* [2001] 1 WLR 567, the failure to follow proper identification procedures in *R v Payne and Quinn, The Times* (15 March 1995), the failure to provide an appropriate adult in *R v Glaves* [1983] Crim LR 685 and *R v Aspinall* [1999] 2 Cr App R 115 and evidence obtained by police deception in *R v Mason* [1987] 3 All ER 481, where false information that the client's fingerprints had been found at the crime scene was given to the solicitor, who then advised his client to speak. Here the deception was practised on the solicitor rather than the suspect and interfered with his duty to advise the client. The court has favoured deciding each case on its own facts, rather than formulating rigid guidelines. In considering these issues the court will consider: the vulnerability of the accused and his or her prior experience of police detention and whether the police have acted in good or bad faith.

In *R v Samuel* [1988] 2 All ER 135 the police refused the accused access to a solicitor on the grounds that it would alert other suspects, under the exception to s 58 that provides that access to a particular solicitor may be delayed if the officer has reasonable grounds to believe that the solicitor will, if permitted to consult with his client, interfere with the course of justice, commit a criminal offence or inadvertently do something that would have this effect. But the Court of Appeal stressed in *Samuel* that this is likely to occur only in very rare cases and there needed to be a high probability that the solicitor would alert other suspects which would not be easy for the police to establish. The court also said that if the reason for delaying access was that the solicitor was likely to advise silence, this would not be a sufficient reason for refusal. So the court exercised its discretion in Samuel's favour because he was denied one of the most fundamental rights of the citizen. It was clear that if the solicitor had been present he would have advised silence and Samuel would not have confessed.

But we also find cases where evidence has been admitted despite breaches of the Codes. In *Dunn* [1990] Crim LR 572, the Court of Appeal upheld the admission of confession evidence despite the failure to contemporaneously record an interview. Here it was held that the presence of a solicitor's clerk meant that the accused was not disadvantaged by the breach of the Code. Minor breaches are unlikely to lead to exclusion, especially if the lawyer is present or the accused is already familiar with interrogation procedures. Even the denial of the right to see a solicitor would not automatically lead to exclusion – an additional element such as bad faith would be needed and the overriding issue will be the extent to which the fairness of the trial is compromised. A request to see a solicitor was refused in *Alladice* (1988) 87 Cr App R 380, but the confession was still admitted. The court ruled that a breach of s 58 delaying access to a solicitor would not by itself entail exclusion of admissions made in the absence of legal advice. In *R v Anderson* [1993] Crim LR 47 the Court of Appeal expressed reluctance to interfere with the discretion of a trial judge who had admitted a confession in breach of s 58, because, they said, even if the solicitor had been present and advised silence, it was unlikely the accused would have followed that advice. In *R v Delaney* [1998] 2 All ER 135, the Court of Appeal said it would not exclude evidence just because the suspect had been wrongfully denied legal advice or to punish or discipline the police. A failure to caution did not justify exclusion in *R v Gill* [2003] EWCA Crim 2256. Here the court stressed the absence of bad faith on the part of the police and the fact that even if the caution had been given, it would not have made any difference. In *Dunford* (1990) 91 Cr App R 150 an admission made in the absence of a solicitor was admitted on the grounds that the solicitor's advice would not have added to the accused's understanding of his legal rights.

Legal advice is clearly crucial as the individual is vulnerable during interrogation, in quite intimidating surroundings subject to interrogation by experienced interviewers, so there is a strong pressure on him to speak. In some of the worst miscarriages of justice, including the Guildford Four and the *Confait* and *Evans* cases, false admissions were made in the absence of legal advice. Without a solicitor present the suspect may be more at risk of false confession. Breaches of PACE and the Codes may also be addressed through police complaints procedures which have been revised several times since the 1980s in the light of concerns over the role of the police in miscarriages of justice. But is exclusionary discretion sufficient to protect the suspect? Obviously a discretionary approach allows the court to distinguish between minor and more serious breaches, but may also give the police more latitude in approaching the borderlines of impropriety. A further protection is provided by the abuse of process doctrine and of course by the increasing importance of Convention rights, which have increasingly influenced criminal procedure.

In any event, given that the majority of defendants plead guilty, the nature of the interrogation, including any impropriety, may not come under the scrutiny of the court. A guilty plea may be a consequence of informal plea bargaining where the defence agrees to plead guilty in exchange for being charged with a lesser offence, which may be particularly attractive to a defendant with previous convictions. It may also be a response to the potentially substantial sentence discount for guilty pleas currently set at a maximum of one-third, depending on the stage in the process when it is offered.

Vulnerable suspects

PACE and the PACE Codes also include a number of provisions to protect the vulnerable suspect during interrogation. Suspects may be vulnerable because of their age, learning disabilities, or other impairments and mental disorders. The class of suspects or interviewees is broad and will include professional criminals, but also vulnerable groups, children and young persons, individuals with learning disabilities as well as those lying on the boundary of needing an appropriate adult, and individuals who are at particular risk of making unreliable statements. Suspects may also be vulnerable because of hearing or speaking problems or because of difficulty in understanding English. The challenge for criminal procedure is to make rules which accommodate the whole range of suspects.

Annex G to Code C provides guidance to police and health care professionals on fitness to be interviewed. A detainee may be at risk if conducting the interview would significantly harm the person's physical or mental state, or if anything the detainee says about his involvement or suspected involvement in the offence might be considered unreliable in subsequent court proceedings because of his mental state (Annex G.2(a) and G.2(b)). The assessment should evaluate how the person's mental state may affect his ability to understand the nature and purpose of the interview, to comprehend what is being asked, and to appreciate the significance of any answers given to what is being asked and to make a rational decision about whether they want to speak. The extent to which the detainee's replies may be affected by his condition, rather than representing an accurate and rational statement of his involvement in the offence, and how the nature of the interview might affect the detainee, should also be considered (Annex G.3) The focus should be on the functional ability of the detainee, rather than a medical diagnosis, as a person suffering from a severe mental illness may still be fit to be interviewed.

PACE introduced new requirements for the assistance of an appropriate adult in cases of vulnerability because of age or mental vulnerability. Code C.11.15 specifies that: 'A juvenile or a person who is mentally disordered or otherwise mentally vulnerable, must not be interviewed or asked to provide or sign a written statement in the absence of an appropriate adult' unless delays will lead to harm to property or persons and an officer of rank of superintendent or above is satisfied the interview would not significantly harm the person's physical or mental state. Mental vulnerability is defined as applicable to any person who because of their mental state or capacity may not understand the significance of what is said, of questions or their replies, while the definition of mental disorder is that used in s 1(2) of the Mental Health Act 1983, namely 'any disorder or disability of mind' (Codes C, Notes for Guidance 1G). If the custody officer has any doubt about the mental state or capacity of a detainee, that detainee should be treated as mentally vulnerable and an appropriate adult should be called.

The police should ask the appropriate adult to come to the police station if they believe the suspect falls within the above definition or is a juvenile, which was originally under the age of 17 (PACE s 37(15), but now is under 18. The role of the appropriate adult is protect the suspect's rights, to advise him or her and to ensure that the interview is conducted fairly. The Code also notes that although juveniles or people who are mentally disordered or otherwise mentally vulnerable are often capable of providing reliable evidence, they may, without knowing or wishing to do so, be particularly prone in certain circumstances, to provide information which is unreliable, misleading or self-incriminating. Special care should always be taken in questioning such a person, and the appropriate adult should be involved if there is any doubt about a person's age, mental state or capacity. Because of the risk of unreliable evidence it is also important to obtain corroboration of any facts admitted whenever possible.

(Notes for Guidance 11.C)

A juvenile or person who is mentally disordered or otherwise mentally vulnerable should not be interviewed regarding their involvement or suspected involvement in an offence, or asked to provide or sign a written statement or record of interview, in the absence of the appropriate adult (Code C.11.15).

The exceptions are very limited, namely where delay will lead to interference with, or harm to, evidence connected with an offence, interference with or physical harm to persons or serious loss or damage to property, lead to alerting others suspected of committing an offence but not yet arrested, or hinder the recovery of property obtained on consequence of the commission of the offence (C 11.1). Vulnerable suspects should not be interviewed unless an officer of superintendent rank or above is satisfied that the interview would not significantly harm the person's physical or mental state (C.11.18). This provision also applies to anyone who at the time of the interview is unable to appreciate the significance of questions and their answers or understand what is happening, because of the effects of drink, drugs, ailment or condition, or has a hearing disability, or has difficulty understanding English, and if, at the time of the interview, the interpreter is not present.

A mentally disordered, or otherwise mentally vulnerable, person detained under the Mental Health Act 1983 s 136 should be assessed as soon as possible by an approved social worker and registered medical practitioner (Code C.3.16). Once arrangements have been made for their treatment or care they can no longer be detained under s 136, but if the assessment determines that they are not mentally disordered within the meaning of the Act, they must be immediately discharged. For a person who is mentally disordered or mentally vulnerable, the appropriate adult would be a relative, guardian or other person responsible for their care or custody, or someone experienced in dealing with mentally disordered or mentally vulnerable people, or other responsible adult and who is not a police officer or employed by the police (Code C.1.7). For a juvenile an appropriate adult would be the parent or guardian or person representing the local authority if he or she is in care, a social worker or responsible adult aged over 18 who is not a police officer or employed by the police. If a custody officer is told a suspect may be mentally disordered or otherwise mentally vulnerable, he must request an appropriate adult, or use an adult from the local AA service if available. In *Morse* [1991] Crim LR 195 the Court of Appeal said that a person of low intelligence who is not capable of advising a juvenile cannot count as an appropriate adult.

Research conducted soon after PACE was enacted found that juveniles spent long periods in detention because of delays waiting for an appropriate adult to arrive (Maguire 1988; Brown 1989). The later research by Skinns (2011b) and Kemp *et al.* (2012) found that those under 16 spent less time than adults at the police station in the day, but a little longer when arrested at night and think this could be due in part to problems finding an appropriate adult late at night.

Research for the Runciman Commission also found that the appropriate adults accompanying juveniles were passive and unsure of their role rather than actively involved or supporting the suspects (Evans, 1993). The Code was therefore revised so that the appropriate adult is advised as follows:

- they are not expected to act simply as an observer; and
- the purposes of their presence is to:
  - advise the person being interviewed;
  - observe whether or not the interview is being conducted properly and fairly;
  - facilitate communication with the person being interviewed. (C.11.17).

The Royal Commission on Criminal Justice (1993) said it was dissatisfied with the arrangements for the advice and protection of vulnerable suspects in interrogation and recommended a review of the role, functions and training of appropriate adults. It also emphasised the need for clearer guidelines for officers on the criteria to use in deciding whether an appropriate adult is necessary and for better training. It anticipated an increase in the number of vulnerable suspects as more mentally disordered individuals moved into the community. A Home Office Review Group in 1995 made several recommendations including better training and guidance, improving the advice in the PACE Codes on who might fulfil the role of the AA in appropriate cases, and setting up appropriate adult panels. They also recommended that appropriate adults should be entitled to confidential interviews with suspects and these changes were subsequently implemented.

The function of the appropriate adult is now set out in the Home Office Guide for Appropriate Adults (Home Office 2011). The role of the appropriate adult is to assist the detainee so that he understands what is happening during the interviewing and investigative stages, so they should support, advise and assist the detainee, ensure that the police act fairly and respect the rights of the detainee and help communication between the detainee and the police and others. The suspect must be informed of his rights in the presence of the appropriate adult and should be advised that he may speak privately to the appropriate adult at any time. The caution should be given in the presence of the appropriate adult, who has a right to be told why the detainee is being held and to be present during the interview. The appropriate adult should intervene if it is necessary to help the detainee communicate effectively with the police or if he feels that the questioning is confusing, repetitive or oppressive, and may ask for a break if it is felt that the detainee needs a rest or legal advice or wishes to speak to him or her in private. The appropriate adult should also be present during any fingerprinting or photographing of the detainee, or during any searches or identification procedures. Even if the detainee refuses legal advice the appropriate adult can request that a solicitor be called and, in cases where the detainee is eligible for assistance from an appropriate adult, the legal adviser should attend the police station in person.

One problem is recognising and identifying suspects to see if they fall within the appropriate adult provisions, particularly in borderline cases. Gudjonsson *et al.* (1993) assessed 173 suspects at the police station before they were interviewed by the police, monitoring a range of issues including suggestibility, anxiety, understanding of their legal rights, mental state, intellectual functioning and reading ability. They found that 35 per cent of the suspects had problems that might interfere with their functioning during interrogation or their ability to cope with it. On the basis of this they concluded that an appropriate adult was necessary for 15 per cent of the suspects in the sample, but the police subsequently identified the need in only 4 per cent of cases. The authors note that suspects who were depressed and suicidal were most likely to be missed. There were also problems in identifying intellectual impairment if it did not impede social functioning. Moreover, some suspects may not wish to admit to an impairment. Most of the detainees had previous convictions so had some understanding of their legal rights, but only one-third said they had read the Notice to Detained Persons. The majority also had low IQ scores and the authors argue that it is unlikely that the average IQ of detainees is much over 85. They also surmise that earlier studies had underestimated the incidence of significant intellectual impairment among suspects interviewed at the police station. The authors highlight the need for appropriate training to identify vulnerable individuals. Similar problems were identified in Brown's study (Brown 1989). He found that officers in his sample considered that an appropriate adult was required in only 1 per cent of cases because of mental illness or learning disabilities, but this is much lower than one would expect to find within the population of suspects as a whole. The problem will be particularly acute in relation to borderline cases.

Further reviews of appropriate adult provision in England and Wales were undertaken by the National Appropriate Adult Network (NAAN) in 2006 and 2010. A cross-departmental report, *Improving Health, Supporting Justice*, was published in response to the Bradley Report, to improve health care and other services for vulnerable individuals in the criminal justice system and the NAAN report was conducted as part of this strategy (Perks, 2010). Information was obtained from all police forces and the data showed the majority of requests for appropriate adults were for juveniles. The number of adults identified as vulnerable varied from area to area and it was noted that the prevalence of mental health and learning disability/difficulty identified in prison is higher than the apparent levels of need indicated in police custody (2010: 4). This may mean opportunities are lost to divert these vulnerable adults from the criminal justice system. The majority of appropriate adult services for juveniles are provided by Youth Offending Teams who have a statutory responsibility to provide AA services to juveniles under the 1998 Crime and Disorder Act, but most of the services for vulnerable adults are subcontracted to other or private sector organisations. The survey found satisfaction with the services provided for juveniles during office hours, but the majority of respondents 'expressed frustration at the lack of any statutory responsibility for AA services for vulnerable adults' (2010: 13). Many vulnerable adults were charged without an appropriate adult present. The Report recommends that a statutory responsibility for AA services should be given to local authorities. A combined service for both vulnerable adults and juveniles would be preferable and it might offer another opportunity to refer vulnerable adults to other services and divert them from the criminal justice system and ultimately from prison.

A further concern has been the treatment of 17-year-old suspects who, until recently, were treated as adults under PACE when in custody, so did not have an automatic right to an appropriate adult. This was anomalous as under the Children Act 2004, 17-year-olds are treated as children with cases heard in the Youth Court, and special measures to support child witnesses in court have now been extended to 17-year-olds. In Northern Ireland 17-year-olds are treated as juveniles and are entitled to an appropriate adult; 17-year-olds are also treated as children under the UN Convention on the Rights of the Child. In two recent cases, two 17-year-olds, Joe Lowton and Edward Thornber, committed suicide following contact with the police. Joe Lowton killed himself in 2012 after being charged and bailed on a drink-driving charge. Edward Thornber killed himself when he received a letter from the police telling him he would be charged with possession of cannabis. But demands and petitions for an increase in the age were resisted by the Home Secretary until the case of *R on the application of HC v Secretary of State for the Home Department and Commissioner of Police for the Metropolis* [2013] EWHC 982 (Admin). In this case a 17-year-old was arrested and held in custody for 11 hours; his mother found out about his detention 4½ hours after his arrest but he was never charged with the offence regarding which he had been questioned. He was offered a solicitor but declined. Here the High Court ruled that the relevant provision in the PACE Code failed to treat the child's best interest as a primary consideration and breached the Article 8 rights of the child and the parents. The court ordered the Home Secretary to amend it. It noted the inconsistencies between PACE and other relevant provisions and said that Article 8 and the UN Convention require that a 17-year-old in detention should be treated in conformity with the principle that his best interests are the primary consideration. The court said that the rights of both parent and child are engaged when the young person is in custody. As Mr Justice Moses said, 'Many 17-year olds do not believe they need any guidance at all. They demonstrate the youthful arrogance of which many parents are aware. All the more need then, for help and assistance from someone with whom they are familiar' (para 94). A Consultation on this and other revisions was undertaken and this amendment has now been made in the revised Code C.1.5A which came into effect on 27 October 2013. So the 17-year-old is now entitled to have an appropriate adult present and the police have to inform the suspect's parents of the grounds of the arrest.

There are also challenges facing vulnerable defendants in court. The Youth Justice and Criminal Evidence Act 1999 provided an array of special measures to assist vulnerable witnesses including those with learning disabilities. Defendants were not treated as eligible for special measures at trial under the original Act available to witnesses, under s 19(1) of the YJCEA. However, the court was able to use its discretion to offer measures available before the 1999 Act and would do so where assistance was necessary for the defendant to have a fair trial (CPS, 2011: para 5.54). In addition, while defendants are not normally able to give evidence via a live link, vulnerable defendants may now be allowed to do so if it enables them to participate fully in their trial (ss 33A-C YJCEA, inserted by the Police and Justice Act 2006, s 47). This applies to defendants under 18 where their ability to participate in the proceedings as a witness giving oral evidence in court is affected by their level of intellectual ability or social functioning (CPS, 2011: para 5.55). For defendants over 18 the court may direct that evidence be given by live link if the person is unable to participate effectively in the proceedings as a witness because of a mental disorder or significant impairment of intelligence and social functioning. Vulnerable defendants may also be assisted by an intermediary if giving evidence in court if it is necessary to ensure a fair trial (ss 33AA and 33BB YJCEA, inserted by Coroners and Justice Act 2009 s 104).

Section 77(1) of PACE also provides specific protection for suspects with learning disabilities who make confessions, where:

(a) the case against the accused depends wholly or substantially on a confession by him;

      and

(b) the court is satisfied –
      (i)   that he is mentally handicapped; and
      (ii) that the confession was not made in the presence of an independent person,

the court shall warn the jury that there is special need for caution before convicting the accused in reliance on the confession, and shall explain that the need arises because of the circumstances mentioned in paragraphs (a) and (b) above.

In *R v McKenzie* [1993] 1 WLR 453, the Court of Appeal said that where the prosecution case depends wholly upon a confession and the accused has a significant degree of mental handicap and the confession is unconvincing to the point where a properly directed jury could not properly convict upon it, then the judge, if he has not excluded the confession already, should withdraw the case from the jury. Usually confessions in such cases are more likely to be excluded under s 76 or 78.

It is also clear that defendants with learning disabilities experience problems in custody and in coping with confinement. Studies of prisoners with learning disabilities, by the Prison Reform Trust, have found that they are more likely to be segregated or subject to control or restraint (Loucks, 2007; Talbot and Riley 2007; Talbot 2008). This differential treatment may raise equality issues as public authorities, including the police and prison service, are under a duty imposed by the Equality Act 2010 to promote equality and not to discriminate on grounds of race, sex, disability, religion or belief, sexual orientation, gender reassignment or age, marriage or civil partnership.

Despite the above measures, individuals with mental health problems and with learning disabilities still face problems in the criminal justice system as the Bradley Report showed (Department of Health 2009). It highlighted the problems of identifying, assessing, and treating individuals with learning disabilities and stressed the need for early identification and assessment of their problems to divert them from the criminal justice system. The Report's findings, including the need to avoid prosecution but instead to deal with these individuals through the health-care system, were supported by the House of Commons Justice Committee, as well as those working with offenders and by the Government. Keeping them within the criminal justice system poses substantial problems for the administration of the prisons as well as for other prisoners. However, in practice diversion is often not achieved because of insufficient resources available for mental health care as well as problems of identification.

Code C of PACE makes clear that a police station should be used as place of safety as a last resort for a mentally disordered or otherwise vulnerable person detained under the Mental Health Act 1983 (C.3.16). Under s 136 of the Mental Health Act 1983 a person can be held in a police cell for up to 72 hours, much longer than permitted under PACE, which is 24 hours. A recent review by HMIC, HMIP and the Care Quality Commission and Healthcare Inspectorate Wales of the use of police cells as a place of safety for people with mental health needs found that police custody was still being used, due to a range of reasons, including insufficient staff at health-based places of safety or the lack of available beds (HMIC *et al.* 2013). This review recommends reducing the maximum period of detention in police custody under the MHA to 24 hours. If a person is already mentally ill, the experience of being confined in a police cell can exacerbate the mental health problems, while for a severely intoxicated person custody may not constitute a place of safety. Concerns have been raised over the lack of risk assessment of detainees and the level of checks, even where a risk has been identified, as well as the failure to identify those suffering from mental health problems, or those at risk of suicide.

The information we have on deaths in custody has highlighted the vulnerability of the accused in interrogation and the particular problems facing vulnerable suspects. Over half of those who died in police custody in 2011/12 were people with mental illness. We also know that offenders as a group have higher rates of mental illness than the public at large. The police have a statutory duty under the Police Reform Act 2002 to refer to the IPCC any complaint or incident regarding a death that has occurred during or following police contact and where there is an allegation or indication that the police contact contributed to the death. There has also been an obligation on HMRC, SOCA and UKBA to refer fatalities to the IPCC since April 2006. The latest figures available on deaths during or following police interrogation for 2012/13 show 30 road traffic fatalities (deaths of motorists, police cyclists or pedestrians arising from police pursuit or police vehicles responding to emergencies and other police-related traffic activity), no fatal police shootings, 15 deaths in or following police custody, 64 apparent suicides following police custody (that is, within two days of release from custody) and 21 other deaths following police contact (Grace 2013). The category 'deaths in or following police custody' includes deaths while the person is being arrested or taken into detention and may occur on police, private or medical premises, in a public place or in a police or other vehicle, and includes persons detained by the police under the Mental Health Act 1983.

Of the 15 who died in or following custody, seven of the group were identified as having mental health issues, including long-term mental health disorders, depression and previous suicide attempts, and nine members of the group had links to alcohol or drugs, having recently consumed them, or were in possession of drugs or alcohol at the time of arrest or were intoxicated. The most common reason for detention related to antisocial behaviour or public order offences. Four of the 15 fatalities involved some form of restraint by the police.

Concerns have been raised over the use of illegal holds and inappropriate restraints, the problems of dealing with people with alcohol or drug problems and the treatment of black and minority ethnic suspects. High-profile cases of BME suspects, such as Sean Rigg, who was suffering from schizophrenia, have focused attention on this issue of illegal holds and inappropriate restraint. Sean Rigg died after he was restrained and arrested in London in 2008. He collapsed while being held in the police van after being pinned down and held in a prone position for 8 minutes. No checks were made on him while he was held in the police van. An IPCC report in 2010 into his death found that police officers acted reasonably and proportionately in restraining him, but the inquest into his death found that unnecessary force had contributed to his death. The IPCC then announced an external review to inquire into the death in 2012 which reported in 2013 (Casale 2013). The external review recommended a reconsideration of the conduct of the officers involved in the apprehension, restraint and detention of Mr Rigg in relation to possible breaches of their duty of care and with a view to determining whether to bring misconduct proceedings. It also recommended reconsideration of the use of restraint including the duration of restraint in the prone position (Casale, 2013, p. 3). It was also critical of the forensic medical examiner involved in Mr Rigg's care. It also highlighted the need for effective monitoring in custody, including maintaining CCTV systems in proper working order, and greater communication with the deceased's family. The IPCC has now published its own review of its work investigating deaths, in response to these criticisms, and has formulated a plan of action, including greater contact with families of the deceased (IPCC 2014).

An IPCC study examined 333 deaths in or following custody over an 11-year period from 1998/99 to 2008/09 (Hannan *et al.* 2010). There were 49 deaths in 1998 but this had fallen to 15 in 2008/9. The composition of the deceased in the sample was 90 per cent male, 76 per cent White, 7 per cent Black, 5 per cent Asian, 2 per cent Mixed Race and 1 per cent Chinese/Other. The majority were arrested in a public place and the most common reasons for arrest were being drunk and incapable or disorderly, public order, driving and drug offences. The researchers found that 'The most common causes of death were natural causes, overdoses, suicide and injuries received prior to detention' (ibid.: vi). Twenty-six per cent of the sample were physically restrained by officers on arrest, during transportation or while in custody or in hospital. People in the age group 25–34 were more likely to be restrained than other age groups and members of BME groups were 'significantly more likely to be restrained than White people' (ibid.). Sixteen people in the sample were classified as restraint-related deaths, 12 of whom were White, 3 were Black and 1 was Asian.

In March 2012 ACPO updated its *Guidance on the Safer Detention and Handling of Persons in Police Custody*, first published in 2006 in response to concerns raised by the IPCC, as well as by the Inspector of Prisons and Inspector of Constabulary (ACPO 2012). It recommended enhanced risk assessments, particularly for detainees suffering from alcohol or drug intoxication or under restraint, and formulating new protocols for dealing with suspects who are drunk or incapable and a new policy for dealing with diabetics. It also emphasised the importance of engaging health-care professionals in diagnosis and treatment of vulnerable detainees. Violent detainees should not be left unsupervised in vehicles. Suspects should be risk-assessed prior to custody, regarding health or injury, and if necessary taken directly to hospital. In custody there should be proper monitoring of cells for those under the influence of drugs or alcohol and greater use should be made of CCTV. Adequate health care should be provided as appropriate and any force or restraint should be proportionate and lawful and the prone position should be avoided. Proper training should be given to staff. Those who have consumed drugs or alcohol and who are at higher risk should be roused every 30 minutes. If a detainee cannot be roused, an appropriate health-care professional or ambulance must be called. There is also advice on dealing with mental disorders and the mentally vulnerable, as a person could react badly to custody even if not being treated for mental illness, while a person with learning disabilities may be more suggestible. For mentally disordered offenders, where possible their diversion should be considered before charging is made.

The IPCC Report (2014) also raised concerns over the use of restraints and recommended a number of changes, including improved training in restraint techniques, and greater awareness of the risk of head injuries associated with intoxication, the use of CCTV in cells holding high risk individuals and the adoption by police forces of procedures to ensure that Custody Officers comply with PACE Code C when assessing, checking and rousing detainees (IPCC 2014). It also raises the question of whether those with mental health problems who are severely intoxicated should be held at the police station and recommends that alternative facilities should be made available.

Addressing concerns over the treatment in detention is clearly important for the legitimacy of the police and for particular communities where confidence in the police may be low. A transparent procedure for the reporting and investigation of deaths in custody is also essential.

Miranda v Arizona and its legacy

As we have seen there are still issues of concerns over the treatment of suspects and evidence obtained by interrogation and these issues have also received considerable attention in the United States, where the Supreme Court jurisprudence has highlighted the need for protection for suspects during interrogation. In *Miranda v Arizona* 384 US 436 (1966) where the police had failed to inform Ernesto Miranda of his right to see a lawyer, the US Supreme Court dealt robustly with the challenge of preventing the abuse of police powers. This decision of the Warren Court in that case constituted a landmark in the protection of the suspect during interrogation and specified new guidelines for the police to provide protection against improper police practices on the part of state and federal law enforcers.

Chief Justice Warren stressed in *Miranda* that procedural safeguards must be used to protect the privilege and stipulated the following procedure:

> He must be warned prior to any questioning that he has the right to remain silent, that anything he says can be used against him in a court of law, that he has the right to the presence of an attorney, and that if he cannot afford an attorney one will be appointed for him prior to any questioning if he so desires. Opportunity to exercise these rights must be afforded to him throughout the interrogation. After such warnings have been given, and such opportunity afforded him, the individual may knowingly and intelligently waive these rights and agree to answer questions or make a statement. But unless and until such warnings and waiver are demonstrated by the prosecution at trial, no evidence obtained as a result of interrogation can be used against him.
>
> (ibid.: at 478–9)

So the suspect had to be warned by the police of his right to silence, and his right to a lawyer at the police station and at trial. The police should tell him that he has the right to stop the interrogation at any point and have access to a lawyer on demand. This was supported by an exclusionary rule: confessions could not be admitted unless these safeguards had been observed and the defendant had waived these rights in full knowledge and voluntarily. So the *Miranda* guidelines went further than PACE in informing the accused that the interrogation may be stopped at any time, in giving access to counsel without exceptions, and in the automatic exclusion of admissions obtained in violation of the requirements, in contrast to the discretionary exclusion of admissions obtained in breach of the PACE Codes. At that time there had been a line of cases that raised concerns over unacceptable police tactics, the bullying of suspects and their isolation for long periods (see, for example, *Davis v California* 348 US 737 (1966)).

The *Miranda* guidelines aimed to prevent the physical and mental abuse of suspects at the police station and to prevent the suspect from being tricked into making admissions. The suspect should make a free, rational and informed choice whether or not to speak, and the decision should not be made under pressure, in the hope of advantage or fear of detriment. 'Knowingly' means in awareness of the right to silence and 'intelligently' signifies that a rational decision is made. Although the Fifth Amendment itself does not refer to warnings or waiver, these were read into it by the court in *Miranda*. This case therefore reaffirmed the right to silence and the right to make an informed choice whether or not to exercise that right. It also expressed the Supreme Court's recognition of the importance of judicial integrity in preventing abuse.

As the court said:

> The privilege against self-incrimination, which has had a long and expansive historical development, is the essential mainstay of our adversary system and guarantees to the individual 'the right to remain silent unless he chooses to speak in the unfettered exercise of his own free will', during a period of custodial interrogation as well as in the courts or during the course of other official investigations.
>
> (ibid.: at 458)

If an individual waives his right to silence he must do so 'knowingly and intelligently' or his answers will be inadmissible. A statement given in interrogation while in custody should be excluded unless the state can show the suspect was told before questioning that he has the right to remain silent and have the presence of lawyer before and during questioning. He should also be told that if he does speak that anything said can and will be used against him in court. The prosecution has to show that the warning was given and the right has been expressly waived either orally or by signing waiver forms. After *Miranda* the suspect held in custody could not be questioned in the absence of a lawyer unless he had been informed of his right to silence and his right to counsel and had waived these rights. In applying the guidelines, issues have arisen in relation to what constitutes 'custody' and in determining the point at which the warning should be given and when a waiver has been made.

In practice, determining a knowing and intelligent waiver may be problematic and the courts have been willing to imply a waiver in borderline cases. For example, in *Michigan v Mosley* 423 US 96 (1975) an initial refusal to be questioned was deemed not to prohibit further questioning and in the second interrogation the subject's response could be construed as a waiver. It was also held in *Colorado v Spring* 479 US 564 (1987) that a waiver in relation to particular offences can be construed as a general waiver so that the police may then question the suspect in relation to more serious offences.

Although under the original *Miranda* decision any statements obtained in breach of *Miranda* requirements should be excluded, as we shall see, some post-Miranda rulings by the Supreme Court weakened its protective value. In *Miranda* the court said a warning was required where 'the individual is taken into custody or otherwise deprived of his freedom by the authorities in any significant way and subjected to questioning' (at 444). *Miranda* left open whether it applies to the situation prior to arrest where a suspect makes a statement voluntarily, or where questioning occurs outside the police station. A suspect could see himself as deprived of his freedom even if at home if he is surrounded by police and thinks that any resistance or flight will be construed adversely. In *Miranda* 'custody' seemed to be conceived broadly and the early cases included the suspect's home as in the case of *Orozco v Texas* 394 US 324 (1969), where the suspect was questioned at home initially regarding a murder at a restaurant the previous evening. Here the Supreme Court held that the *Miranda* requirements applied when the suspect had been questioned outside the police station. He admitted going to the restaurant and owning a gun, which was later found and from which the shot was fired which killed the victim. Orozco was convicted but because the questioning had not been preceded by a *Miranda* warning his conviction was quashed. This decision was criticised by commentators as over-extending *Miranda*.

It is 48 years since the *Miranda* decision and during that time significant inroads have been made into the *Miranda* protections. These changes reflect the changing composition of the Supreme Court and changes in the political climate as well as the 'war' on drug crime. Initially *Miranda* was applied robustly but in the 1970s and 1980s, during the Reagan and Bush administrations, the court retreated from this position, failing to automatically exclude evidence obtained in breach of the *Miranda* requirements and adopting a more narrow technical approach to them, and in so doing moved closer to the discretionary approach in the UK, and this has continued in the last two decades. In *Harris v New York* 401 US 222 (1971), one of the first cases to retreat from a vigorous interpretation of *Miranda*, incriminating statements made to the police, before Harris had been Mirandized, conflicted with his testimony in court and the court held that he could be cross-examined on them to undermine his testimony and credibility at trial. The trial judge had stressed that *Miranda* should not be used as a licence to commit perjury safe in the knowledge that one would not face the embarrassment of being confronted by one's previous inconsistent statements at trial and this decision was upheld by the Supreme Court.

A 'balancing' approach in which the public interest was weighed against the suspect's rights developed in the 1980s. In *Rhode Island v Innis* 446 US 291 (1980) the suspect made it clear on his way to the police station that he did not wish to speak before seeing a lawyer. In the course of the journey, the officers spoke among themselves and discussed the possibility of a child finding the missing murder weapon, a shotgun, or shells, with possible tragic consequences. In response to this, the accused volunteered to show them where the weapon was concealed and took them to the site. The Supreme Court held that the discovery of the weapon as well as the accompanying statements were admissible because the conversation with the officers did not amount to an interrogation for the purpose of the *Miranda* rules, as the comments were not intended to produce such a reaction. 'Interrogation' means expressly asking questions and actions or words of the police that they knew were reasonably likely to produce that reaction and here the police could not have known their comments would have that effect. Yet one might equally argue that most reasonable people would very likely be affected by such an appeal to child safety and excluding such tactics is drawing the boundaries too narrowly. *Innis* was similar to the earlier case of *Brewer v Williams* 30 US 387 (1977) where the court had excluded the suspect's incriminating statement, but because of a denial of his right to counsel under the Sixth Amendment rather than the Fifth Amendment privilege. In *Brewer* the police officer had referred to the fact that the victim would not receive a Christian burial if her body was not discovered soon as snow was falling, following which the accused showed the police where the body could be found.

In *New York v Quarles* 467 US 649 (1984) the court ruled that the *Miranda* warning could be omitted in emergencies. A suspect was pursued and detained by the police in a supermarket. The police thought he had a gun and so questioned him to find it before giving a *Miranda* warning. Quarles directed them to some boxes where the gun was found. He was then arrested, Mirandized and charged with possession of the gun. At first instance, the trial judge excluded his statement locating the gun and its discovery because he had not received the warning. But the Supreme Court argued that given the immediate danger to the public, the possibility of a passer-by finding the gun and harming himself or others, the *Miranda* warning need not be given, and the statements of the accused were admissible despite the failure to warn. The aim of *Miranda* – to protect the suspect's Fifth Amendment rights – was balanced and outweighed here by the objective danger to the public. But it would still have been open to the court to permit the police to question a suspect in an emergency without a warning to obtain information urgently to protect the public, and to then exclude the statement at trial. In *Oregon v Elstad* 470 US 298 (1985), the court similarly declined to exclude evidence obtained in the context of a *Miranda* violation. In *Warden v Williams* 467 US (1984) the court took the view that if real evidence obtained by violating the *Miranda* requirements would have been discovered in any event, then it may be admitted in evidence.

In *Moran v Burbine* 475 US 412 (1986), when the suspect was detained by the police, a lawyer obtained for him by his sister rang the station and asked if his client would be further questioned that day. The answer given was 'no', but in fact Burbine was questioned later that night without being informed that he had a lawyer or that the lawyer had rung. He received his *Miranda* warnings and confessed. The court concluded that the police were not obliged to disclose this information, even though it might have affected his decision to talk. Provided that he understood his right to silence his waiver was valid. Yet, as Stuntz (1989) notes, the tactics in *Moran v Burbine* and *Rhode Island v Innis* were precisely the kind of tactics *Miranda* was intended to protect against. The effect of these decisions is that *Miranda* is a shield only against police coercion, but not against police deception and undermines the principle that the waiver must be a result of the individual's rational choice. Deception in the course of interrogation has arguably become a more important element of criminal investigations as the use of coercion has become more strongly controlled, as Leo (1992) observes. Moreover, as Amar and Lettow (1995) note, as interrogation becomes more tightly controlled, the extremes of the interrogation process may be driven underground, into unregulated police interview rooms, surprise searches, wiretapping and invasions of privacy. Given this they advocate pretrial interrogation by judicial examination to prevent police misconduct. A similar argument for greater judicial involvement was also proposed in the context of Northern Ireland as we saw in Chapter 4, but was resisted by the UK Government. Attempts have also been made to extend waiver from express to implied waiver, inferred from the individual's conduct or actions. In *North Carolina v Butler* 441 US 369 (1979) Butler made incriminating statements and wanted them excluded at trial because he had not at that time waived his right to counsel. The court stressed that the waiver issue must be determined by the particular facts in each case and refused to rule out the possibility that waiver could be implicit.

By the 1990s the public, politicians and the media were displaying an increasingly punitive attitude, resulting in a substantial increase in incarceration and a move towards what has been described as mass imprisonment, with the United States having the highest imprisonment rate in the world. Being tough on crime became an essential element of political strategy for the Clinton administration, as it had for the Reagan and George H.W. Bush administrations which preceded it. Moreover, following 9/11 public anxieties over crime and demands for punishment were further fuelled by the war on terror and concern over home-grown terrorists as well as external threats and were reflected in the policies of the George W. Bush administration. Budgetary constraints are now limiting further penal expansion and Obama has been more supportive of rehabilitative rather than simply punitive measures.

However, there has been an erosion of the ability of *Miranda* to protect suspects, in relation to the limits placed on *Miranda*'s definition of custody and with a reduction in the requirements for an effective waiver as Fairlie (2013) observes. She cites the case of *California v Beheler* 463 US 1121 (1983) where custody for *Miranda* purposes was confined to the restraint of freedom of movement to the degree associated with formal arrest. So the police can tactically advise the suspect he is not under arrest, even though the situation is clearly coercive, and tell him that he is free to leave at any time and the courts would not treat this as a custodial interrogation. In *Howes v Fields* (2012) 113 S. Ct. 118 the suspect was taken out of his cell in the evening and questioned at length by two armed guards for seven hours in a conference room and not Mirandized, but told if he did not want to cooperate he could leave at any time. He was questioned at length despite telling his interrogators he did not want to speak anymore and being deprived of his medication. At the end of this period, in the early hours of the morning, he confessed. Yet the court ruled this was not a custodial situation for the purposes of *Miranda* and he was not entitled to a *Miranda* warning. The interpretation of waiver has also been broadened as in *Miranda* it was clear that the burden on the state to show waiver was a heavy one and would not be presumed simply from the fact of obtaining a confession, but waiver required an explicit statement. It had to be made specifically after the warning was given and the standard at the very least was the intermediate standard of clear and convincing evidence. *Miranda* specifically said a waiver could not be inferred either from silence of the accused after warnings given, or from the fact that a confession was eventually obtained. But in *Colorado v Connolly* 479 US 157 (1986) the standard was reduced to preponderance of the evidence and in *Berghuis v Thompkins* 560 US 370 (2010) the court found the suspect had waived his rights through confessing, even though he refused to sign a waiver form and for most of the lengthy interrogation he said virtually nothing. Moreover, because statements obtained in breach of *Miranda* have been used at trial whenever a public safety exception applied, as in the *Quarles* case discussed above, the disincentive to improper conduct has been lost, and Romano (2011) has argued that *Miranda* is on the verge of extinction.

The weakening of *Miranda*'s protective value by the Roberts court is contrasted by Fairlie with the more rights-protective demands of international criminal justice, which reflects more faithfully than US domestic practice the original aim of the *Miranda* opinion. In the international criminal courts, where suspects' rights have been breached, this has 'consistently resulted in exclusion' (Fairlie 2013: 37). This has been seen as essential in achieving the legitimacy of the new courts.

Recent cases have continued this trend to restrict *Miranda*'s application. For example, in *Salinas v Texas* 570 US (2013), the appellant, without being placed in custody or receiving a *Miranda* warning, answered voluntarily some of the police questions regarding a murder but remained silent when asked whether ballistic testing would match his shotgun to shell casings found at the scene of the crime. At trial the prosecutor used his failure to answer the question as evidence of guilt and he was convicted. On appeal he argued that the use of his silence violated the Fifth Amendment. But his appeal was rejected by the state appellate court and this was affirmed by the Supreme Court on the ground that he had not expressly invoked the privilege when asked the question. The court followed the earlier case of *Minnesota v Murphy* 465 US 420 (1980) where it had ruled that the witness who wants the protection of the privilege must claim it at the time he relies on it. In *Murphy* admissions had been made to a probation officer in the course of a sexual offender treatment course where the offender was obliged to respond truthfully to questions that were used in evidence against him.

However, the spirit of *Miranda* has been reasserted in some post-millennium cases. For example, in *Dickerson v United States* 530 US 428 (2000) the Supreme Court upheld the warning and waiver requirements and asserted the constitutional foundation for *Miranda* and said, '*Miranda* has become embedded in routine police practice to the point where the warnings have become part of our national culture'. In *Missouri v Seibert* 542 US 600 (2004) the court also excluded a post-warning confession when an earlier confession was obtained prior to a warning.

The experience of Canada

Canadian jurisprudence also shows a tension between the formal acknowledgement of rights of detainees and limits on their scope imposed by the courts in response to Charter challenges. The right to counsel is protected by s 10(b) of the Charter: 'Everyone has the right on arrest or detention to retain and instruct counsel without delay and to be informed of that right'. There must be a free choice whether or not to speak (*R v Hebert* [1990 2 SCR 151). Although the police are not required to inform suspects of right to silence before questioning, in practice most police forces deliver both counsel and silence cautions. They should be informed of their right to retain and instruct counsel without delay, told about access to counsel free of charge if they meet legal aid requirements, and be given information about access to immediate legal advice regardless of financial status, as well as information on the duty solicitor scheme.

However, while there is a right to consult counsel, in *R v Sinclair* [2010] 2 SCR 310 the Canadian Supreme Court ruled that there was no general right to counsel during interrogation, so this is clearly a weaker right than in England and Wales, the United States, or the International Criminal Court. Here Sinclair had an initial conversation with his lawyer but wanted to consult again during interrogation, but the court said the right to counsel was a one-time-only opportunity with few exceptions and a request to consult counsel again during questioning can be denied. Sinclair, who was charged with murder and convicted of manslaughter, had spoken twice by phone to his lawyer when arrested, but wanted to speak to him again during his interrogation in which he had initially remained silent. But the police refused to allow him to do so. He then made an admission later in the interview, as well as incriminating statements to an undercover officer placed in his cell. He also took the police to the scene of the murder and took part in a re-enactment. The trial judge ruled that the statement from the interview and to the undercover officer and the re-enactment were all admissible and this was upheld by the Court of Appeal and the Supreme Court. The majority of the court, in a 5:4 decision, said that during an interview there is no right to re-consult a lawyer or to consult a specific lawyer if he cannot be reached within a reasonable time. The court said that:

> In the context of a custodial interrogation, the purpose of s. 10(*b*) is to support detainees' right to choose whether to cooperate with the police investigation or not, by giving them access to legal advice on the situation they are facing. This is achieved by requiring that they be informed of the right to consult counsel and, if a detainee so requests, that he or she be given an opportunity to consult counsel. Achieving this purpose may require that the detainee be given an opportunity to reconsult counsel where developments make this necessary, but it does not demand the continued presence of counsel throughout the interview process. There is of course nothing to prevent counsel from being present at an interrogation where all sides consent, as already occurs. The police remain free to facilitate such an arrangement if they so choose, and the detainee may wish to make counsel's presence a precondition of giving a statement.
>
> (at 310)

The court also said that while the police must respect the individual's Charter rights, a rule requiring the police to automatically retreat when detainees state that they have nothing to say 'would not strike the proper balance between the public interest in the investigation of crimes and the suspect's interest in being left alone'. The police may continue questioning after the suspect has made clear that he wishes to remain silent. In *Singh* (2007) 3 SCR 405 the Canadian Supreme court approved persistent questioning by the police, although the detainee had said he did not wish to speak 18 times. There is no right not to be spoken to by the police and it is hard for the suspect to resist if his wishes are ignored by the police who carry on questioning. Even though Singh repeatedly asserted his right to silence, the police persisted and obtained an incriminating admission which the court deemed was voluntary. If the police were obliged to refrain from questioning where the suspect has said he does not want to speak to police, the court said, the state's interests would be ignored and this would overshoot the protection afforded to the individual's freedom of choice at common law and under the Charter.

In Canada any confession obtained in interrogation should be made voluntarily and not as a result of threats, inducements, oppressive behaviour or trickery and the burden is on the Crown to show voluntariness. The prosecution will need to show that the suspect was treated fairly and had an opportunity to consult counsel and, if not, this may mean any admissions are excluded, even if they were made voluntarily. However, in *R v Oickle* [2000] 2 SCR 3 and subsequent cases, the courts have been construing voluntariness very loosely. So in *Oickle* a statement was found to be voluntary despite police language minimising the significance of the crime, the introduction of 'failed' polygraph results and inducements and promises not to investigate his fiancée if he confessed. In a subsequent case, *R v Khansaiyasith* [2008] O.J. No. 1477 (S.C.J.), the defendant said he wanted to remain silent 47 times but was interviewed after being tasered and after saying he was ill, having just taken heroin. Hospital records also showed he was bruised after being hit by a police vehicle, but his statements were admitted as voluntary statements. The court also said in *R v Spencer* (2007) SCC 11 that if inducements are offered, they will look at the strength of the inducement, so an inducement may not be seen as sufficient to impair the will of the accused. Yet, as we shall see in Chapter 6, inducements may be an ingredient in the production of false confessions. The Supreme Court said in *Oickle* that there is no legal requirement of video recording but the failure to record may be viewed suspiciously and it will be hard for the Crown to prove beyond reasonable doubt that it is voluntary. Visual recording is now widely used in custodial interviews of suspects at police facilities in Canada.

Conclusion

It is clear that the position of suspects in England and Wales has also been improved through the procedural protections in the PACE Codes, the Duty Solicitor Scheme and the accreditation scheme for legal advisers. The measures in PACE that provide more protection for suspects have been supplemented subsequently by improved protections at the trial stage for vulnerable suspects, so we now have many safeguards to protect suspects from over-zealous interrogators and prosecutors. The changes in PACE paved the way for an enhanced spirit of professionalism in the conduct of interrogations and to less confrontational interviewing techniques, as noted by Williamson and Moston (1990). New skills training and stricter supervision have been introduced and there has been a greater emphasis on ethical investigation and interviewing. From the police standpoint, the police can be confident that if an interview is conducted properly, it will be admitted in evidence.

Although PACE was intended to improve the protection of the suspect and to boost the public's confidence in the police, there is some evidence that strategies and tactics used by the police initially sought to maintain the position prior to PACE (McConville *et al.* 1991). As PACE has increased regulation of the interrogation process and the account-ability of the police and improved the balance between state and citizen, the police looked for ways of recovering their diminished powers, for example, by increasing pressures on suspects they believe to be guilty. Despite the formal changes of PACE, police culture adapted to use the formal procedures to preserve that culture (Reiner, 2010). We noted earlier the number of appeals based on the failure to properly observe the PACE Codes.

So far we have considered the legal framework and guidance for the interrogation of suspects and the formal protection for vulnerable suspects. However, the practice and experience of the interviewing process may generate risks of wrongful conviction, even where officers are acting lawfully, because of the dynamics of interrogation and partic-ular vulnerabilities of suspects. While overtly oppressive behaviour is controlled by PACE, it has been argued that it does not sufficiently protect those highly suggestible individuals most at risk of false confes-sions. Moreover, the majority of suspects in the UK and the United States do waive their right to silence and speak even if they do not fully under-stand the caution. The dynamics of interrogation and the experience of vulnerable witnesses will be further considered in Chapter 6.

6
False Confessions

Introduction

The framework of formal due process rights to protect the suspect was considered in Chapter 5 but the question remains of whether they offer sufficient safeguards against false confessions and wrongful convictions given the number of miscarriages of justice. Recurring features have been found in the miscarriage of justice cases, including problems with forensic evidence, police misconduct, unreliable and uncorroborated confessions, perjury of witnesses or co-defendants, mistaken identifications, the fabrication of evidence and tunnel vision on the part of the investigating officers, oppressive conduct by the police, extended detention under antiterrorist law, and nondisclosure of evidence, including forensic evidence.

Examples may be found of overzealous interrogation and improper behaviour but, as we shall see, false confessions are still possible where interviews are conducted properly but suspects may confess because of vulnerability or a desire to escape. Miscarriages may also occur because honest and well-intentioned witnesses misidentify suspects or give erroneous testimony. Misidentification by eyewitnesses has been a recurring feature of wrongful convictions here and in the United States. The Innocence Project in the United States found that 75 per cent of wrongful convictions confirmed with DNA diagnosis involved eyewitness misidentification; in 50 per cent unvalidated or improper forensic science played a role; false confessions were implicated in 25 per cent; and unreliable informants in 15 per cent (http://www.innocenceproject.org/). Other issues included prosecutorial misconduct, ineffective defence, police misconduct and racism, factors which are harder to quantify but evident in some of the miscarriages of justice overturned by DNA testing. Little

(2008) proposes that the problems of wrongful convictions should be addressed in capital cases by the exclusion of four categories of evidence which are known sources of wrongful convictions, namely eyewitness misidentifications, false confessions, criminal informants and unvalidated or 'junk' science.

At trial juries have in the past accepted uncritically police testimony. Jurors are also influenced by how confident witnesses are, so if the police say a suspect is lying the jury is more likely to believe them than the defendant (Cutler 2011). Cumbersome appeal procedures and the reluctance of the Court of Appeal to overturn jury verdicts have also figured.

Issues to be considered in this chapter will include the circumstances in which individuals may make false confessions, problems in detecting deception in practice and the groups of suspects at higher risk of making false confessions. The relevant social scientific research on lie detection and effective interviewing will be reviewed and the most promising developments in eliciting true rather than false confessions will be discussed.

Miscarriages of justice

Although the term 'miscarriage of justice' has been used principally to refer to wrongful conviction of the innocent, it also includes wrongful acquittals of the guilty, and obviously for each person wrongfully convicted, the guilty party has escaped justice. There may also be miscarriages of justice where the person is guilty but the integrity of the process has been undermined. Lord Justice Mantell said in *R v Davis, Rowe and Johnson* [2011] 1 Cr App R 115 that 'A conviction can never be safe if there is doubt about guilt. However, the converse is not true. A conviction may be unsafe even where there is no doubt about guilt but the trial process has been vitiated by serious unfairness or significant legal misdirection' (at 131–2). Examples would be the case of *Mullen* (1999) 2 Cr App R 143, where the way the appellant had been unlawfully removed from Zimbabwe amounted to an abuse of process; the case should not have proceeded irrespective of his guilt because of the 'blatant and extremely serious failure to adhere to the rule of law' (at 156). So the focus here is on the integrity of the process.

We also need to consider the political and social context of the convictions, particularly in relation to suspects detained on suspicion of terrorist offences during the Northern Ireland conflict. The detention and questioning of suspects in holding centres in Northern Ireland was discussed in Chapter 4, but the treatment in interrogation of Irish suspects detained in England and Wales following bombings on the mainland was also problematic. The suspects were held in connection with incidents that had generated public outrage, where there was intense media coverage and considerable pressure on the police to get a conviction. It has also been argued that the communities themselves were seen as the suspect, an issue we will consider in Chapter 7.

The Birmingham Six were convicted in 1975 of murder and causing an explosion and their conviction was not quashed until 1991 (*R v McIlkenny and others* (1991) 93 Cr App R 287). They said their written confession was obtained by coercion. The Guildford Four were imprisoned in 1975 for the pub bombings in Woolwich and Guildford; their conviction was not quashed until 1989 so they spent 14 years in prison (*R v Richardson, Conlon, Armstrong and Hill, The Times* (20 October 1989)). Hill confessed within 24 hours and implicated the others who then confessed. The forensic tests used by the prosecution expert witness Frank Skuse in the trials of the Birmingham Six and Judith Ward were found to be unreliable. Evidence was fabricated in the cases of the Guildford Four and the Maguires and there was also a failure to disclose prosecution evidence in the case of Judith Ward and the Maguires.

Judith Ward was convicted in 1974 for murder and causing an explosion and held in prison for 18 years until her conviction was quashed in 1992 by the Court of Appeal who said that because she had a personality disorder, no reliance could be placed on her confession (*R v Ward (Judith)* (1993) 96 Cr App R 1). She fantasised about her relations with the IRA and made a false confession. Medical evidence on her condition had not been disclosed at trial and fresh medical evidence was admitted on appeal. The Court of Appeal also found that test results favouring the defence had not been disclosed by the Forensic Science Service and other information relevant to the defence had not been disclosed by the DPP and prosecuting counsel.

The Maguires were convicted in 1976 for possession of explosive substances, also in connection with the Guildford and London bombings. Leave to appeal was initially refused in 1977. They spent many years in prison and one of them died there. But after the Guildford Four's convictions were quashed, the Maguires' case was referred back to the Court of Appeal. The court quashed the Maguires' convictions in 1991 because the prosecution did not disclose crucial scientific evidence to the defence, namely the notebooks of the forensic scientists indicating an innocent source of the nitro-glycerine found on them and at their premises (*R v Maguire et al.* (1992) 94 Cr App R 133).

Many of the defendants in these miscarriages of justice, including the Guildford Four and Birmingham Six, were interrogated under anti-terrorist legislation which at that time allowed greater power to detain suspects. However, while the rights of suspects have been strengthened substantially since the 1980s, counter-terrorism provisions have continued to allow for extended detention for those suspected of terrorist offences. There are now improved procedural safeguards, including visual recording not available in the 1970s and 1980s, with the requirement for recording of interviews of persons detained under the Terrorism Act and the Counter-Terrorism Act now inserted into Code H of PACE, but those suspected of terrorist offences may be held for longer than ordinary suspects to obtain information. Section 41 of and Schedule 8 to the Terrorism Act 2000 originally allowed extended detention pre-charge of 7 days. This was increased from 7 to 14 days by the Criminal Justice Act 2003. The Terrorism Act 2006 (ss 23–26) amended the 2000 Act and extended the maximum to 28 days, although the Act also gave new procedural protections. In 2007 the Labour Government tried to increase pre-charge detention to 42 days in its Counter-Terrorism Bill, but was defeated in the House of Lords. The Coalition Government also tried to extend it further, but it has now reverted to 14 days since January 2011, but could be increased again if an emergency arose. Under PACE nonterrorist suspects may be detained prior to charge for 24 hours with extension to 36 hours following a review and authorisation by an officer of the rank of superintendent or above (s 42(1). A further extension of detention to a maximum of 96 hours is possible only if authorised by a magistrates' court (s 43). Suspects should be charged as soon as possible or released.

For ordinary suspects not questioned in connection for offences related to terrorism, the PACE provisions will govern their treatment, but while PACE has had a significant and beneficial impact on their treatment, we find cases of wrongful convictions and miscarriages of justice both before and after its enactment. Stefan Kiszko was convicted in 1976 of the murder and sexual assault of an 11-year-old girl, Lesley Molseed. Here there was a failure to disclose exculpatory evidence which the prosecution had at the time, namely that heads of sperm were found on the victim's clothing yet the accused was infertile. His conviction was quashed by the Court of Appeal in 1992 when it heard evidence not disclosed at trial (*R v Kiszko, The Times* (18 February 1992)). During his time in prison he was attacked by other prisoners and died two years after his release.

The Bridgewater Four were convicted in 1979 for murdering a newspaper boy, Carl Bridgewater, who had been attacked when he disturbed burglars at Yew Tree Farm. Their convictions were finally quashed in 1997 because of the fabrication of the interview evidence. Patrick Molloy of the Bridgewater Four said he confessed after physical maltreatment, as well as sleep and food deprivation. Gerry Conlon, one of the Guildford Four, said he had confessed after being deprived of sleep and food as well as being refused access to a lawyer. Some of the worst miscarriages of justice were associated with the West Midlands Serious Crime Squad, which was disbanded in 1989. It had been involved in both the Bridgewater Four and Birmingham Six cases. The suspects were deprived of food and sleep and subjected to threats and violence to obtain confessions. In the case of *Twitchell* [2000] 1 Cr App R 373, Keith Twitchell 'confessed' following mistreatment by the Squad, including being handcuffed to a chair and having a plastic bag placed over his head. He was suffocated until he agreed to sign a confession to the murder of a security guard. Following his conviction, he spent nearly 19 years in prison before winning his appeal.

Recording of interviews is obviously a key step forward. However, in the case of the Cardiff Three, wrongly convicted for the murder of Lynne White, the interview was recorded but they were still subjected to bullying, hectoring and intimidation. Their confessions, however, were not excluded at their trial in 1990 and they were not released until 1992 (*R v Paris, Abdullahi and Miller* (1993) 97 Cr App R 99). Concerns were raised over the actions of members of the South Wales police in the 1980s and 1990s, including allegations of fabrication of evidence and intimidation of witnesses. In the Cardiff Newsagent Three case, Michael O'Brien, Darren Hall and Ellis Sherwood were convicted of the murder of a newsagent in 1988 and were not released until 1999. They claimed mistreatment by the South Wales police, denial of access to legal advice and fabrication of evidence. Hall's confession, which implicated his co-defendants, was found to be unreliable because of a personality disorder (*R v O'Brien, Hall and Sherwood* [2000] EWCA Crim 3). The South Wales police were asked in 2010 to examine the investigation and publish a report on it, but to date this has still not been delivered. Failure to disclose evidence that would assist the defence has been a recurring feature in miscarriages of justice. Despite the disclosure regime introduced by the CPIA and discussed in Chapter 3, we still find appeals succeeding because of nondisclosure, as in the cases of *R v Hadley* [2006] EWCA Crim 2544 and *R v Giles* [2009] EWCA Crim 1388.

In some cases convictions have only been quashed after many years because of DNA evidence. Michael Shirley was wrongly convicted of murder and spent 16 years in prison. His conviction was quashed in

2003 when DNA evidence showed his conviction was unsafe (*R v Shirley* [2003] EWCA Crim 1976). Sean Hodgson was also wrongfully convicted of murder and spent 27 years in prison claiming his innocence (*R v Hodgson* [2009] EWCA Crim 490). DNA testing of the crime scene sample eventually exonerated him. After his appeal, DNA testing of the exhumed body of David Lace, the original suspect, showed a match with crime scene samples. The DNA testing had been available for some time before Hodgson was exonerated, but when an initial request for samples had been made the Forensic Science Service had said, incorrectly, that the exhibits in the case had been destroyed. The implications and issues surrounding DNA evidence are discussed further in Chapter 8.

But flawed forensic evidence has also figured in miscarriages of justice. A study by Garrett and Neufeld (2009) in the United States of innocents who were convicted of serious crimes, but later exonerated by post-conviction DNA testing, found that in the majority of the trials the forensic analysts giving evidence for the prosecution gave invalid testimony, that is, testimony that gave conclusions that misstated empirical data or which were unsupported by empirical data. The trials involved 72 forensic analysts employed by 52 laboratories, practices or hospitals from 25 states and, as the authors point out, the adversarial process did not effectively police this invalid testimony. The experts were rarely cross-examined by defence counsel who also rarely obtained their own experts. They emphasise the need for the scientific community to develop appropriate standards to ensure valid presentation of forensic evidence in the criminal courts and to maintain the integrity of the criminal process.

The Report of the Canadian Lamer Commission of Inquiry into the wrongful conviction of Gregory Parsons for the murder of Catherine Carroll also commented on the effects of inadequate interviews on failures in criminal investigation (Lamer 2006). They identify recurring features in wrongful conviction cases: a shocking crime with a high profile in the community, where there is public pressure to find and convict the perpetrator immediately; an absence of direct evidence, leading to reliance on circumstances that are subjectively interpreted to draw inferences of guilt; reliance on questionable evidence, such as prisoner informants; the demonisation of a suspect who may be a loner, outsider or a member of a minority group; and the

> exaggeration of adversarial roles on the part of police and prosecutors leading to 'noble cause corruption'. This involves the justification of improper practices in order to achieve the perceived 'correct result'.

All of these features may contribute to the malaise of tunnel vision which, in turn, may reinforce them, creating a vicious circle.

(Lamer 2006: 71)

But while there are clear cases of impropriety leading to miscarriages of justice, we also find false confessions where interviews are conducted properly and due process rights observed, as well as cases where eyewitnesses or other witnesses in good faith make false allegations. False confessions may be made in the police station, with or without a lawyer present. Those situations where the person has confessed but the interview was conducted properly may be harder to challenge. As Ventress *et al.* note: 'A steady trickle of "post-PACE" cases going to appeal indicates that the safeguards created by PACE are not completely effective or are not always properly applied' (Ventress *et al.* 2008: 369). There are also cases where expert witnesses may unintentionally give flawed evidence, for example, in the case of Kevin Callan in the UK, who was wrongfully convicted of the murder of his 4-year-old disabled daughter in 1991 and spent four years in prison, during which time he acquired a knowledge of neurology to challenge his conviction (Callan 1997). There may also be problems with the legal advice given so that the appropriate defence is not submitted at trial as happened in the cases of *Ahluwahlia* (1993) 96 Cr App Rep 133 and *Humphreys* [1995] 3 All ER 108.

There are now fewer wrongful convictions based on oppressive interviewing, but there is still the problem of inequality of arms between the state and the suspect in terms of access to DNA testing services. Naughton and Tan (2010) argue that convicted persons maintaining their innocence should have access to the latest DNA techniques. They refer to Article 27(1) of the UNDHR which says that everyone has the right to share in scientific advancement and its benefits. When they were writing, in 2010, 249 individuals in the United States had been exonerated through DNA evidence, including 17 who had been on Death Row. Awareness of the problem of wrongful convictions exonerated through DNA evidence has been one reason for the decline in public support for the death penalty in the United States (Baumgartner *et al.* 2008). There the federal Innocence Protection Act 2004 allows all prisoners convicted of federal offences who are maintaining their innocence access to DNA testing if specific evidence has not previously been tested or where newer and more reliable methods of testing are now available and the proposed testing raises a reasonable probability that the applicant did not commit the offence. Although the courts have treated this as a matter for individual states, rather than a constitutional right, the majority of states have made provisions for such testing. It also requires preservation of biological evidence from criminal cases. But in the UK the DNA database has been used mostly to identify potential suspects rather than deal with post-conviction challenges and there is more scope for the destruction of biological material.

While it is difficult for any system to completely prevent miscarriages of justice, what is needed is a reliable and efficient system for detecting and rectifying such miscarriages of justice. The experience of the Birmingham Six and Guildford Four highlighted difficulties and delays in mounting a successful appeal by those asserting a wrongful conviction. There has also been criticism of the failure to prosecute and convict officers involved in the miscarriages of justice. A delay in bringing prosecutions in the Kiszko case, where the detective in the case died, made it difficult to proceed against others involved in the case. In the Birmingham Six case, a prosecution for perjury and conspiracy to pervert the course of justice was halted on the grounds that the intense publicity in the case meant it was not possible for the officers concerned to receive a fair trial. It is clearly important to have a speedy and efficient process, as even with the improvements in disclosure and forensic techniques it is still possible in any enhanced system that miscarriages of justice may occur.

Reviewing miscarriages of justice

The experiences of the Birmingham Six and Guildford Four highlighted the problems with the appeals procedure at that time, including the narrowness of the grounds of appeal, as well as problems of disclosure, problems of access to the Appeal Court and delays resulting in the innocent spending lengthy periods in custody. The role of the Court of Appeal in dealing with wrongful convictions had been criticised as some of the key cases had been referred to them by the Home Secretary several times before the convictions were quashed. At that time the court seemed reluctant to recognise failures on the part of the police and other bodies, particularly in the case of the Birmingham Six where there were claims of physical abuse. Malleson (1993) reviewed the appeal process for the Royal Commission on Criminal Justice and found that although the court had wide powers under the Criminal Appeal Act, it was reluctant to exercise them very often, partly because of its fear of usurping the role of the jury and partly the fear of the floodgates opening if it allowed too many appeals. It also lacked sufficient resources to examine the circumstances surrounding the case or to assess the integrity of the police and forensic experts. Many claims did not reach the court and those who were unassisted were far less likely to be granted leave to appeal. Even if they did reach the court, the results were uncertain. Time-loss rules introduced in 1970, designed as a penalty to deter frivolous appeals, also deterred complainants and applications fell dramatically after their introduction. The Appeal Court had limited resources and seemed more at ease dealing with cases raising technical or procedural issues which could be resolved quickly, rather than those that required investigation of pre-trial errors by the police or lawyers. Plotnikoff and Woolfson (1993) found that the service provided by lawyers to their clients post-conviction and sentencing was variable and advice was often not in writing. Some prisoners decided not to appeal on the basis of inaccurate information given by their advisers. Clients who did not speak English encountered particular problems.

In response to these concerns the Royal Commission on Criminal Justice recommended that prisoners should be given written advice on any grounds for appeal and on whether an application for leave to appeal to the full court should be renewed. This should be covered by legal aid and interpreters should be provided where appropriate for non-English speakers (RCCJ 1993). It also recommended the introduction of a new criminal cases review body, the Criminal Cases Review Commission. The May Report (1990) was also critical of the delays on the part of the court in dealing with the Maguires. It also noted that neither the court nor the Home Office had the power or expertise needed to investigate alleged miscarriages of justice and argues that a new independent body was needed to deal with such cases.

The 1995 Criminal Appeal Act reflected the recommendations of the RCCJ. It amended the grounds of appeal in the 1968 Act and abolished the proviso in s 2(1) of the 1968 Criminal Appeals Act that allowed the court to dismiss an appeal even if the point raised by the appellant is decided in his favour, but the court considers no miscarriage of justice has occurred. Under the 1995 Act the Court of Appeal: (a) shall allow an appeal against conviction if they think the conviction is unsafe, and (b) shall dismiss an appeal in any other case. The court may still order a retrial where the interests of justice so require.

The Criminal Cases Review Commission (CCRC) was established in 1997 under the Criminal Appeal Act 1995. Both the Royal Commission and May Reports thought that the Home Secretary should not be involved in the consideration of the investigation of alleged miscarriages of justice. The purpose of the CCRC is to review possible miscarriages of justice by the courts in England, Wales and Northern Ireland.

It should consider claims and refer cases to the Court of Appeal where there is a 'real possibility' that the court will find the conviction, verdict or finding unsafe, or the sentence excessive. There will need to be new arguments, or new evidence not previously considered since it was not available, or could not be presented at the time of the original trial, and where there are exceptional circumstances why it was not submitted at that time. It will consider whether any fresh evidence affects the safety of the conviction and, if so, will quash the conviction. The CCRC Report (2013) notes that most miscarriages of justice occur because investigators and lawyers make quite basic errors; for example, they do not follow up obvious areas of inquiry or fail to take account of evidence already in their possession. Experts may be wrong and witnesses may err, but most of the errors are made by professionals.

In 2012/13 the CCRC received 1,625 applications compared to 1040 in 2011/12 (CCRC:7). On average they have received about 900 applications a year (CCRC 2013: 11). Since they commenced in 1997, they have referred 324 cases to the appellate court, a referral rate of 3.47 per cent. The number of referrals in 2012/13 was lower, at 1.2 per cent, as 21 cases were referred. In 2012/13 69.2 per cent of the Commission's referrals were upheld by the court. Since 1997, 70.2 per cent of appeals following the Commission's referrals have been allowed. The CCRC's work over its first decade was reviewed by Elks (2009), who found one-quarter of its applications concerned sexual offences and one-third of referrals were convictions for murder; 13 per cent of applications related to sentence.

However, despite these changes problems still remain for prisoners who maintain their innocence in dealing with the Parole Board, as Naughton (2013) argues. Although the Parole Board should not discriminate against prisoners maintaining their innocence, in practice it may be difficult to obtain parole. Successful completion of relevant offending behaviour programmes will be a key factor in persuading the Board to approve release, but some may require acknowledgement of guilt before commencing the course. Moreover, as he points out, lawyers may advise their clients not to begin the courses as it implies an admission of guilt. Compensation for those who successfully prove a miscarriage of justice has also been cut by the Criminal Justice and Immigration Act 2008 (Naughton 2013). The wider effects of wrongful imprisonment – often for longer periods – may be very damaging in terms of physical and mental health and detrimental to prisoners' families (Roberts 2003). In some cases the public may still perceive them as guilty despite their release. Naughton has advocated the development of Innocence Projects as the best strategy in dealing with miscarriages of justice and has been closely involved with the work of Innocence UK. However, this route has been questioned by Quirk (2007) because of the limited funding and lack of review mechanisms available to Innocence Projects compared to the CCRC. In the United States they have fulfilled an important role because of the lack of state support for alternatives, but in the UK the CCRC fulfils a key function. Moreover, she argues, they only focus on the innocent, but many of the issues raised regarding unsafe convictions may be important, even if the appellants are guilty, because of the integrity of the process and both the guilty and the innocent need the protection of a remedy when their due process rights are infringed.

Waiver: the dangers of speaking

In the debate on the right to silence, the corollary of the argument that the right protects the guilty was the assumption that loss of the right would not harm the innocent, because speaking would enable the suspect to clear up matters more quickly and, provided that adequate procedural safeguards are in place, including restrictions on admissibility of involuntary or improperly obtained confessions, then the innocent will not be at risk. So the Criminal Law Revision Committee (CLRC) (1972) argued that advising the suspect to remain silent could prejudice the innocent suspect as it could discourage him from making an exculpatory statement. Advance disclosure of an explanation that establishes innocence could allow for earlier verification. But if the detainee remains silent, then the prosecution may be less willing to drop the charge, so he could spend longer on remand. The assumption that silence harms the innocent was also advanced by Friendly (1968) and by Williams (1987) who argued that failing to speak in interrogation would greatly increase the risk of a wrongful conviction and referred to examples where defendants with a valid defence were convicted because they had been wrongly advised not to give evidence.

But this argument that silence will harm the innocent is difficult to prove, not least because the number of cases remaining silent are few, silence is rarely advised as we have seen and is the exception rather than the rule. Before 1994 advisers rarely advised silence (McConville *et al.* 1991) and the post-1994 research suggests a similar pattern (Bucke, Street and Brown 2000). We also know that there are cases where the innocent are wrongfully convicted because the guilty party remains silent, for example, the Sacco and Vanzetti case. But the waiver of the right to silence has featured in many miscarriages of justice, including Judith Ward, the Bridgewater Four, Stefan Kiszko, the Birmingham Six and the Guildford Four. Some of the worst miscarriages of justice have occurred where the defendants have made false admissions.

We also lack evidence of the number who do waive their right and speak, but still do not achieve an early release from detention. We know that large numbers of defendants spend time on remand; remand prisoners constitute about 15 per cent of the prison population – between 12,000 and 13,000 – in England and Wales and that they may, in some cases, experience poorer treatment than sentenced prisoners (HMIP 2012).

As we saw in Chapter 3, the majority of suspects in the UK waive their right to silence (Moston 1993; Softley 1980; Bucke, Street and Brown 2000) and similar patterns have been found in the United States. Leo (1996) found that four out of five suspects waived their rights and Kassin *et al.* (2007) found that 81 per cent of suspects in their study waived their rights. Research on wrongful convictions shows the suspect's own false admissions may be crucial to conviction in many cases. For most suspects being in detention and under interrogation is quite stressful and this stress may be exacerbated for those with vulnerabilities.

As we have seen, innocent people may be wrongfully convicted for a variety of reasons, but we also need to consider why the majority of suspects waive their right to remain silent. A number of factors may influence the decision, including the way the caution is administered. Suspects may not understand their rights. The police are skilled at eliciting waivers by establishing rapport with suspects and innocent suspects may believe that by speaking they will show they are innocent. Some research studies indicate that those without criminal records are more likely to waive their rights than those with prior criminal histories. For example, Kassin and Norwick (2004) found that innocent suspects were more likely to waive their *Miranda* rights than guilty suspects. The innocent may think there is nothing to fear if they speak as they have nothing to hide and think their innocence will protect them. Kassin (2005) notes that the innocent are more likely to waive their rights to silence and counsel and more willing to cooperate with polygraphs and searches if they think that by speaking they will clear their name.

Even if suspects are reminded that they do not have to speak they may not fully understand the caution when they waive that right. Research in the UK by Baldwin on police interrogations in the West Midlands, West Mercia and Metropolitan police areas found that in over one-tenth of the cases observed and in one-third of the police stations studied, the caution was given in such a garbled way it was impossible to understand and in some cases it was not given at all (Baldwin 1994). If the caution is given in a casual, rushed or bureaucratic way, then this may downgrade the content of the warning (see Griffiths and Ayres 1967). Moreover, as we saw in Chapter 5, the courts in the United States have been more willing, in recent years, to imply waivers.

Suspects may have a poor understanding of the extent of their rights despite the warning, because of a lack of awareness of what the rights mean or entail. They may not understand what would be good reasons for remaining silent or acceptable to the court. When they do speak, they may lack awareness of the prejudicial effect of statements, for example, in cases of secondary liability or inchoate offences. The understanding of the caution will be affected by the suspect's age, mental and physical condition and grasp of English. Administering a caution of itself does not mean the recipient has fully understood the implications of speaking or silence. Canadian research also shows younger offenders and adults with learning disabilities may have problems understanding their rights in interrogation when cautioned, but the lack of understanding also may be found among students. The Canadian caution says that the suspect is not obliged to speak unless he wishes to do so, but whatever is said may be given in evidence, with some slight variations in wording between states. The right should be explained in language appropriate to the person's age and understanding. Moore and Gagnier's (2008) study of Canadian students found only 43 per cent fully understood the right to silence caution. Eastwood and Snook (2009) explored the understanding of both the right to silence and right to counsel cautions among a sample of university students and few of the students fully understood either caution. Unfamiliar words may make it difficult to understand if it is given quickly or if the rights are presented by the police as formalities. Eastwood *et al.* (2010) found that university students understood only approximately one-third of cautions when presented verbally, regardless of the varying complexity of the cautions given. They conclude that the fact that university students only understood one third of the information in the caution 'suggests that suspects and accused persons would also struggle to comprehend fully the information contained in police cautions', especially as the conditions of an experimental study would be less stressful than a real police interview (466). The majority of respondents understood that they could retain or talk to a lawyer and almost half understood that there was a number they could ring that would be a source of free legal advice. But most did not understand that they could have access to legal help immediately or that their right to legal aid depended on their being charged with a crime. Cautions in Canada vary between police organisations. Usually they give the right to silence caution first, followed by the right to counsel caution. Legal counsel cautions in Canada are more complex than silence ones and Eastwood and Snook recommend a standardised police caution across Canada, keeping them shorter and avoiding multiple syllabic words and legal language.

Studies of the comprehension of the *Miranda* warning in the United States have also found problems in understanding. The value of a *Miranda* warning or caution properly given may still be insufficient to protect a suspect who is vulnerable because of age, IQ, mental health issues, and so may not be able to fully understand those rights or give effect to them. Grisso (1981) found only 21 per cent of juveniles and 42 per cent of adults understood the *Miranda* warning. Goldstein *et al.*'s research (2003) highlighted the lack of understanding of adolescents of their *Miranda* rights. Later studies also found it was unusual for suspects to understand all their rights given in a *Miranda* warning (Viljoen, Zapf and Roesch 2007). Rogers *et al.* (2008) note that the complexity of the words and sentences in the caution that may require a relatively high level of education – for *Miranda* at least a seventh-grade education – but most prisoners are at the level of or below sixth grade. We know that there are high levels of learning disabilities and difficulties in the prison population compared to outside.

Research on the understanding of the suspect's key rights, that has also been conducted in the UK, has found similar problems of comprehension. In the UK an arrestee must be told at the police station of his right to have some one informed of his arrest, the right to consult privately with a solicitor and that free independent legal advice is available, and the right to consult the PACE Codes of Practice (PACE Code C.3.1). The detainee must also be given a written notice setting out these rights, the arrangements for obtaining legal advice and the caution (C.3.2). The caution on the right to silence and the implications of remaining silent will also, of course, be given at the beginning of the interview. Gudjonsson, Clare and Cross (1992) found that the Notice to Detained Persons could only be fully understood by a person with an IQ of 105 or above, which meant that 40 per cent of the general population were unable to understand all of it. Fifty-two per cent of the subjects understood the right to silence as set out in the revised Notice. Clare and Gudjonsson (1993a) designed and tested a more simplified version for the Runciman Commission which did increase the numbers understanding the right to silence to 81 per cent. They also found a significant number of subjects whom they identified as having difficulties with reading or intellectual impairments, but who did not request special help, and as we saw in Chapter 5, this still remains a problem.

Their research was conducted when a simpler caution was used, so we would expect increased difficulty in understanding the more complex caution used following the Criminal Evidence Order in Northern Ireland and the CJPOA. The ambiguity of the caution may mean that suspects do not fully understand either the implications of silence or the fact that they may still remain silent. A study of the new caution in Northern Ireland by JUSTICE and the Committee on the Administration of Justice found that only 5 per cent of suspects could understand its significance or meaning (JUSTICE 1994). The police also often administered the caution with comments such as 'Now is the time to speak' and 'You have to speak to us or we will charge you.' The lawyers interviewed were critical of some officers for misrepresenting the meaning of the Order and thought that only a small minority of suspects understood the significance of the caution even when they professed to do so. Most clients thought they were obliged to answer questions. In Bucke, Street and Brown's (2000) study, police officers and legal advisers were doubtful whether suspects did fully understand the new caution, particularly those without prior experience of the interrogation process.

Fenner, Gudjonsson and Clare (2002) examined understanding of the right to silence caution among police station suspects and individuals attending a job centre who were matched for intellectual ability. In both cases they found understanding of the caution was extremely limited. Only 11 per cent of the participants demonstrated a full understanding of its meaning, and while the majority claimed to understand the caution when presented to them as it would have been by the police, it was clear that they did not fully understand it. Cooke and Philip's (1998) study in Scotland found that while 89 per cent of the participants in their sample of 100 convicted young offenders *claimed* to have fully understood the caution, in fact only 11 per cent had fully understood it. In Scotland adverse inferences are not permitted from silence so their simpler caution should be easier to understand.

As we saw in Chapter 3, relatively few suspects exercise their right to silence. Regardless of any formal pressures to speak, such as those now enshrined in s 34 of the CJPOA, there are also informal pressures on suspects to speak as well as fears of adverse inferences from non-cooperation. Moreover, those most likely to be persuaded to speak when warned of adverse inferences from silence may not be sophisticated terrorists or racketeers who may be very familiar with interrogation procedures and who may want to establish an alibi, but rather those less well informed on criminal procedure. The pressure on suspects to speak is intense, not least because it is deeply grounded in the rules of everyday conversational discourse and these pressures will be intensified in interrogation. Questions can and will be asked even if it is clear that the person does not intend to speak and the purpose of repeated questioning is to undermine the will to remain silent. Remaining silent when confronted with sustained questioning in a police interview room demands considerable fortitude and self-discipline. These pressures are built into normal conversational discourse and these are increased when confronted by an authority figure. Psychological experiments on obedience have shown that the presence of an authority figure can have a powerful effect on the individual's actions and his free will and that the individual's sense of responsibility for his own actions may be impaired (Milgram 1963). As it is so difficult to resist talking in everyday discourse, it is not surprising that these pressures intensify in the context of a police interview and that individuals under pressure may doubt their own judgement and may even, in some cases, falsely confess (Gudjonsson 1992).

While the PACE Codes, as we have seen, exert formal controls over the police and provide much greater protection for the suspect than previously, they cannot deal with these pressures built into social exchanges, where an individual feels obliged to speak when spoken to and not to interrupt those who do not speak. Even if the accused says he wishes to exercise his right to silence, the police still have the right to question him (ACPO 2002).

A skilled interrogator can exploit the normal rules of conversational discourse to initiate a story that the speaker feels obliged to finish by encouraging discussion on an apparently unrelated topic, or by remaining silent after a response which may encourage the interviewee to say more than originally intended. The law on confessions stresses voluntariness in communicating information and in choosing to speak or remain silent. But social discourse and social interaction incorporate a strong social duty to speak so that most people would feel that remaining silent is rude or boorish. The suspect may also be arrested in the early hours of the morning, spend time waiting for his solicitor to arrive, while his interrogator is clearly in a position of strength, in familiar surroundings and is in control of the interview.

False confessions

False confessions are not a new phenomenon. The twentieth-century show trials illustrated vividly the dangers, but the persecution of witches in Europe and the Salem witch trials in Massachusetts in the seventeenth century highlighted the problem of pressuring individuals to confess and of obtaining reliable evidence, as dramatically configured in Arthur Miller's *The Crucible*. We know that under pressure individuals may confess to crimes that they have not committed. The discovery of DNA evidence and subsequent DNA exonerations have thrown light on the problem of wrongful convictions and have highlighted the fact that false confessions are present in many of those convictions. Research from the Innocence Project in the United States found that false convictions figured in 51 of 225 post-conviction DNA exonerations (http://www.innocenceproject.org; see also Scheck *et al*. 2000; Garrett 2008). Confessions may also be found to be false in some cases because it is physically impossible for the person to have committed the crime, for example, because the suspect was found to be at another location when the offence was committed or because of a physical factor, as in the *Kiszko* case.

The actual number of false confessions may be difficult to ascertain, but may be greater than suggested by the number of appeals, as not all cases may come to light if there is no appeal. Confessions elicited outside the criminal justice system, for example in military investigations or corporate investigations, may not be publicised. False confessions may be made in some cases, but the case does not proceed to trial. But we can get some information from self-report studies. In Sigurdsson and Gudjonsson's (1996) study of prison inmates in Iceland in 1994, 12 per cent of the sample said that they had made a false confession at some point.

A confession is defined in s 82(1) of PACE as a 'statement wholly or partly adverse to the person who made it, whether made to a person in authority or not and whether made in words or otherwise', so it is a statement against a person's interest and as such assumed to be reliable. For this reason a confession has long been accepted as a legitimate exception to the hearsay rule. Because the notion of confessing to a crime you did not commit seems so irrational and hard to believe, it is not surprising that juries may be reluctant to accept a confession is false. Yet as the Canadian Supreme Court acknowledged in *R. v Oickle* [2000] 2 SCR 3, 'innocent people are induced to make false confessions more frequently than those unacquainted with the phenomenon might expect' (at paras 34–45). This claim is supported by self-reporting and experimental studies.

Moreover, if a confession appears to have been made voluntarily and the interview was conducted properly and the suspect had access to legal advice, then miscarriages of justice following guilty pleas will be even harder to rectify. The courts may assume people will not confess to crimes they have not committed if they are properly cautioned and noncoercive techniques were used in interview. Confessions are very powerful and may influence jurors even if concerns are raised regarding their provenance or the way they are obtained. At trial a confession is so powerful in persuading the jury that even contradictory evidence may have little impact on the jury. A confession may also contains details that will be convincing to the jury but may have been imparted by the police during interrogation or picked up from newspaper reports.

As Leo and Drizin (2004) note, a confession is 'highly prejudicial and highly damaging to a defendant, even if it is the product of coercive interrogation, even if it is supported by no other evidence, and even if it is ultimately proven false beyond any reasonable doubt' (2004, at 959). Their review of actual cases involving *proven* false confessions found a conviction rate of 81 per cent.

Even if a confession is made involuntarily and under oppression and this is made clear to the court, it will not necessarily mean that the jury will discount it. Kassin and Sukel (1997) found in a mock jury study that where it was clear a confession was obtained oppressively and jurors were told to disregard it because it was involuntary, and they said it had not influenced their decision, in fact the conviction rate increased despite knowledge of that oppression. In *Arizona v Fulminante* 499 US 271 (1991), the majority of the Supreme Court accepted that a confession was coerced in this case but affirmed the 'harmless error' rule adopted in *Chapman v California* 368 US 18, in relation to the admissibility of involuntary confessions. The admission of such a confession will be assessed in the context of other evidence presented in the case to determine whether its admission is harmless beyond reasonable doubt. So it may be that in certain situations the error may be rendered harmless, for example because there is sufficient other evidence and it can be treated like other trial errors. If there is evidence of a confession the courts are more likely to presume guilt. Confessions may taint other evidence and can have a great impact on the jury. An experimental study of eyewitness evidence found witnesses changed their initial identifications once told the suspect had confessed, so a confirmation bias operated (Hasel and Kassin 2009). Even a contested confession may be boosted by other weak evidence or flawed forensic evidence.

False confessions and convictions based on them undermine confidence in the criminal justice system and are wasteful of resources and clearly leave the guilty free to commit more crimes. False confessions raise a number of issues, including whether the police are able to recognise them, whether they will be 'caught' at later stages of the criminal justice process, and whether formal due process rights are sufficient to protect the suspect.

Pressures built into the criminal justice process, including the sentence discount for guilty pleas, may mean that dubious evidence is not tested in court, but the trial moves quickly to the sentencing stage. Suspects may also be persuaded by their lawyers to plead guilty to a lesser offence for a lighter sentence (McConville and Mirsky 2005). Credit is given for guilty pleas at the sentencing stage because it saves time and expense for the court and may mean vulnerable witnesses do not have to give evidence and shorter sentences relieve pressure on an overcrowded prison system. At present the maximum discount is one-third and efforts to increase this have been resisted. The Coalition Government proposed an increase of 50 percent in *Breaking the Cycle* (Ministry of Justice 2010) but in the face of this criticism it was not included in the Legal Aid, Sentencing and Punishment of Offenders Act 2012. The sentence discount is currently governed by s 144 of the Criminal Justice Act 2003, which states that where the offender has pleaded guilty then the court must take into account the stage in the proceedings in which he indicated his guilty plea and the circumstances in which it was given. A very late plea given for a tactical reason may not attract a discount. So a greater reduction will be earned by an early plea at the first reasonable opportunity. Whatever the merits of sentence discounts, it means that bargaining is built into the criminal justice system. Research on acceptance of police cautions that require an admission of guilt has also found that:

> suspects do indeed feel pressured, for a multitude of reasons, including a desire to leave the police station as soon as possible – which is very often the primary concern. If the offer of a caution is made to a suspect in this state of mind, particularly when they lack experience of the criminal justice system and may therefore be a good candidate for a caution, they are very likely to seize it as a way of securing immediate release from an unpleasant situation. It may take days, weeks or even months before clear reflection is possible, almost always too late. The acute pressure felt by a suspect may be such that it is almost impossible for a well balanced decision to be made there and then in the police station.
>
> (Hynes and Elkins 2013: 971)

Police cautions are intended as a means of disposal to deal with minor offences, so where more serious offences are involved the pressures on the suspect may be even greater.

The fact that someone would confess to involvement in, for example, a murder to escape short-term detention would seem irrational but shows how interrogation may affect suspects who are vulnerable and uncertain how long they will be detained. Our understanding of this phenomenon has been enhanced by research on false confessions and on miscarriages of justice. Mental illness, personality disorders and medical problems such as diabetes or epilepsy may all affect judgement. Research on false confessions, including the work of Gudjonsson (2003), Vrij (1997, 2008, 2010), Kassin and Wrightsman (1985) and Kassin (2008a), has furthered our understanding of this issue.

False confessions may occur for a number of reasons, for example, as a result of bullying or hectoring by the interrogator, but also because of the person's mental state. As we have seen, s 76 of PACE is intended to deter and prevent oppressive conduct in interrogation but this does not prevent a false confession where a person is interviewed properly and confesses voluntarily, but nonetheless the confession is false. As we saw in Chapter 5, oppressive interviewing and inducements or threats will render any confessions obtained inadmissible if the prosecution is unable to prove otherwise and any deprivation of food or sleep or bullying will be prohibited. PACE also imposes requirements for juveniles and those with learning disabilities to have an appropriate adult present, but does not eliminate the problem of suggestibility, or the desire to escape of adults who would not be immediately identified as vulnerable. Moreover, as we saw in Chapter 5, the numbers identified as requiring an appropriate adult in interrogation are lower than would be expected in terms of the numbers in the wider population or in the prison population.

The phenomenon of false confessions cuts across class, age and other lines, although some groups are more at risk than others. Leo and Drizin (2004) found that 93 per cent of false confessors in their analysis of 125 of proven interrogation-induced false confessions were men. False confessions were more commonly found in relation to cases of murder, so suspects seemed more likely to confess to more serious crimes; these confessions were subsequently shown to be false when the real perpetrator was identified or new scientific evidence was found. Younger suspects may be particularly vulnerable to making false confessions. A later experimental study by Gudjonsson *et al.* (2006) of college students found the numbers making false confessions ranged from 3.7 to 7 per cent. A major European study of over 23,000 juveniles found 14 per cent reported having given false confessions (Gudjonsson *et al.* 2009). Gudjonsson *et al.* argue that youthfulness is a high risk factor in false confessions, as clearly youths are less mature and more impulsive. They are less able to consider long-term consequences and more susceptible to outside influences, and more likely to focus on short-term advantages rather than longer-term implications, which renders them vulnerable in the interrogation context. A study of hypothetical mock interrogations by Grisso *et al.* (2003) also found that juveniles were more likely to say that they would confess rather than deny an accusation or remain silent.

Gudjonsson's extensive research has found correlations between personal characteristics of suggestibility and the tendency to confess (1994, 2003). Individuals with learning disabilities are over-represented in false confessions and may be more suggestible than other subjects. They may also be less aware of their rights or how to use them, and may not understand their rights or know how to apply them and may seek approval from authority figures. Compliant individuals may be more anxious to please their interrogators and to avoid confrontation. Gudjonsson (2003), Kassin and Wrightsman (1985) and Kassin and Kiechel (1996) have shown the significance of vulnerabilities, including suggestibility and compliance with persons in authority, in the production of false confessions. Suspects with learning difficulties, or suffering from mental health problems, are particularly vulnerable and we know that they may confess to serious crimes even with a lawyer and appropriate adult present and where the interview is recorded. As we saw earlier, the legal advisers may also be marginalised in interrogation.

Innocent suspects who are mentally impaired, because of mental illness, learning disabilities or personality disorders may confess in response to relatively little pressure. Vulnerable individuals may be at greater risk of making false confessions. Gudjonsson defines psychological vulnerability as 'psychological characteristics or mental states which (a) impair suspects' ability to understand their legal rights, (b) render suspects prone, in certain circumstances, to provide information which is unreliable or misleading' (Gudjonsson 1994: 94). He has developed the Gudjonsson Suggestibility Scales (GSS1 and GSS2) to assist in identifying those vulnerable to giving erroneous responses to questions. They can be used on suspects, witnesses and victims by measuring the response to leading questions and to pressure from negative feedback (Gujdonnson 1997).

Whether an individual will falsely confess may depend on a number of factors, including their vulnerability, and mental state at the time of the interrogation and the manner in which they are treated by their interviewers. As we saw when discussing appropriate adults in Chapter 5, more training is needed to identify vulnerability and suggestibility. In the case of *R v Aspinall* [1999] 2 Cr App R 115, a schizophrenic suspect was held for 13 hours without an appropriate adult or solicitor present and the Court of Appeal ruled that his answers should have been excluded under s 78.

There may also be cases where a learning disability may lead to boasting and exaggerations which may place the individual at risk. There are some indications that false confessions occur in lengthier interrogations. In Leo and Drizin's (2004) study the mean was 16.3 hours, and some were up to 24 hours. In the United States most interrogations last from half an hour to two hours but some may last much longer as in the case of Randall Lee Fields (see *Howes v Fields* [2012] 113 S.Ct. 118). In interrogation there may be a conflict between the police interest in clearing up the crime by extracting a confession and the citizen's right not to incriminate himself. But extensions to detention are usually sought on the assumption that the longer a person is in custody the more he will be encouraged to speak and, as we have seen, extensions may be permissible in the UK, subject to the requirements in PACE and the Terrorism Act.

Research on the length of time in detention in England and Wales found that PACE initially reduced the length of time spent in detention when it was first introduced, but the duration then increased (Brown 1989; Phillips and Brown 1998). Maguire (1988) and Bottomley *et al.* (1991) found that there were variations between police stations and similar variations were identified in a later study by Kemp *et al.* (2012) based on 25,000 custody records from 44 police stations in four police force areas. Kemp *et al.* found that 17 per cent of detentions were under two hours, 47 per cent of detainees were released within 6 hours, 34 per cent were released between 6 hours and 15 hours, 14 per cent were released between 15 and 24 hours and 5 per cent were held over 24 hours. The mean duration for suspects was 8 hours and 55 minutes and for suspects and for other detainees (including those detained regarding immigration offences and under the Mental Health Act) it was 9 hours and 18 minutes. This compared to an average of 6 hours and 40 minutes in Phillips and Brown's earlier study, although there were some differences in data collection methods.

Factors associated with an increase in detention time in Kemp *et al.*'s study were a request for a solicitor and, even when this was controlled for the seriousness of offence, there was still a significant variation. A request for an interpreter also correlated with an increase. Juveniles had a shorter duration, except at night. White Irish and White Other and Chinese detainees also had a higher duration. Chinese detainees were more likely to request a solicitor or interpreter and to be detained for non-PACE offences, such as immigration offences. There were also longer durations for those detained under s 136 of the Mental Health Act 1983, which may reflect the lack of availability of suitable alternative places of safety as we saw in Chapter 5 (see also Docking *et al.* 2008). Women in the Kemp study were detained for shorter periods than men, but they also committed less serious offences. Duration also increased outside the period from 8 a.m. to 8 p.m. Longer periods of time were spent where individuals were detained for immigration offences and under mental health law, or for administrative matters such as bail breaches, or where they were detained for more serious offences.

The typology of false confessions

Three types of false confessions are identified by Kassin and Wrightsman (1985): voluntary, coerced-compliant and coerced-internalised. A voluntary false confession is where the person spontaneously confesses without prompting by police. In the case of the kidnapping of the Lindbergh baby in 1932, over 50 people confessed. People may voluntarily confess for a variety of reasons, including because they want attention, have misplaced feelings of guilt, suffer from delusions, or if they think it advantageous, or to protect someone else. There may be cases where false admissions are made because of guilt feelings about matters unrelated to the offence. There are also serial confessants who regularly confess to the police when crimes are reported in the media. There may be psychological problems such as a desire for notoriety, as in the case of George King who had narcissistic and antisocial personality disorders and falsely confessed to murder (*State of New Jersey v George King*, No. A-2665–10T1 (23 March 2012). There was no suggestion that the confession had been coerced, but expert evidence suggested his grandiosity and need for admiration made him vulnerable to making a false confession (Watson *et al.* 2010).

In the case of coerced compliant false confessions, the suspect may react badly to the experience of interrogation and confinement and confess to escape the stress of interrogation, or may simply want to go home, or to obtain drugs if suffering withdrawal symptoms, or other short-term benefits. In the notorious Central Park jogger case in 1989, five black and Latino teenage boys aged 14 to 16 confessed to the rape and assault of the victim, after a long interrogation, and thought they would be allowed to go home after they confessed. In this case, *New York v Wise, Richardson, McCray, Salaam and Santana* 194 Misc. 2d. 481 (2002), five false confessions emerged from a single investigation. They were convicted and jailed in 1989, and spent 13 years in prison until 2002, when the perpetrator confessed and his confession was supported by DNA evidence.

If the suspect's denial makes the interrogation more unpleasant, then he may be more willing to confess. A suspect may be vulnerable to the risk of false confession because he or she is unable to cope with interrogation or has fears of being confined. Anxiety, fear and depression may make it difficult to make a rational choice whether or not to speak, and then if he does speak, he may give false information if he believes it will hasten his release through being bailed. Gudjonsson and MacKeith (1982) argue that for some suspects the experience of interrogation by the police may lead to psychiatric disorders and post-traumatic stress. Being in an alien environment and isolated, combined with uncertainty about the future and the presence of an authority figure, may be stressful and the suspect may display symptoms of anxiety, verbal incoherence and hyperventilation. The suspect may be taken to the police station in the middle of the night. During extended periods of detention, eating and sleeping patterns may be disrupted and the effect of this may undermine the ability to make a rational choice over speaking or silence. In such circumstances if the suspect does speak, the reliability of the statements may be questionable.

A psychologist's report on the men wrongfully convicted for the murder of PC Blakelock, the Broadwater Farm case, argued that Braithwaite had confessed following an acute anxiety attack due to claustrophobia when confined to a cell. Psychologists showed how factors of suggestibility, compliance and low IQ may lead to false admissions. In this case Engin Raghip was aged 19 when interviewed regarding the murder, without a solicitor present, and said he signed an admission because he was afraid following threats made by the police. He also said he had a mental age of 10 or 11. His initial appeal failed, but later the convictions of the three were quashed (*R v Silcott, Braithwaite and Raghip, The Times* (9 December 1991)). The court found some parts of the interview were written at different times. It was shown on appeal that he had an IQ of 77. The Court of Appeal stressed that decisions on cases brought under s 76(2) should not be made on whether the IQ of the accused falls above or below an arbitrary figure and assessments of a person's mental state at the time of the interview should be based on medical evidence. Moreover, if the suspect is used to an authoritarian structure where he is routinely rewarded for cooperation, for example, if a person has been institutionalised, then his ability to make rational decisions may be undermined in an interrogation context.

Uncorroborated confessions were also significant in the *Confait* case where three boys were convicted of offences, including the murder of Maxwell Confait, manslaughter and arson with intent to endanger life, on the basis of confessions unsupported by independent evidence. The confessions had been obtained in the absence of legal advice (*R v Lattimore, Leighton and Salih* (1976) 62 Cr App R 53). One of the boys, Lattimore, was aged 18 but with a mental age of 8 and described by a medical expert as highly suggestible. Leighton was aged 15 with an IQ of 75, which is classified as borderline subnormal. The third defendant, Salih, was 14 at the time. Lattimore said he confessed because he wanted to go home and the other two said they confessed because they wanted to escape. The Fisher Report on this case highlighted the vulnerability of suspects in interrogation and showed the need for special provisions for interrogating vulnerable suspects which were later incorporated into PACE (Fisher 1977).

An internalised false confession is where a person believes he has committed a crime and thinks he is speaking the truth and may distrust his own memories. Some suspects are highly suggestible and respond to leading questions. They may believe they are guilty because at the time of the event in question they were intoxicated or under the influence of drugs. There may also be cases where at the outset of the interview they are confident they are innocent of the accusations put to them, but the interviewing process leads them to doubt their own judgment and they are vulnerable to manipulation by an authority figure. An example here would be Michael Crowe, a 14-year-old youth who was subjected to a lengthy interrogation over his sister's death where the police lied and said they had physical evidence of his guilt. They also suggested he had a split personality with a good and bad Michael and had blotted out the killing. He confessed but the case was not pursued because DNA evidence linked another man, Richard Tuite, to the crime, who was convicted of the murder. Some suspects may answer in the affirmative when have not really understood the question. Some individuals suffering from personality disorders may fill in gaps in their memory with imagined material, and some suspects are unable to distinguish fact from fantasy (Clare and Gudjonsson 1993b; Gudjonsson 2005). The production of false memories without deliberate intent to lie is referred to as confabulation. It has been associated *inter alia* with neurological disease and with schizophrenia and it may be scored by a variety of tests (Lorente-Rovira *et al.* 2010).

Experimental studies have shown that people can change visual perception, behaviour and emotions when confronted with false evidence, which may sway them. An individual subjected to group pressure may doubt his own judgement (Asch 1951, 1956). In some circumstances the suspect may genuinely come to be believe he has committed the offences; in the Canadian case of Joel Labadie, the suspect was convinced by the police that he had blacked out which was why he could not remember committing the murder of which he was accused.

If suspects are confronted with false evidence such as forensic evidence, this may lead some vulnerable suspects to think they have committed the crime and induce false confessions. This effect is supported by experimental research on the impact of false evidence (Kassin and Kiechel 1996). The research of Wade *et al.* (2010) also showed that doctored video taped evidence could induce people to provide false eyewitness testimony against others, to falsely confess themselves, and to believe they had stolen money. False information has figured in some miscarriages of justice. It was given by the police to the suspect in the case of Martin Tankleff to elicit a confession and in this case the suspect spent 17 years in prison before successfully challenging his conviction for the murder of his parents (*People v Tankleff* 84 NY 2d 999 (1994)).

McConville *et al.* (1991) have referred to a further category of false confessions, namely the 'coerced passive confession', where suspects may adopt words which amount to a confession without even being aware that they have made an admission.

What is clear from the above that innocent people may be induced to confess through police pressure, but also, in some cases, in noncoercive interviews. We also know that the majority of suspects waive their right to silence and many also waive their right to counsel, so both these rights offer limited protection. We now need to consider the other side of the coin, namely whether particular types of interviewing methods are more likely to produce false confessions and the ability of interviewers to detect lies in the course of interrogation.

Tunnel vision in interrogations

Once a confession is obtained during the interrogation process, then the police may not pursue other evidence, or other suspects, but may close an investigation. Tunnel vision is the tendency of criminal investigations to run in a single groove once under way and to dismiss conflicting evidence. It has been described as the 'single-minded and overly narrow focus on a particular investigative or prosecutorial theory, so as to unreasonably colour the evaluation of information received and one's conduct in response to that information' (Lamer 2006: 71). The Lamer Report said that the investigation and prosecution of Gregory Parsons, wrongfully convicted for the murder of Catherine Carroll, 'became a "runaway train", fuelled by tunnel vision and picking up many passengers along the way' (2006: 171). This problem of tunnel vision was also highlighted by the Royal Commission Report in the UK which stressed the need for the police to gather all relevant evidence including that which exonerates the suspect: 'the police should see it as their duty in conducting investigations to gather and consider all the relevant evidence, including any which may exonerate the suspect', instead of rushing too quickly to the conclusion that they have arrested the offender (RCCJ 1993: 2.5, 2.7). The new disclosure regime recommended by the Commission and introduced by the Criminal Procedure and Investigations Act 1996, discussed in Chapter 2, partly reflected these concerns.

Police training, particularly the Reid method, may encourage tunnel vision, so if the police do not obtain a confession at once, they may redouble their efforts; the interrogation is therefore guilt-presumptive. Evidence is sought to confirm the original hypothesis of guilt rather than assessing the evidence to see what might have happened. In the *Confait* case, for example, because of the preoccupation with the admissions of the defendants, little attention was paid to the relevant medical and forensic evidence concerning the time of the victim's death or the starting of the fire. Efforts were made to focus the jury's attention on the admissions, even though the other evidence would have been crucial in assessing the probative value of alibi evidence. Other potential suspects were given cursory attention. In the later case of Angela Cannings, wrongly convicted for the murder of her children, potential innocent explanations for the death of her children were not considered and instead the police relied on circumstantial evidence supported by an expert witness, Roy Meadows, whose credibility would later be questioned (*R v Cannings* [2004] EWCA Crim 1).

If officers approach the investigation with preconceived ideas, this will shape the results of the interview in terms of the information elicited. A particular line of investigation may be pursued to the exclusion of other lines of inquiry, thereby obscuring the search for the truth. As McConville *et al.* (1991) argue, criminal cases are constructed by the police according to their own view of who is guilty, so instead of searching for the full facts of the case, they may focus on a narrow section of the population, defined by class, gender and ethnicity; they then place them in the hostile environment of the police station and, having reached a prior decision on their guilt, proceed to confirm guilt by interrogation designed to obtain a confession. The case is constructed out of incidents which may be ambiguous, and on the basis of the beliefs and goals of the officers, rather than an objective set of facts:

> Police practice is not, therefore, designed to ensure that the maximum possible reliance for evidential purposes can be placed upon suspects' statements in all cases where they are made, but instead to ensure that statements of confession are made in the maximum number of cases. Through experience, the police have learned that statements are more likely to be made when the suspect is psychologically vulnerable, a state best achieved by compulsory confinement, isolation and manipulation of self-esteem. It is to these features that they direct their attention rather than to questions of the reliability of statements....Contrary to the rhetoric of law, which depicts the police as neutral investigators earnestly seeking 'the truth' in an impartial setting, the first concern of the police is to place the suspect into an environment which is hostile for the suspect and favourable to the police themselves. In this way, the police lay the foundations for the construction of a case *against* the suspect rather than for an impartial inquiry.
>
> (McConville, Sanders and Leng 1991: 54–5)

The authors found that the police rarely checked suspects' accounts and the interviewing officer may treat the suspect as presumptively guilty, the aim of the interview is to produce a confession so any lines of defence offered by the suspect will be ignored or dismissed, as allowing contradictory evidence will undermine the attempt to build a case for the prosecution (McConville *et al.* 1991). With limited resources the police may want to narrow the scope of their inquiries. McConville (1992) also found that pressure on resources may result in poor investigative work and a failure to review the investigation early on may lead to delays and loss of evidence. Once time has elapsed, it may be harder to trace witnesses and obtain forensic evidence. Baldwin and Moloney (1992) also found insufficient supervision of investigations with too much pressure on lower-ranking officers and that the procedures at that time contained the potential for laxity if not abuse. Many officers were determined to obtain a confession, presuming guilt prior to interview. However, there have been significant changes since the early 1990s in the interviewing methods used in the UK.

The dynamics of interrogation

The methods used by the police may be significant as they may use tactics which are deemed legitimate and lawful and are designed to elicit confessions, but which may result in false confessions from vulnerable suspects. The structure of police interrogation and the psychological effects of interrogation may explain why the majority of suspects elect to speak regardless of any penalties attached to silence. The context of the police station and design of the interview reflects the authority of the police and the vulnerability of the suspect. Given these pressures, the notion of a free choice to speak and a free and autonomous individual making a rational decision does not reflect the reality of interrogation in many cases, despite the fact that voluntariness, as we have seen, is an issue for the courts to consider in assessing the reliability of any admissions. A variety of tactics may be used by the police to encourage the suspect to talk, which do not constitute oppression, but which may undermine the right to silence. McConville *et al.* (1994) studied police interviews and found that when the solicitor told the police the client did not intend to answer questions, they were not deterred from initiating an interrogation. A range of strategies were used, including asserting police authority over the lawyer by treating him or her in an offhand way or marginalising them by arranging the room so that the police and suspect were physically close and eye contact between adviser and client was impossible. Sometimes the suspect would be told that silence implied guilt or that guilt would be inferred from silence during interrogation.

The dynamics of interrogation therefore need to be considered in making sense of false confessions and experimental research has contributed to this understanding. The accusatorial approach, favoured in the United States, focuses on accusation, confrontations, control of the suspect, psychological manipulation and disallowing denials, and is guilt-presumptive. The Inbau–Reid Manual *Criminal Interrogation and Confessions* clearly instructs interrogators in psychological techniques designed to encourage suspects to speak (Inbau, Reed *et al.* 2001). Similar handbooks were produced for the UK market, for example by Walkley (1987). The Inbau–Reid Manual focuses on 23 areas which are part of the Reid technique, including the behavioural indicators of deception, the Behavior Analysis Interview (BAI) which is also used to elicit deception, and the 9-step interrogation technique. The BAI protocol, devised by the US firm of John E. Reid and Associates, aims to distinguish different responses from guilty and innocent suspects. It comprises asking background questions to collect information on the suspect and investigative questions relating to the specific case and obtaining information on the suspect's involvement in the crime. It also includes behaviour-provoking questions designed to evoke distinct reactions in innocent and guilty suspects, for example, a greater willingness to help the police among innocent suspects. If, after the BAI, the interrogator thinks the person is lying, he or she may then use the 9-step technique to get a confession.

So in the United States interrogation is two stages.The first is to establish whether the person is a suspect and should be formally interrogated. To determine guilt in this first stage there will also be a reliance on nonverbal behavioural cues. When that is established, the second stage of the formal interview begins, using a variety of manipulative tactics, including isolation, confrontation and minimisation, designed to elicit confessions that confirm the belief of the suspect's guilt. This belief in guilt may also lead to longer interviews.

The suspect should first be isolated in a small room to increase anxiety and then a 9-step procedure is recommended, including confronting him with strong accusations of guilt with no opportunity of denial, minimising and normalising the crime, encouraging suspects to see a confession as a means of escape, and then once the admission has been made, converting it into a detailed and full-narrative confession. This approach has been widely used in the United States and Canada. Typical tactics include isolation, looking for contradictions, establishing rapport and appeal to self-interest. The use of the minimisation technique may also mean that suspects lower their expectations of a harsh sentence and are more likely to confess in expectation of leniency. The 9-step process incorporates negative and positive incentives, on the one hand confronting the suspect with accusation of guilt, refusing to accept a denial, but also offering sympathy, moral justification, or minimising the crime. Here the police might suggest, for example, that it was an accident, or there was provocation, or that the suspect will be treated with leniency.

But the processes of confrontation and minimisation used in the Reid technique may trigger behaviours that are then seen as confirming the guilt of suspects, so their distress may be viewed as resistance to admitting guilt, and the isolation of suspects may generate fear and exhaustion, so they want to extricate themselves. Psychological experiments have shown that students are more likely to confess falsely when minimisation and maximisation techniques are used (Russano *et al.* 2005). Placing the suspect in a small room may increase anxiety and wish to escape. Moore and Fitzsimmons (2011) point out that while the current test for scientific techniques after *Daubert* focuses on the reliability of principles and methods underpinning scientific evidence, 'There is no scientific basis from which to conclude that the Reid approach is reliable and diagnostic' (Moore and Fitzsimmons 2011: 520). The absence of a scientific basis for the Reid technique raises the question of whether, as Gallini (2010) argues, confessions arising from it should be declared inadmissible. While the Inbau-Reid manual states that none of the nine steps would induce an innocent person to confess, no empirical evidence to support this is given.

The development of the Inbau–Reid protocol was seen as an improvement on earlier coercive methods of interrogation and facilitating a more professional approach, but it may involve deception and control. There has also been criticism of the behavioural indicators of deception specified in the Inbau–Reid manual which are not supported by scientific evidence. Vrij (2005) found empirical evidence that conflicts with the Inbau–Reid view that the innocent are more likely than the guilty to cooperate with the police. The Reid technique, previously widely used in Canada, was criticised as too coercive and oppressive in the case of *R v Chappl*e (2012) AJ No. 881, where the judge said that the use of this technique in Chapple's interrogation meant the interview was guilt-presumptive and undermined Chapple's presumption of innocence and right to silence. Judge Dinkel noted that the use of the Reid technique 'can lead to overwhelmingly oppressive situations that can render false confessions and cause innocent people to be wrongfully imprisoned' (at para 122).

The Inbau–Reid technique has also been criticised as more likely to lead to false confessions than the alternative PEACE approach (Kassin 2008a; Moore and Fitzsimmons 2011). One element of the Reid technique is a focus on developing rapport, through using compliments and false praise and Moore and Fitzsimmons (2011) argue that those with low levels of education may be vulnerable to this. Suspects with learning disabilities and difficulties who want to please the interviewer also may be more likely to change their story.

Investigators in the United States are trained in using the BAI protocol and many have attended workshops training them in the Reid technique since 1974. Masip *et al.* (2010) argue that the BAI recommendations are in line with common sense thinking, but are inaccurate. They argue that 'the BAI is an example of common-sense beliefs that have pervaded the police' (2010: 2) yet empirical research shows that the ideas underpinning BAI are not supported by scientific evidence. These interview techniques were also very influential in the UK in the 1980s when PACE was enacted and PACE did not fully address the psychological pressures inherent in interrogation or in the techniques accepted by the police as legitimate.

A further problem is the reliance on nonverbal cues in the Inbau–Reid model. The Reid technique contains within its protocol assumptions that lack empirical support, namely that we can reliably distinguish deceit from innocence from behavioural cues, such as the suspect's uncooperativeness and lack of eye contact. Many of the signs seen as guilt indicators in the BAI, such as crossing one's legs, or shifting in the chair, may also be signs of nervousness, shame or withdrawal. This means that the innocent but nervous suspect may be more likely to be subjected to full interrogation.

Moreover, if these beliefs are 'common sense', then suspects may also share those beliefs and try to avoid displaying guilty reactions, and the guilty may be able to manipulate their behaviour to a greater extent than innocent suspects. Although reliance on nonverbal cues is encouraged in the Inbau–Reid manual, as Kassin notes, these 'are not empirically diagnostic of truth and deception' (Kassin 2008b: 1310). Detecting when a suspect is lying is obviously an important skill in detecting both false confessions and false alibis, but it is not always easy to do so and both the police and the public may find it difficult to detect lies. Inbau claims that the Reid training has a high level of accuracy in detecting truth and lies, but this is not borne out by scientific research, which shows that police officers do not possess a greater ability to detect liars than ordinary people and in some studies fare worse. Moreover, the training given may also encourage professional observers to pick up on signs that are unreliable and to overestimate their ability to detect liars. Most of the signs, such as being more anxious or less helpful, are not a reliable guide to distinguishing liars from truth tellers. Some people are more proficient liars and do not feel guilty about lying, so may not display any unusual behaviours. Although both police manuals and common-sense thinking may assume that liars will appear more nervous, there are no obvious physical signs comparable to Pinnochio's nose. People also may behave differently in the stressful context of an interview which may affect their behaviour, irrespective of guilt.

Vrij *et al.* (2010) highlight the fact that there may be no obvious outward physical signs of lies, or very small differences between liars and non-liars. Proficient liars may adopt strategies to evade detection, as sometimes lies may be embedded in otherwise truthful statements, apart from one crucial detail, which give the account plausibility.

Many of the beliefs widespread among the police on nonverbal cues are misleading, such as reliance on stereotypes of deceptive behaviour such as avoiding eye contact, fidgeting and gaze aversion, when the available research indicates these are not reliable indicators and signs of nervousness and may be prevalent in the behaviour of innocent interviewees. This has been described by Ekman (2001) as the Othello error. Some studies suggest that certain physical characteristics, including attractiveness, a baby-faced appearance and a symmetrical face, may evoke trustworthiness yet bear no relation to the reality of trustworthiness (Porter *et al.* 2008). Speech-related cues may be more useful than nonverbal ones.

Moreover, investigators do not routinely receive feedback on their judgements on whether they are correct or not. As Luke *et al.* point out, 'Decades of research on deception have consistently found that humans are mediocre at detecting deceit. Across hundreds of studies, the average accuracy of human lie judgments is only marginally higher than chance, a finding that holds true even for presumed lie experts such as police officers' (Luke *et al.* 2013: 54). One study found that psychology students performed better than officers trained in lie detection (Vrij and Graham 1997). Vrij and Graham stress that there is no typical deceptive behaviour despite police officers' misperceptions of liars' typical behaviour. Studies of the police as lie detectors range from 45 to 60 per cent accuracy compared to the 50 per cent accuracy expected by chance. While the police are more confident in their ability to detect lies, this confidence is not matched by actual success in lie detection. If observers are very confident they will be less willing to search for other evidence, but rely too heavily on the appearance of suspects and if the suspects are innocent they may be subjected to an even more coercive interview when these cues are interpreted as guilt.

A general reliance on a nervous appearance may also mean that important cultural differences between individuals are overlooked. Studies in the Netherlands found gaze aversion was more common in Turkish and Moroccans and Surinamese people than in Dutch Caucasians (Vrij and Winkel 1991). Making direct eye contact might be seen as rude in Japan or among Aboriginal peoples in Canada, so avoiding it would be seen as respectful, but in the interview context it may interpreted as being untrustworthy. Therefore any training given to officers needs to be aware of these problems and to avoid over-reliance on nonverbal cues and instead to focus carefully on what suspects say.

An alternative approach to interviewing is the PEACE model, which is essentially investigative interviewing, aimed at fact-finding rather than eliciting confessions (Williamson 2006; Clarke and Milne 2001). The PEACE model comprises prepare and plan (organise the evidence and plan the interview), engage and explain (establish a rapport and communicate the purpose of the interview to the suspect), account (conduct a cognitive interview to get the compliant suspect to speak freely and to encourage a noncompliant suspect to open up), closure (address any discrepancies in the suspect's narrative account) and evaluate (compare the final statement to available evidence to resolve inconsistencies and draw conclusions). The PEACE approach is grounded in empirical research and encourages carefully planning the interview, explaining the process to the suspect, and open-ended questions.

This approach was endorsed by the RCCJ in 1993 as part of a number of improvements necessary to prevent miscarriages of justice, while enabling the police to obtain useful information because the interviews are less confrontational. The effect of the new approach is to shift the police role from an adversarial to an inquisitorial one, and to focus on obtaining high-quality evidence from victims, witnesses and suspects to discover the truth about the matter in question. The guidelines stress that the interview should be approached with an open mind and information obtained from the interviewee should be tested against what the officer already knows or what can reasonably be established. The officer must act fairly, is not bound to accept the first answer given and has a right to put questions, even if the suspect declines to comment.

This new approach to interviewing – ethical or investigative interviewing – was first introduced in England and Wales in 1992 in response to findings of impropriety and the poor quality of interviewing highlighted by the empirical research and was intended to professionalise investigations. It was initiated by two Home Office Circulars which set out the principles of investigative interviewing and gave guidance on appropriate skills training. It was based on discussions between police, psychologists and lawyers and these principles and recommendations were reflected in new training courses and manuals which were intended to provide an ethical foundation for the police in questioning suspects (see Williamson 1993, 1994 and McGurk *et al.* 1993). PEACE is now the basis of the National Investigatory Strategy and part of the Professionalising Investigation Programme (ACPO 2009).

Officers are trained to explain the purpose of the interview to the suspect and taught how to allow the suspect to give his account, how to end the interview, how to evaluate it and to learn from the experience of interviewing. Vulnerable suspects and witnesses should be treated with special consideration. Those at risk of making a false confession should be identified. Skills training was intended to be backed up by improved supervision of interviews and the use of interactive online programmes. Pilot studies showed an improvement in interviewing skills following the training in PEACE techniques. However, Clarke *et al.* (2011) found that while there has been an improvement in interviewing standards since PEACE was introduced, there were minimal differences in performance between PEACE-trained and non-PEACE-trained officers in their study of 174 interviews from six police forces.

The PEACE approach, now used in the UK, Australia, New Zealand, Western Europe and Canada, emphasises truth-seeking and information gathering, building rapport with the suspect and active listening. Information-gathering aims to elicit information, while the accusatorial method aims to elicit confessions, so the former may generate cognitive cues to deception, while the accusatorial approach focuses on anxiety-based cues. The suspect is allowed to tell his story without interruption and only when he has done so will the interviewee be questioned and presented with any contradictions. More open-ended questions are used to elicit information and deception is prohibited. The PEACE model was used in pilot projects in Newfoundland and Ontario and is now widespread in Canada. Tunnel vision, as we have seen, is encouraged by the Reid training, so a move away from confrontational interrogation towards a cognitive inquisitorial interview, it is hoped, will offset this tendency.

The indications are that the PEACE model is as effective as coercive interrogation in eliciting confessions from offenders without threatening innocents, and because it less stressful for recipients, it may also reduce the risk of eliciting a false confession (Kassin 2008b). Meissner *et al.* (2012) conducted a systematic review of published and non-published experimental and observational studies on the effectiveness of interviewing and interrogation methods, using information-gathering and accusatorial methods, to see which is the most effective in eliciting confessions and in eliciting true confessions, given the concern over the number of proven false confessions. Their analysis included five field studies from the United States, the UK and Canada, and twelve experimental studies, mostly involving college students, which specifically assessed the outcomes of interrogative methods in terms of true and false confessions. They found that the available data supported the effectiveness of the information-gathering approach, although they note the relatively small number of independent samples available for analysis and emphasise the need for further research on this topic. Both accusatory and information-gathering studies produced confessions in the field studies, but the experimental data suggested information-gathering 'increased the likelihood of true confessions, while reducing the likelihood of false confessions' (2012: 8). So the innocent suspect, they argue, is better protected from false confessions by information-gathering, while the ability to elicit confessions from the guilty suspect is preserved. Their meta-analysis of the experimental literature found that:

> while accusatorial methods significantly increased the likelihood of obtaining a true confession (when compared with a no-tactic control condition), these methods also significantly increased the likelihood of obtaining a false confession. ... In contrast to this, information-gathering approaches significantly increased true confession rates, but showed no significant increase in the rate of false confessions. ... In fact, information-gathering approaches appeared to show a numerical decrease in the rate of false confessions obtained. When compared directly against accusatorial methods, information-gathering approaches showed superior diagnosticity by significantly increasing the elicitation of true confessions and significantly reducing the incidence of false confessions.
>
> (Meissner *et al.* 2012: 33–4)

The authors therefore recommend the use of such methods by law enforcement, military and intelligence agencies, and highlight the need for further research on the effects of interrogative practices. While experimental studies may not fully replicate the actual experience of interrogation of real interviewees, they can give us some insights into the process but more research on real subjects would be desirable.

Clearly the training of officers for interview is important, but a review of Canadian officers' experience of interview training by Snook *et al.* (2012) found that officers reported their training was very limited and expressed dissatisfaction with it. There was also a lack of supervision of and feedback given to interviewers although feedback and supervision lead to more skilful interviewing. The training included courses and on-the-job training, but with few opportunities for refresher training. The authors therefore recommend a comprehensive tier-based system of witness-interview training based on the PEACE model and grounded in scientific research.

There are also more effective techniques than those recommended in the BAI for detecting liars, including increasing the cognitive load, asking suspects to give their account in reverse order, withholding information till the end of the interview, and asking unexpected questions to pairs of suspects about alibis to see if they give consistent answers. These procedures may assist in reducing the risk of miscarriages of justice. However, the Reid protocol is still widely used in the United States. Vrij *et al.* (2010) therefore recommend using an information-gathering rather than an accusatory approach and to use devices including asking questions which have not been anticipated. The strategic use of evidence (SUE) encourages suspects to discuss activities while withholding information so that they are unaware the interrogator possesses it to catch out the suspect. Asking questions that are not expected will make it harder for liars to fabricate an instant and consistent response, as will asking suspects to draw a crime scene. Withholding certain crime details, that is, strategic disclosure, may be helpful in some cases, making it harder for suspects to lie with consistency, compared to revealing all the information at the outset. Interviewers trained in SUE appear to fare better in detecting deception (Hartwig *et al.* 2005).

Adding to the cognitive load imposed on interviewees is also useful. Because lying is mentally demanding for suspects, increasing the load may make it harder for them to do so; this may be achieved by asking them to recount events in reverse order and asking them to maintain eye contact with interviewers. These indirect methods may be more productive than aggressive questioning. An information-gathering approach may be more successful in encouraging subjects to talk, and the more information is elicited, the easier it will be to identify inconsistencies, compared to an accusatory interview. The research on SUE suggests that it is effective in eliciting cues to deception (DePaulo *et al.* 2003).

Conclusion

As we have seen, there have been a number of significant improvements here and in other jurisdictions in procedural due process rights as well as improved forensic techniques, which go some way towards the prevention of miscarriages of justice. We also have in the UK better review procedures with the establishment of the Criminal Cases Review Commission. Research is being undertaken on ways of improving the quality of confession evidence and on its assessment in court and on the interview process. Many police forces in the United States now use visual recordings to deter coercive tactics, disable frivolous claims and to give a full record of the transactions; if the court can see the interrogator, they can make a more informed judgement of voluntariness.

However, there still remains a risk of false confessions, especially from vulnerable defendants, with increased pressures to speak, a weakened right to silence and the absence of a formal requirement to corrobo-rate confession evidence. We have also noted that nonverbal behav-iour of suspects in interview may be misinterpreted and the ability of professionals to distinguish liars and truth-tellers may be overrated. The police need to look for internal consistency in the confession, as well as external consistency with known facts and to look for corroboration, so the prosecution does not rely just on the confession. The interest of the media and the public in miscarriages of justice has declined compared to the attention given to the high-profile cases of the Guildford Four and Birmingham Six in the past (Nobles and Schiff 2000). In fact recent media attention has been on the problem of the guilty who succeed in quashing their convictions on technicalities. To keep media attention, engaging celebrities to support one's case may also be helpful, and this has been used in the United States. In the *Tankleff* case, a well-known figure, James Gandolfini, supported the campaign for Tankleff's release and attended the appeal hearing. The number of miscarriages of justice is unknown, as we are aware only of high-profile cases and may only become aware when applications succeed.

There has been disagreement in the United States on whether expert evidence should be admitted on the problem of false confessions, to testify to the fact that innocent suspects may confess under pressure. On the one hand, it is argued that is a matter that ordinary people can understand and an instruction to the jury would be sufficient, while others argue for greater use of expert testimony on false confessions. Expert evidence was admitted in the *King* case and was crucial (Watson *et al.* 2010). But in *US v Belyea* (2005) the District Court would not allow the defence in that case to introduce expert trial testimony on false confessions on the grounds that jurors know that people may lie. However, the Court of Appeals in *Belyea* did say that the court should consider whether it is helpful in a particular case. In the UK experts are now often used as consultants where there are disputed confessions to testify on whether an individual is capable of making a false confession, for example, in *R v Blackburn* [2005] 2 Cr App R 240. Since the *Silcott* case the courts have been more willing to hear expert evidence from psychologists and psychiatrists (*R v Silcott, Braithwaite and Raghip, The Times*, (9 December 1991)).

In Canada the Lamer Report (2006) made a number of recommenda-tions to prevent false confessions, including improving standards for interviewing suspects and witnesses which enhance the reliability of the results of interviews and training for investigators and prosecutors on the existence, causes and psychology of police-induced false confessions. A further feature highlighted by the Lamer Report in the miscarriage of justice cases is a horrific crime creating public outrage and where the public demands the perpetrator be held to account as soon as possible. This was an element of the response to the Guildford and Woolwich bombings in the UK. It also raises the question of whether particular communities may be demonised or treated with suspicion which will now be considered in Chapter 7.

7
Suspects and 'Suspect Communities'

Introduction

We saw in Chapters 5 and 6 the problems experienced by vulnerable individuals in interrogation and the need to ensure an interrogation process that is able to deal with suggestible individuals and to reduce the risk of false confessions. But there may also be issues affecting particular communities that may have implications for their relationships with the police. Attention has focused on the sectarian and religious conflicts in Northern Ireland and on the particular issues faced by black and minority ethnic groups in England and Wales, as well as on particular religious groups post 9/11.

Obviously the experience of terrorism in Northern Ireland raises a number of issues, including whether threats from terrorist groups can be addressed without infringing civil rights, whether it was appropriate to introduce additional emergency powers in Northern Ireland or whether the ordinary criminal law was sufficient to deal with the threat and whether, given the fact of these powers, it was necessary to further weaken the suspect's position through limits on the right to silence in the Criminal Evidence (Northern Ireland) Order. The need for emergency powers during the conflict was also questioned, for example, by Hogan and Walker (1989) and Dickson (2010). Most terrorism-related crimes, including the most serious, arguably can be covered by the ordinary criminal law, for example violence by the offences of homicide and offences against the person and acquisitive crimes to raise funds for terrorist activities by the offences of robbery and theft. Whether a separate parallel criminal justice system, with fewer due process rights, was necessary given the number of terrorism-related incidents was also questioned. Relying on the ordinary criminal law strengthens the rule of law and the legitimacy of the system, and essential to the rule of law is the equal treatment of all suspects regardless of political or religious affiliation. It is preferable to rely on properly drafted and well-thought-out legislation rather than emergency powers. Moreover, over time, emergency temporary provisions may influence the ordinary criminal law leading to more onerous measures for all citizens and temporary provisions may become permanent.

Policing Northern Ireland

The Royal Ulster Constabulary (RUC) had the primary policing role during the conflict, with the army responsible for specific tasks such as border patrols, but obviously there were issues of accountability and legitimacy, as civilians had been injured and killed by the security forces using rubber and plastic baton rounds. Where lethal force was used, the conviction and prosecution rates were low. Human rights violations lay at the heart of the conflict, as Winter (1995) and others have argued, which included the use of emergency provisions, the failure to release prisoners and the use of lethal force. Accusations of a 'shoot to kill' policy on the part of the security forces were fuelled by Bloody Sunday when civilians were killed on a civil rights demonstration in Londonderry, and by the Gibraltar killings. Concerns were also raised over police complaints procedures which, at that time, were investigated by serving police officers. Cases are still being brought regarding the use of torture in interrogation and the admission of unreliable confessions in Northern Ireland. Other problems have included the imposition of exclusion orders, reliance on supergrass evidence and non-jury trials and more recently stops and searches under s 44 of the Terrorism Act 2000. The operation of the criminal justice system in Northern Ireland was excluded from the remit of the Royal Commission on Criminal Justice and we therefore do not have the range of empirical studies on the Northern Ireland criminal justice system comparable to those that were conducted in England and Wales. While some of the worst miscarriages of justice, as we saw in Chapter 6, involved Irish suspects, including the Maguire Seven, the Guildford Four and Birmingham Six, they raised questions regarding treatment by the police and courts in England. However, the Criminal Cases Review Commission now deals with cases from Northern Ireland as well as England and Wales.

Maintaining the integrity of a criminal justice system at times of conflict is difficult, but the protection of human rights and dignity are crucial to the legitimacy of the system. The use of repressive measures may be counterproductive and in Northern Ireland the use of intern-ment increased support for the IRA. Achieving legitimacy in Northern Ireland was problematic during the conflict when the army was involved in policing the civilian population. Furthermore, the Catholic minority was under-represented in the ordinary police force, then the RUC, which was seen at that as primarily a Unionist and Protestant police force policing a mixed population of Catholics and Protestants.

There were also concerns over the collusion of the RUC with loyalist paramilitaries in the killing of civilians, such as the lawyer Pat Finucane, who was shot at home in front of his family in 1989. Although he was not a member of the IRA, he had defended some suspects accused of IRA activities. The loyalist group UFF claimed responsibility for the killing. The failure of the British Government to order a full independent public inquiry into his murder was challenged by the Finucane family and human rights organisations. It was also criticised by the European Court of Human Rights. In *Finucane v UK* App. No. 291788/95 (1 October 2003) the Strasbourg Court ruled that the procedures following his death failed to provide a prompt and effective investigation into allegations of collusion by security personnel and breached Article 2 (at para 84).

We do now have findings from the Stevens Enquiry (2003), the Cory Report (2004a) and the de Silva Review (2102) which considered whether there was any involvement of the army, RUC, security service (MI5) or other UK Government body in the murder of Pat Finucane. The Stevens Enquiry highlighted the role of an RUC informant, William Stobie, in the murder, but he too was shot and a loyalist group claimed responsibility. Stevens also reported on the way his inquiry had been obstructed by the RUC. He found that the RUC did not deal with intelligence from both sides of the community fairly and he was critical of the collusion between the security forces, loyalist paramilitaries, the RUC and the army, and the failure to investigate properly the Finucane murder. The Cory Report (2004a) also found collusion between the security forces and loyalist para-militaries and recommended a public inquiry into the murder. Collusion was also found in relation to the killing in 1999 of Rosemary Nelson, another lawyer involved in high-profile cases (Cory, 2004b).

The Review, conducted by Sir Desmond de Silva, reported in 2012 and concluded that agents of the state were involved in the murder and the killing should have been prevented (de Silva, 2012). The threshold for a finding of collusion was met in this case, and there had been obstruc-tion of the Stevens Enquiry by the army and the RUC. It found that an RUC officer or officers proposed Patrick Finucane as a UDA target when speaking to a loyalist paramilitary (para 74). But while state agents facilitated the murder, there was not an overarching state conspiracy to murder (de Silva, 2012, p. 116). A month before the murder a government minister, Douglas Hogg, had made a speech in Parliament referring to some solicitors being unduly sympathetic to the IRA. The Report thought that while Douglas Hogg's comment had not been intended to encourage an attack on any solicitors, it did increase their vulnerability. The Prime Minister in 2011 acknowledged state collusion and apologised to the family, but has resisted demands for an independent public inquiry. However, the US Congress held its own inquiry into the killing in May 2013.

The Finucane case also raises questions about the role of lawyers during the conflict and of lawyers' professional associations. McEvoy (2011) notes that the Bar Council did not pursue the Finucane case because he was a solicitor. The Law Society condemned the killing and held a public meeting, but took no further action at the time and was opposed to an inquiry, although it did respond more strongly to the later murder of Rosemary Nelson in 1999. Lawyers who felt threatened went to international organizations for help because they did not feel supported by local professional associations. McEvoy castigates lawyers during the emergency regime in Northern Ireland for their collective failure of moral courage. He interviewed 50 lawyers and judges in Northern Ireland after the Good Friday Agreement, in two periods, 2002–3 and 2008–10. Lawyers emphasised that they worked for the entire community and avoided taking a political stance because they were concerned about being seen as sectarian. Lawyers also participated in internment hearings and Diplock trials because they wanted to assist their clients. McEvoy notes the lack of public debate within the legal community over the emergency laws. In fact, most of the critique came from lawyers outside Northern Ireland and human rights organisations such as British Irish Rights Watch and the Haldane Society, although the Committee on the Administration of Justice in Northern Ireland, set up in 1981, offered a critical voice. McEvoy acknowledges the small size of the legal profession in Northern Ireland and the difficulties of working in the conflict of the time, but notes that in other conflicts we find the development of 'cause lawyering' as lawyers seek to use the law to achieve social and political change (see Sarat and Scheingold, 2006).

In the l990s, 93 per cent of the RUC officers were Protestant. Although efforts were made to recruit more widely, there was clearly a shortage of applicants. As McGarry and O'Leary (1999) argued, effective policing demands strong links between the police and the public, but this is impossible if they are overwhelmingly recruited from one group. An

Independent Commission on Policing was set up as part of the Good Friday Agreement in April 1998. It reported in 1999 and highlighted the problems of accountability, transparency and legitimacy within the Catholic community and made a number of recommendations, including a new policing board and improvements in training and transparency. It argued that the force should reflect the population in terms of religion, politics and gender. At that time women accounted for only 12 per cent of the RUC. It recommended 50:50 recruitment of Catholics and Protestants. The RUC was renamed the Police Service of Northern Ireland in 2001 under the Police (Northern Ireland) Act 2000. The force is now 30 per cent drawn from the Catholic population and has new uniforms and badges, including the shamrock, to denote its greater inclusiveness. The latest available figures from the PSNI from 1 November 2013 show the composition is as follows:

Workforce	Perceived Protestant	Perceived Catholic	Female	Ethnic minorities
Police officers	66.9	30.77	27.20	0.54
Police staff	77.43	19.38	63.88	0.57

Detention and questioning in Northern Ireland

The dynamics of interrogation in Northern Ireland during the conflict obviously have to be understood in terms of the political and social context of the time. Although emergency powers were in place, internment had ended in 1975 and efforts to use supergrasses to obtain information had mostly been unsuccessful. So the right to silence became another target for change. The debate over interrogation and concern over the wall of silence in Northern Ireland in the late 1980s centered on the fact that many terrorist suspects hid behind silence, while in mainland Britain the focus was on the use of silence by professional criminals. The actual number remaining silent was unclear as the relevant evidence was not published, but the Republican Press had encouraged silence and members of Republican groups were trained to withstand the pressures of interrogation. Those with more experience of the criminal justice system would be more prepared for the challenges of interrogation and many members had experienced custody during internment and were better able to resist pressures to speak. The Colville Review (1987) of the terrorism provisions recommended abolition of the right to silence which the police saw as a barrier to conviction. The RUC in the 1980s also favoured abolition of the right to silence to encourage suspects to speak.

In the case of *R v Martin and others* [1992] 5 NIJB 40 one of the people involved, Morrison, refused to explain his presence at a house where a man was being held against his will and was about to be shot when he was rescued by the RUC. Morrison said at his trial that he had remained silent because as a Sinn Fein officer he could not speak to the RUC. As a publicity officer he had written pamphlets advising silence during questioning. At trial he admitted his presence at the house, but said he had gone there to organise a press conference to discuss the man's statement that he had been forced to inform by the RUC. The Lord Chief Justice refused to accept the explanation that Morrison had not answered questions on principle and said that he was entitled to draw adverse inferences from his failure to explain his presence and his silence during interrogation, using common sense.

The appeal to common sense, as we have seen, was frequently made by critics of the right to silence, who argued that limiting the right to silence would bring the law closer to common sense thinking. The assumption that the innocent person would want to speak to clear his name and that silence suggests guilt has frequently been made. It is also often claimed that juries will operate with such assumptions, irrespective of judicial direction on this subject. We expect people to take accusations seriously in everyday life and if we confront a person with wrongdoing and receive no response we may well draw an adverse inference. However, common sense may be a poor guide for interpreting responses to interrogation in the context of the police station interview where the questioning is not between equal parties. The relationship between citizens is quite different from the relationship between the police and the accused.

A range of factors other than guilt may account for the failure to speak, including fear, embarrassment, anxiety, confusion, outrage and a refusal to accept the authority or legitimacy of the police. It is especially difficult to interpret silence in the Northern Ireland context where in the past there has been a tradition of non-cooperation with the RUC and also where fears of being seen as an informant are well grounded. As McGrory (1994) observes, what may seem common sense to a trial judge may not seem so to a person from a working-class background living in a community with a history of mutual distrust between the community and the security forces.

At the height of the conflict in the 1970s and 1980s, various repressive measures, including beatings and shootings, were used against informants and suspected informants, for example, kneecapping, that is, shooting in the legs, and breeze-blocking, the dropping of breeze blocks on limbs, as well as tarring and feathering. These informal punishments were meted out by both Republican and loyalist military groups against those suspected of a range of crimes, including being an informer. This parallel system of informal justice has a long history in Northern Ireland, as Monaghan (2002) notes. In the late nineteenth century, for example, during the Land Wars, gangs known as 'Captain Moonlight' would travel around the countryside to punish landlords and agents. Informal justice in Northern Ireland has included retributive and restorative justice, self-policing and people's courts.

So during the 1980s concerns over personal safety or fears for family members, would certainly account for a reluctance to speak, rather than simply guilt. For many suspects during the conflict the risk of being seen as an informant would be far more compelling than the risk of any adverse inferences from silence. As well as the fear of reprisals against them, there may also be the desire to protect families. The failure to respond to questions can be seen as a rational response in these circumstances. So where there is a history of conflict with and distrust of the police, the suspect may be unwilling to speak notwithstanding the threat of adverse inferences, but this will not necessarily be a sign of guilt. The Catholic community had a poor relationship with the RUC at that time. Since then efforts have been made through anti-discrimination law and a range of affirmative action measures to change this situation and now, as noted above, Catholic officers constitute about one-third of the police officers of Northern Ireland.

The use of emergency powers

In the 1970s suspects were often held at interrogation centres, such as Castlereagh Holding Centre in East Belfast, where they were ill treated in some cases, and held in isolation without adequate safeguards, following which they made confessions. At that time some of these confessions were admitted in evidence although it is unlikely that they would be admissible now. Suspects in the 1970s could be held in solitary confinement for long periods in the holding centre at Castlereagh and conditions were criticised by the UN Human Rights Committee (CCCPR/C/79). These issues were litigated in *Ireland v UK* App. No. 5310/71 (18 January

1978), the background to which is discussed by Dickson (2010) and Bonner (2014). The court's approach to extended detention was considered in the cases of *Brogan and others v UK* App. Nos. 11209/84, 11234/84 and 11266/84 (29 November 1988), and *Brannigan and McBride v UK* App. Nos. 14553/89 and 14554/89 (25 May 1993). The court made clear in *Brogan* that the fact that their extended detention was inspired by a legitimate aim to protect the community from terrorism was not, on its own, sufficient to satisfy compliance with the specific requirements of Article 5(3).

The reasons for extended detention cited in evidence to the Colville Inquiry included checking of fingerprints, forensic tests and translation, yet these could have been completed following charging the suspect and are ordinary police activities rather than peculiar to terrorism-related activities (Colville, 1987). Extended detention was clearly a way of increasing pressure on suspects. Also at that time, during questioning under the EPA, access to a lawyer was denied for 48 hours and interviews were not routinely recorded. The recording of interviews was strongly recommended by the Independent Commissioner for Holding Centres in 1993 and has now been implemented. Ordinary suspects are questioned under the PACE provisions extended to Northern Ireland by the Police and Criminal Evidence (Northern Ireland) Order 1989.

Internment Orders were used in the 1970s to detain persons without trial under powers given by the Civil Authorities (Special Powers) Act (Northern Ireland) 1922 and were not phased out until 1985. In the 1970s and 1980s large numbers of people were also detained under the Prevention of Terrorism Act in relation to terrorism in Northern Ireland although the majority were not ultimately charged with any offence. The Act was also used to search and question at ports and airports.

The UN Human Rights Committee was also critical of threats to human rights in the province, including the use of emergency legislation in Northern Ireland and extended powers of detention (CCCPR/C/79, 1995). Modification of the counter-terrorism provisions was an important part of the peace process. An independent review of legislation against terrorism was conducted by Lord Lloyd to see whether counter-terrorism provisions were still necessary in the light of the peace process (Lloyd, 1996). The UK Government in 1995 said it would introduce electronic recording of interviews in holding centres and enhance the granting of compassionate parole for prisoners. There was also a gradual shift towards bringing procedures in the interrogation holding centres closer to those used for 'ordinary suspects' under PACE. Lawyers had been permitted by the Chief Constable of Northern Ireland to attend paramilitary interviews before *Murray* had been decided in Strasbourg in 1996.

Emergency laws were replaced by new UK-wide legislation, the Terrorism Act 2000, following the Lloyd review of counter-terrorist law in the mid-1990s (Lloyd, 1996). The Terrorism Act 2000 combined elements of the Northern Ireland (Emergency Provisions) Act and Prevention of Terrorism (Temporary Provisions) Act, but took account of the Lloyd review recommendations and was intended to be Convention compliant. The Act was accompanied by a Code for Detention and Questioning which allowed the lawyer to attend interviews and visual and audio recording of interviews. It also required judicial permission for an extension of detention beyond 48 hours of persons arrested on suspicion of an act of terrorism, to comply with Article 5 and avoid the need for derogation. In 2002 the PACE tests for the admissibility of confessions, discussed in Chapter 5, were extended to terrorist cases in Northern Ireland. However, as noted earlier, the maximum period for detention rose from 14 to 17 days in 2003, to 28 days in 2006, and now stands at 14 days.

As well as extended detention, other extraordinary measures used in the conflict were exclusion orders, non-jury trials and the use of super-grasses. Northern Ireland was subject to emergency provisions passed under the Northern Ireland (Emergency Provisions) Act 1987. The Prevention of Terrorism (Temporary Provisions) Act 1989 also applied to Northern Ireland as well as England and Wales. The PTA provisions had been in place since 1974 and were renewed annually. The PTA powers included the power to make exclusion orders, so an order could be made by the Secretary of State against a person 'as appears to him expedient to prevent acts of terrorism', as well as including powers to proscribe organisations and powers of arrest, as well as extended powers of detention. The PTA 1976 had also made it an offence to contribute to or solicit contributions towards acts of terrorism in Northern Ireland or to withhold information pertaining to acts of terrorism or about people involved in such acts. So these provisions also increased the pressure to speak and made further encroachments on the right to silence. At that time judicial control of the police and security forces was seen as too weak to provide appropriate safeguards.

The Colville Review (1987) had recommended abolition of exclusion orders but they were retained in the 1989 Prevention of Terrorism Act. In the 1974 PTA the Orders were indefinite; in the 1976 Act they were limited to three years, but with the power to extend them further

(Colville, 1987). Clearly these Orders imposed limits on freedom of movement and constituted a form of internal exile and adversely affected the family rights of citizens of Northern Ireland with families in England, and were seen as discriminatory because of the disparate impact on this group. Following the ceasefire declared by the IRA in 1994, and in the spirit of the peace process, the broadcasting ban was lifted and some exclusion orders were revoked, including those imposed on Sinn Fein President Gerry Adams and on Martin McGuinness, who are now major figures in the post-conflict political landscape.

Non-jury trials, known as Diplock trials, were introduced in Northern Ireland by the EPA 1973 for certain 'scheduled offences', including murder, offences against the person and firearms offences and membership in a proscribed organization as stipulated in the Schedule to the EPA, and were recommended by the Diplock Commission (1972). Some safeguards were given as there was an automatic right of appeal and a requirement for the judge to give reasons for decisions.

The use of these trials was justified in terms of concern over intimidation of jurors, as well as fears of perverse sectarian verdicts by loyalist juries given because of bias for or against the defendant. Greer and White (1986) have claimed, however, that these justifications relied only on anecdotal evidence, but if jurors were afraid they could have been given anonymity and protection. The development of the Diplock Courts might be viewed as a disproportionate response to a perceived problem that affected many suspects lying outside the class for whom it was intended. One study found that 40 per cent of the cases heard in the Diplock Courts had no connection with terrorist activities (Haldane Society, 1992). Jackson and Doran (1995) in their study of 43 Diplock and jury trials in Belfast Crown Court from 1989–91 found that there was far less scope for participation by the defendant in jury than nonjury trials and their use clearly moved the criminal justice system closer to an inquisitorial one. The majority of convictions in relation to scheduled offences relied on confessional evidence. The use of this measure also paved the way for the use of non-jury trials in England and Wales in complex cases and where there is a clear and present danger of jury tampering.

A review of the courts was conducted in 2006 which favoured a presumption of jury trial but noted that there remained a risk of juror intimidation and perverse verdicts, so that it should still be possible to use the courts where appropriate (Northern Ireland Office, 2006). The Justice and Security (Northern Ireland) Act 2007 stipulates that the

Director of Public Prosecution for Northern Ireland may permit a non-jury trial if it satisfies the conditions set out in the Act and there is a risk of impairment of the administration of justice. Although the scheduling of offences is now removed, as Jackson (2009) notes, the conditions remain broad, including if the offence is committed in response to religious or political hostility or the defendant is an associate of a member of a paramilitary group. The use of these courts has been extended every two years and was extended for a further two years until 31 July 2015 by the Justice and Security (Northern Ireland) Act 2007 (Extension of Duration of Non-Jury Trial Provisions) Order 2013. Under the 2007 Act, a certificate may be given where the DPP is satisfied that the defendant is, or has been at any time, a member of a proscribed organisation, the offence was committed on behalf of a proscribed organisation or that organisation was involved with or assisted in carrying out the offence, an attempt has been made to prejudice the investigation or prosecution of the offence on behalf of the proscribed organisation or that organisation was involved in that attempt, or the offence was committed in response to religious or political hostility of one person or group towards another person or group, and, in the above cases, that there is a risk that the administration of justice might be impaired if the trial were to be conducted with a jury (s 1).

In the 1970s supergrass evidence had been admitted in England at trials of gangs of bank robbers in London, but juries were reluctant to convict defendants on the uncorroborated evidence of supergrasses and judges had expressed reservations about such convictions. But they were used in Northern Ireland in the early 1980s in the Diplock Courts. Greer (1995) argues that the increased reliance on informers resulted in part from the loss of internment and stronger due process controls on interrogation, which made it harder to extract confessions from suspects. These supergrasses were given immunity, reduced sentences, or resources to start a new life elsewhere. Convictions based on the uncorroborated evidence of supergrasses in Northern Ireland mostly involved Republican supergrasses, reinforcing claims of sectarian justice. From 1981 to 1983, 7 loyalist and 19 Republican supergrasses were responsible for nearly 600 people being arrested and charged in Northern Ireland, based on figures given to Parliament by the Junior Minister for Northern Ireland, Nicholas Scott (HC Deb Vol 73, 100, 1985). Gifford's (1984) study of the use of supergrass evidence found that 54 per cent of the defendants in the supergrass trials he examined were convicted on the basis of uncorroborated evidence.

Initially some Diplock judges showed a willingness to use supergrass evidence but few convictions based on this evidence survived on appeal (see, for example, *R v Graham* [1983] 7 NIJB 36). They came under criticism from lawyers and judges inside and outside Northern Ireland. However, when the Northern Ireland Court of Appeal made clear that the dangers of supergrass evidence was greater than that of normal accomplices, their use stopped in 1986. They were not used again until 2012, when an attempt was made to rely on supergrass evidence to obtain a conviction for the murder of UDA leader Tommy English. But this failed when all the accused were acquitted of the murder charges. In the 1980s accomplice evidence was subject to a mandatory corroboration warning which reflected concerns over the risk of fabrication and of a cut-throat defence in the hope of favourable treatment and the avoidance of a heavy sentence, and because the accomplice's knowledge of the offence could mislead the jury. However, a formal warning is now deemed inappropriate and was abolished by s 32 of the Criminal Justice and Public Order Act 1994, because it treats the accomplice as part of a general class of witnesses, rather than assessing the individual risk in each case. Instead a caution warning may now be given if there is an evidential basis for concern (*R v Makanjuola* [1996] Crim LR 44). During the 1980s and 1990s, the focus of the security forces shifted from the use of supergrasses towards the infiltration of paramilitary groups which raised new problems of secrecy and a reluctance to disclose sources of the intelligence obtained.

British troops were withdrawn from Northern Ireland in August 2007 after 38 years. But sectarian hate crimes and paramilitary attacks and shootings persisted and despite substantial progress, clearly deep divisions remain. The riots in 2013 over the refusal to allow Protestant marches through Catholic streets and the continuing resentments over the display of national emblems give some indication of the depth of conflict and volatility of the situation, and lack of confidence in the police from both sides of the conflict. In addition, lethal violence has continued to be inflicted by dissident sectarian groups.

Contemporary counter-terrorism measures

The concern with security has dominated debates on law and order in recent years, supplanting the traditional concern with crime control, and has meant that rights have been under greater threat and the focus has shifted away from Northern Ireland towards international terrorism, and particularly Islamist extremism. Policing has been shaped by terrorist threats and terrorism has been seen as a new form of criminality. Terrorism is defined in s 1 of the Terrorism Act 2000 as

(1) the use or threat of action where –
    (a) the action falls within subsection (2),
    (b) the use or threat is designed to influence the government [or an international governmental organisation] or to intimidate the public or a section of the public, and
    (c) the use or threat is made for the purpose of advancing a political, religious, racial, or ideological cause.
(2) Action falls within this subsection if it –
    (a) involves serious violence against a person,
    (b) involves serious damage to property,
    (c) endangers a person's life, other than that of the person committing the action,
    (d) creates a serious risk to the health or safety of the public or a section of the public, or
    (e) is designed seriously to interfere with or seriously to disrupt an electronic system.
(3) The use or threat of action falling within subsection (2) which involves the use of firearms or explosives is terrorism whether or not subsection (1)(b) is satisfied.
(4) In this section –
    (f) "action" includes action outside the United Kingdom,
    (g) a reference to any person or to property is a reference to any person, or to property, wherever situated,
    (h) a reference to the public includes a reference to the public of a country other than the United Kingdom, and
    (i) "the government" means the government of the United Kingdom, of a Part of the United Kingdom or of a country other than the United Kingdom.
(5) In this Act a reference to action taken for the purposes of terrorism includes a reference to action taken for the benefit of a proscribed organisation.

The threat of terrorism has been used to justify increases in police powers, with an expansion of antiterrorism measures, including Control Orders, as well as the wide powers under Schedule 7 of the Terrorism Act 2000, criticised by civil libertarians. The Terrorism Act 2006 addressed *inter alia* the encouragement of terrorism, dissemination of publications, the preparation of terrorist acts and terrorist training, and extended detention for a maximum of 28 days. The 2008 Counter-Terrorism Act also included provisions on the gathering and sharing of information for counter-terrorism and other purposes, including the disclosure of information to and by the intelligence services; post-charge questioning of terrorism suspects; the prosecution of terrorism offences and punishment of convicted terrorists; notification requirements for persons convicted of terrorism-related offences; and powers to act against terrorist financing, money laundering and certain other activities. The Protection of Freedoms Act 2012 reduced the maximum period of pre-charge detention from 28 to 14 days.

Control Orders and TPIMs

Control orders were also introduced in 2005 and were more onerous than the current Terrorism Prevention and Investigation Measures (TPIMs). Those subject to a Control Order could be relocated away from their homes, banned from meeting certain people and from using mobile phones or the internet. There were also restrictions on visitors. Their phone calls were monitored and they could be subject to curfews of 16 hours a day. They were electronically tagged and had to report regularly to the police. It was a form of house arrest and as such affected the family of the suspect and their homes could be searched. Control orders made it hard for the suspect to live a normal life, engage in work or education and were stigmatising. They were also were based on secret evidence. Control orders could be used against UK nationals as well as foreign nationals. Orders lasted one year but could be renewed.

Control orders were replaced by TPIMs in 2012 under the Terrorism Prevention and Investigation Measures Act 2011, which, while restricting the movements of those under surveillance, impose fewer constraints than Control Orders. Proceedings for both Control Orders and TPIMs may be held without the suspect and his lawyer present, although a special advocate will be appointed to represent the individual in those proceedings. Information regarding the reasons for the TPIM can be withheld from the suspect and the lawyer on public interest grounds. Control Orders were given on the basis of reasonable suspicion but TPIMs are based on reasonable belief. TPIMs are initiated by the Home Secretary with the permission of the High Court. MI5 can apply to the Home Secretary for a TPIM to be placed on a suspect where, following an assessment, there is a reasonable belief that he or she is engaged in terrorism-related activities. Although Control Orders were reviewed by Parliament annually, TPIMs are reviewed every five years.

TPIMs are designed to deal with those who are perceived as dangerous but where it is difficult to charge them and put them on trial. Suspects wear electronic tags and are subject to a curfew of a maximum of ten hours and must report regularly to the police. Usually they will be required to live at home and stay the night there unless permission has been given for a change of location. Suspects are allowed access to mobile phones and the Internet. They can be prohibited from visiting certain locations, including overseas, or accessing certain websites. TPIMs last two years following which suspects must be released from them unless there is evidence of new terrorism-related activity. In 2013 there were nine men subject to a TPIM, including suspects believed to have links to al-Shabab, the Somalian-based terrorist group.

But critics have argued they are less effective than Control Orders as some of those under surveillance have absconded and not been traced. Ibrahim Magag hired a black cab and disappeared in 2012 and Mohammed Mohamed escaped from a mosque in November 2013 dressed in a burka. Usually their names are protected although in these cases names were released because they had absconded. Civil libertarians have questioned the fact that the allegations against them may be kept secret and that they have not been subjected to a criminal trial. Effectively they have been punished without the safeguards of a criminal trial. The Independent Reviewer of Terrorism Legislation has said that there should be a higher standard of proof required before the government can apply to the courts to impose an order (Anderson, 2013).

Liberty (2012) has campaigned against these controls on movement on the basis that they are unfair because they restrain people without trial and conviction, and make it difficult for people to clear their name and are unsafe because some people have disappeared. If restrictions on the admissibility of intercept evidence were admissible in criminal proceedings, it is often argued, this would be a better alternative. Police bail could also be applied to terror suspects with appropriate restrictions, but also with essential safeguards. The Strasbourg Court also stressed in *A & Others v UK* App. No. 3455/05 (19 February 2009) that the right to protection against non-degrading treatment must be maintained despite the most challenging conditions facing modern societies.

The use of Schedule 7 and Section 44

Schedule 7 of the Terrorism Act has also been extensively used as part of counter-terrorism strategy. Under Schedule 7 of the Terrorism Act 2000 a person may be questioned at ports or border areas and 'must give the examining officer any information in his possession which the examining officer requests' (Schedule 7, para 5(A)). The person commits an offence if he fails to comply with a duty under the Schedule and on conviction may receive a fine and/or a maximum of three months' imprisonment (para 18). So here the failure to speak is expressly criminalized and penalized. He can be questioned whether or not the officer has grounds for reasonable suspicion of an involvement in terrorism, can be detained and questioned for up to nine hours, can be searched and commits an offence if he refuses to answer questions (para 18, Schedule 7). There were powers to detain people at ports and borders on the basis of reasonable suspicion in Northern Ireland and in the context of a response to a specific terrorist threat in the 1980s. But Schedule 7 lacks the requirement of reasonable suspicion and gives a generalised power to stop and search. Liberty reports that in 2012–13 there were 56,257 examinations under Schedule 7 and 63,902 in 2011–12 (Sankey, 2013: 4). The powers have been used primarily against members of ethnic minorities, principally persons of Asian origin. In 2012–3 79 per cent of those detained were non-White (which includes Black, Asian, Mixed, Chinese and Other).

Schedule 7 has been attacked for being too broad and too intrusive. In September 2012 the Home Office published a Consultation on Schedule 7 and this review was stimulated in part because of its impact on Muslim communities, as well as issues raised by the Independent Reviewer of counter-terrorism law (Anderson, 2011). The majority of respondents to the Consultation thought the powers were too wide and unfair. Amendments to Schedule 7 were introduced by the Anti-social Behaviour, Crime and Policing Act 2014 (Schedule 9). The Act limits questioning to an initial maximum of one hour with an extension to a maximum of six hours with reviews of detention and access to a solicitor. These safeguards apply in all places of detention, not just the police station. A strip search can only be conducted where there is reasonable suspicion that an item is being concealed. Schedule 9 also requires Codes of Practice to be issued to reflect these new requirements. But Schedule 7 still does not have a requirement of reasonable suspicion for the detention. It is also questionable whether Schedule 7 is still needed as the new s 47A of the Act gives sufficient powers and has the advantage of being based on reasonable suspicion and addressing the Strasbourg Court's criticism of s 44 of the Act, expressed in the case of *Gillan and Quinton v UK* App. No. 4158/05 (12 January 2010).

Schedule 7 will also be considered in Strasbourg as the case of *Malik v UK* App. No. 32968/11, brought by Liberty, is pending at the Strasbourg Court, where it has been deemed admissible. The detention of David

Miranda under Schedule 7, which is under investigation, also focused media and public attention in its use. The High Court in *Sylvie Beghal v DPP* [2013] EWHC 2573 (Admin) has also urged consideration of a legislative amendment for a statutory ban on the introduction of admissions made in a Schedule 7 examination in a subsequent criminal trial and this is now under consideration.

Individuals may be stopped and searched by the police and other state officials under several statutes, but attention has focused on s 44 of the Terrorism Act, recently repealed and replaced, which was used disproportionately against Asian, Muslim and young black males, although White suspects constituted the numerical majority of s 44 stop and searches. Although reasonable suspicion is required for stops and searches under PACE, it was not required under s 44 of the Terrorism Act 2000 which gives powers to stop and search to look for articles that might be used in connection with terrorism. The powers were limited to a 48-hour period. Under s 44 a senior police officer was empowered to authorise any constable to stop and search a pedestrian if he considered it expedient for the prevention of acts of terrorism. The reform group JUSTICE reports that from 2000–8 108,714 people were stopped and searched under s 44, of whom 1,442 were arrested and of these only 147 people were arrested for a terrorist offence, and since 2000 nobody has been convicted of a terrorist offence following a search under s 44 (http://www.justice.org.uk/pages/stop-and-search-under-the-terrorism-act-2000.html). One in three people arrested under s 44 were members of an ethnic minority group. In 2007–8 there were 117,278 stops and searches under s 44. The Carlisle Review also noted that while arrests had followed searches under the Act they were not always for offences connected with terrorism (Carlisle, 2008).

The use of these powers was challenged in the Strasbourg Court in *Gillan and Quinton v UK* App. No. 4158/05 (12 January 2010) where the court concluded that the use of stop and search powers under the Act infringed Article 8. Section 44 was too broad and could potentially be misused against certain black and minority ethnic groups. The blanket deployment of s 44 across the whole of London was unlawful and the authorisation was not signed off properly. The applicants had been stopped and searched on their way to a demonstration in East London, under ss 44–7 of the Terrorism Act 2000. The court noted that while the applicants were not BME there was a danger the powers would be used arbitrarily against BME groups and that there were insufficient safeguards under the Act.

Most police forces stopped using these powers after *Gillan*. The Counter-Terrorism Review recommended that stop and search powers under ss 44–7 be repealed and replaced by more limited powers. So s 59 of the Protection of Freedoms Act 2012 repeals ss 44–7 (stop and search powers under the Terrorism Act 2000) and replaces them with powers based on a higher threshold for authorisation of reasonable suspicion in s 47A. The power to stop and search is limited to an area where specific intelligence of a possible attack is known. Authorisation would be given under s 47A where there is reasonable suspicion an act of terrorism will take place and the powers are considered necessary to prevent such an act. Authorisation can last no longer and cover no greater an area than is necessary to prevent such an act. New Codes of Practice were also required to accompany these changes. The Protection of Freedoms Act 2012 also reduced the maximum period of pre-charge detention from 28 to 14 days.

Section 117 of the Coroners and Justice Act 2009 also strengthened the oversight of terrorism law by extending the statutory Independent Custody Visitor scheme to terrorist detainees under the Terrorism Act 2000 and strengthens the role of the Independent Reviewer of terrorist legislation in reporting on the treatment of detainees.

The latest report from the Independent Reviewer of the operation of the Terrorism Acts recommends improvements in the process for proscribing and de-proscribing groups and more safeguards regarding the use of anti-terrorist powers in the ports (Anderson, 2013). In response the government has said it does not plan any wholesale review of counter-terrorism policing structures until the National Crime Agency is well established, but it is considering issues of proscription (Home Office, 2013a). It also notes the latest data on charging, sentence length and seriousness of offence, and convictions following terrorism-related arrests, which showed no statistically significant differences between Muslim offenders and those from other or no religions in the proportions charged, sentence length or the seriousness of the offence in the period September 2001 to August 2012 (Home Office, 2013b).

The disparate impact of counter-terrorism measures

While there have been some improvements in response to the above criticisms, the question of disparate impact of counter-terrorism measures is still being raised. A report by Choudhury and Fenwick (2011) for the Equality and Human Rights Commission on the impact of counter-terrorism measures on Muslim communities found respondents felt that they were being stopped because they were Muslim. The focus of counter-terrorism has now shifted away from sectarian groups in Northern Ireland towards other sources, principally Islamist extremism, which has generated a debate on whether the Muslim community has now become a 'suspect community'. Security has become a key part of the law and order agenda since 9/11 and the July 2005 London bombings, with attention focused on the terrorist threat from within the UK, on the activities of home-grown terrorists and their potential and actual participation in terrorist activities here and outside the UK and in armed struggles overseas, as well on the threat from outside the UK. As the participants may include, in some cases, individuals with no prior criminal history, so-called clean skins, this has made it harder to police, which has generated further increases in the powers of the state and the police, and focused more attention on particular communities. Prisons have also come under closer scrutiny as a further potential source of radicalisation and extremism and concerns raised over the intimidation of prisoners by Muslim gangs and also tensions between Muslims and other prisoners (House of Commons Home Affairs Committee, 2012).

Pantazis and Pemberton (2009) argue that Muslims have been construed as the 'enemy within' and counter-terrorism measures directed primarily against them have led to the construction of Muslims as a 'suspect community' which has replaced the Irish community as the focus of counter-terrorism and security measures. A suspect community is a subgroup singled out by the state as 'problematic' and which is then targeted by the police, so an individual may become suspect simply by being a member of the group. The term is borrowed from the work of Hillyard (1993) who examined the impact of the PTA on the treatment of Irish people in the UK, who were regularly stopped and searched and 'trawled' for information. Yet 86 per cent of suspects detained under the PTA in the period 1974 to 1991 were released without charge. The widespread use of the powers under the PTA, he argued, contributed at that time to bringing the whole Irish community under suspicion. Greer (1994), however, was very critical of Hillyard's view of the Irish community as a suspect community, arguing that it was based on a very small unrepresentative sample from which it was difficult to generalise.

Pantazis and Pemberton acknowledge the differences within the Muslim community, which is not a monolithic group, but emphasise the fact that they share a common identity and experiences, including being the object of suspicion. They highlight the fact that a disproportionate number of young Asian males are stopped and searched under counter-terrorism provisions, although they note that the religion of suspects has not been recorded. As we have seen, searches could be made without reasonable suspicion under counter-terrorism law. While the majority of suspects stopped and searched are White, in terms of the proportions of the population, a disproportionate number of Asian and black individuals are searched. They argue that defining Muslim communities as suspect can increase and legitimate the fear of Muslims and point to the increase in hate crimes against them. It may also be counterproductive in that it can undermine relations between police and Muslims, just as the targeting of Irish communities in the past increased support for the IRA. Studies, including that of Spalek *et al.* (2008), have highlighted a sense of grievance among young Muslim males, impeding good relations with the police. Similar findings were made in Choudhury and Fenwick's recent study for the Equality and Human Rights Commission (2011).

However, Greer (2010) has strongly challenged Pantazis and Pemberton's thesis, arguing that it lacks empirical support. He is very critical of the notion of a suspect community and argues for a more nuanced multidimensional approach to understanding the relationship between Muslims and antiterror laws. He questions whether these provisions have turned the whole Muslim community into a suspect community and whether Islamophobia is generated by these laws. Counter-terrorism stop-and-search laws had existed before 9/11 and none of the major pieces of antiterror law post-2001 have been targeted specifically against Muslims. Research on the use of s 44 has primarily shown a racial rather than a religious profiling. The Preventing Violent Extremism programme was based on the assumption that the majority of Muslims do oppose violent extremism and the programme was supported by many Muslims. Where specific areas, such as High Wycombe, have been targeted it is because of specific evidence about particular radical individuals or groups, rather than because of suspicions of Muslims generally. As Muslims were involved in 7/7 terrorism, inevitably there will be a disproportionate impact on Muslims, but this is not the same as saying that all Muslims are under suspicion. Moreover, feeling under suspicion is not the same as being under suspicion. New legislation also protects against hate crimes grounded in religious hatred. Greer stresses that Muslims are not a homogenous group and not all Muslims think they have been treated unfairly. While Pantazis and Pemberton focus on labelling, Greer notes that as there is a real threat from Islamist extremism, this inevitably means some Muslim networks will fall under suspicion, but does not mean that Muslims in general become a suspect community. If the human rights of particular individuals are breached, then this needs to be addressed, but it is not a matter of the community as a whole becoming suspect.

However, Pantazis and Pemberton (2011) stress that what is important is people's experiences and perceptions which suggests a sense of being treated as suspect. Moreover, despite differences between Muslims, they share a common experience in terms of the differential impact of counter-terrorism measures. Choudhury and Fenwick (2011) interviewed Muslims and non-Muslims in Birmingham, London, Glasgow and Leicester. They found that Muslims were more aware than non-Muslims of the impact of counter-terrorism measures and in a sense led parallel lives. They note that:

> Experience from Northern Ireland teaches us that counter-terrorism measures have the potential to stigmatise whole communities, to fuel resentment and even to bolster support for terrorist movements. There is a danger that the Muslims in contemporary Britain can become the new suspect community.
>
> (2011, p. 9)

They recognise that it is problematic for policymakers and governments because 'it is an inescapable fact that the majority of those suspected of terrorist activities are Muslim, and that counter-terrorist measures are likely to target Muslims' (ibid.). They also acknowledge the real threat of terrorist violence. But such measures may be counterproductive if they lead ordinary Muslims to feel that they are constantly under suspicion. Interviewees thought that the measures were also contributing to anti-Muslim hostility and increasing fear and suspicion of them. They also resented the fact that other problems within the communities such as drugs, gangs and racist violence were not being given sufficient attention. Concern was expressed over the use of Schedule 7 and stop-and-search powers on the street, being questioned about their religious beliefs and which mosque they attend, as well as the use of CCTV surveillance in Muslim areas of Birmingham, all of which increased their sense of alienation. Muslim respondents were more likely than non-Muslims to report experiences concerning the use of counter-terrorism measures involving themselves, their friends or acquaintances. The fact that funding and measures under the Prevent programme were directed at Muslim communities also reinforced the association of Muslim communities with extremism. The House of Commons Communities and Local Government Committee also thought that the focus on Muslims in the

Prevent programme was unhelpful on the basis of evidence received from respondents (House of Commons, 2010).

We do now have more research studies available of the Prevent programme which involves engaging with communities to address the risk of terrorism, working with sectors where there is a risk of radicalisation and seeking to gain the trust of the community (Innes *et al.*, 2011, Bahadur Lamb, 2013). Innes *et al.* (2011) reviewed Prevent policing in four areas and showed there was some support for the police intervention. Moreover, British Crime Survey data suggested a mostly positive view of the police from Muslim communities, although younger Muslims were less positive than older Muslims. So the findings suggest a more complex picture than indicated by the notion of the suspect community.

The policing of black and minority ethnic communities

Attention has also been given to the relationship between black and minority ethnic communities and the police. The Macpherson Report (1999) on the murder of Stephen Lawrence highlighted the problems of institutional racism within the police force. It defined institutional racism as:

> The collective failure of an organisation to provide an appropriate and professional service to people because of their colour, culture or ethnic origin. It can be seen or detected in processes, attitudes and behaviour which amount to discrimination through unwitting prejudice, ignorance, thoughtlessness and racist stereotyping which disadvantage minority ethnic people.
>
> (Macpherson, 1999: para 6.34)

Bias may operate overtly, unconsciously or be institutionalized. Racism is not static but may change over time. Racism may be direct or indirect or institutional in the sense that is embedded within the culture and practices of an institution. It may also be experienced by BME staff (Holdaway, 2009). The Macpherson Report had a wide-ranging impact leading to greater awareness of and efforts to combat racism and also influenced changes to police complaints procedures, contributing to the introduction of the IPCC. After the Macpherson Report there were some indications that direct and overt racism has declined (Foster *et al.*, 2005). However, a covert film of police recruits for a BBC documentary, *The Secret Policeman*, showed its persistence. Policing entails that a high level of discretion is given to officers which makes it harder to control and influence than many other occupations. The traditional occupational culture of the police is also resistant to change (Loftus, 2009; Reiner, 2010). However, we should be wary of seeing the police as a monolithic entity, as there may be differences among different levels of the organisation and also among forces.

Concerns have been raised over the use of stop-and-search powers against young black people, as well as cases of violence and deaths in custody and in the context of police pursuits, as in the *Duggan* case, which precipitated the London riots in 2011. As we saw in Chapter 5, a disproportionate number of black and minority ethnic individuals have died in custody. Although there has been an increase in the number of black police officers since Macpherson, the proportion is still relatively low so BME communities are under-represented and make up only 5 per cent of police officers (Ministry of Justice, 2013).

The available data makes clear that black citizens are more likely to be treated as suspects, and subject to stop and search under powers given in s 1 of PACE and in s 60 of the Criminal Justice and Public Order Act, which allows the police the power to stop and search in anticipation of violence (EHRC, 2010, 2014). Following a consultation the Home Secretary announced in April 2014 a package of measures to reform the use of stop and search, including revisions to Code A of PACE. There is also a disproportionate number of black and minority ethnic prisoners, about one-quarter of the prisoner population. However, this figure will include foreign national prisoners and white ethnic minorities, for example, East European and Irish prisoners. Inside prison we also find differentials, with black and minority ethnic prisoners more likely to be subject to disciplinary charges, and to make complaints and to experience racial harassment and abuse. It has been said that BME and white prisoners live in 'parallel worlds' inside prison and black prisoners believe that they receive worse treatment in prison than White prisoners (HMCIP, 2008). The Mubarek Report, following the death of Zahid Mubarek, murdered by his cellmate in a racist attack, has also highlighted the problems of safety within prison (Keith, 2006). Data issued under s 95 of the Criminal Justice Act 1991 has furnished data on ethnicity in relation to arrest, caution, conviction and imprisonment. There are also statutory duties on public authorities, including the police, to promote equality under the Equality Act 2010 and this has also given us more information on equality measures and their impact.

Black, Asian and minority ethnic groups are also over-represented as victims, with the highest victimization rates for mixed groups, followed by Chinese/Other, Asian and Black, with the white rate being the lowest. Black males have the highest homicide victimisation rates (Ministry of Justice, 2013). Fear of crime is also greater amongst BME groups (Chaplin *et al.*, 2011). A debate has ensued for some time on whether the differential crime rates reflect policing practices which may be discriminatory, as well as moral panics created by the media based on negative stereotypes which mean the police focus on black suspects.

Others have focused on the deprivation and social exclusion of ethnic minority urban communities which provide fewer opportunities for legitimate sources of income and status and therefore may be more criminogenic. If suspects are treated and labelled as criminal, they may find it harder to obtain work in the legitimate economy. Demographic factors also may be relevant. Of course official crime statistics may not give the full representation of crime patterns, but we can obtain a more detailed picture when supplementing official statistics with the Crime Survey, self-report studies and qualitative research. We also need to distinguish differences within the broad BME category as there may be differences between ethnic groups, as well as differences of class, age, culture and religion and gender. The analysis of discrimination may therefore require an intersectional analysis which focuses on the multiple levels of discrimination that may result from class, ethnicity, gender and other factors. Social exclusion is primarily associated with class, but also intersects with ethnicity and gender, so young women within some minority ethnic communities may be the most marginalised group.

Nonetheless, to understand the disproportionate number of BME persons in custody we need to consider earlier stages in the criminal justice process, from policing, particularly stop and search, and cautioning, to the trial process. BME suspects are more likely be remanded in custody, although they are more likely be acquitted in the Magistrates' and Crown Courts than white defendants, so the picture is complex. When sentenced, they are more likely to receive longer sentences but this may reflect the types of offences with which they are charged. A substantial literature has examined the reasons for over-representation in prison, including the fact that black defendants are less likely to plead guilty than others, so will not benefit from sentence discounts and so will receive longer sentences on conviction. Hood's (1992) major study of Birmingham Crown Court found that the differentials were mostly attributable to factors in relation to the type of offence and that black defendants were more likely to elect jury trial, but found that about 20 per cent of the differential could be due to differential treatment. A later study of the Crown Court found little evidence to suggest verdicts based on ethnicity but did find a greater perception of unfairness on the part of BME defendants (Thomas, 2010). This reflects earlier findings which showed that black people had less confidence that they would be treated fairly by the criminal justice system as defendants (Mirrlees-Black, 2001).

A range of criminological theories, including left realist, critical and radical criminology, labelling theories, and subcultural and control theories, have sought to explain the disproportionate number of BME persons in custody. Particular ethnic groups may favour particular types of offending and may lack the opportunities to commit particular crimes, so street crime is more likely in groups who spend time on the street and is more visible than other types of crime so is more likely to be detected and processed. Crimes of those in deprived areas may be more visible than white-collar crimes as there is more police activity in black urban areas which means that offences are more likely to be noticed. It may also be difficult for young people to move out of their area, to find work or cheap housing, which may make it harder to escape becoming involved in gangs or gun crime. Nonetheless, as realist criminologists have argued, crime is a real and ongoing problem for black communities and gun crime and drugs have had a widespread and damaging impact on them. Black crime has to be considered in the broader context of the deprivation and social exclusion of black communities and the cumulative disadvantage experienced by them.

These issues have been extensively researched and a key issue is the relationship between the police and black communities and here attention has focused on differential stop and search and arrest rates. These figures are calculated per 1,000 of population and for black people have varied between six and seven times more than the white population over recent years. The latest available statistics on race and the criminal justice system, published in November 2013, demonstrate the persistence of these trends: black people aged ten or over in 2011/12 were 6 times more likely than white persons to be stopped and searched under PACE, and Asian and mixed persons were two and half times more likely to be searched than white persons. There have also been higher arrest rates for black, Asian and minority ethnic groups except for Chinese/Other (Ministry of Justice, 2013). In 2011/12 black people were 3.3 times more likely to be arrested than white people, per 1,000 of the population, and those from mixed ethnicity groups 2.3 times more likely than white people, but there was no difference between white and Asian people (ibid.). Black defendants were also less likely to receive an out-of-court disposal. Black and minority ethnic offenders were given longer sentences although there were differences between offences. Average custodial sentences increased for all ethnic groups from 2010 to 2012, although the distribution among ethnic groups varies according to offence groups.

Although much attention has been given to stop and search figures, when they are examined in terms of the available population on the streets when patrols are made, compared to the resident population, the differential between BME and white people is not significant and the former are not over-represented (Waddington *et al.*, 2004). Younger people are more likely to be out on the street so demographic factors may be relevant. However, it could also be argued that the police direct patrols into areas where there is a concentration of black people (see, Bowling and Phillips, 2007).

Interestingly, despite the history of poor relations between the police and BME communities, the IPCC has received fewer complaints from black than white citizens. However, this may reflect a lack of confidence in the IPCC rather than a greater level of satisfaction. Also overall confidence in the police is higher than for the criminal justice system as a whole (Chaplin *et al.*, 2011, p. 91). However, public confidence in the police was dented by the deaths of Mark Duggan, Sean Rigg and Ian Tomlinson. The Independent Police Complaints Commission was set up by the Police Reform Act 2002 to improve public confidence in the police complaints procedure, but Smith (2009) questions whether it has achieved this aim.

The need to improve relations between the police and the public was stressed in the Consultation Paper *Policing in the 21st Century: Reconnecting police and the people* (Home Office, 2010). Several changes were introduced, including the election of Police and Crime Commissioners, intended to improve the accountability of local police forces to the local community and the creation of a National Crime Agency to strengthen the fight against organised crime and security at the borders, replacing the Serious Organised Crime Agency. These modifications were implemented in the Police Reform and Social Responsibility Act 2011 and the Protection of Freedoms Act 2012. The National Crime Agency became operational in 2013.

Conclusion

The relationship between the police and particular communities, as we have seen, may be shaped by a number of influences. Perceptions of the police show variations between black and minority ethnic groups, between different age groups and different religions. So there are problems in characterising communities as suspect communities. The relationships between these groups and the police are complex and have changed over time. At the same time, we have seen that perceptions of differential treatment may affect the relationships between some members of the community and the police.

We have also noted the tension between security and the defence of due process rights of suspects and the ease with which rights may be infringed in the context of concerns over terrorism. Since the 1980s the emphasis has been on striking a balance between the rights of the accused and the duty of the police to protect the public. But once rights are weighed against the interests of security, they can more easily be eroded.

8
The Body as Evidence

Introduction

The body may be used in evidence in a number of ways, through samples of bodily fluids, blood, urine, semen as well as fingerprints and DNA evidence. Exterior marks, such as tattoos, scars or signs of physical injury, may also be used in evidence, as well as footprints, and it is likely that greater use will be made of biometric identifications of irises in the future. The use of the body as a source of evidence has become more important with technological and scientific advances, notably DNA profiling. However, the use of bodily samples as evidence raises a number of issues, namely the relationship between the privilege against self-incrimination and bodily samples, issues of privacy and bodily integrity, and the equality of arms principle.

Problems relating to forensic evidence have figured in miscarriages of justice, including the cases of the Guildford Four, the Birmingham Six, the Maguires and Judith Ward. These cases have highlighted problems regarding the failure to disclose forensic evidence to the defence, the need for defence access to exculpatory forensic evidence and the importance of quality controls on forensic evidence. In the Birmingham Six case there was a failure to disclose a possible innocent reason for what appeared to be traces of explosives on the defendants. They were convicted in 1975, but their first appeal failed in 1987. Their case was referred again to the Court of Appeal by the Home Secretary in 1990 and their conviction was finally quashed in 1991. This time the court was persuaded by the discovery that the Forensic Science Service (FSS) had failed to disclose relevant evidence and the results of an ESDA test, which showed that some notes from the 'interview' were not made contemporaneously (*R v McIlkenny and others* (1991) 93 Cr

App R 287). As well as disclosure failures, the defence in the cases of the Birmingham Six, the Maguires and Judith Ward lacked the necessary resources to challenge prosecution evidence, as they did not have the expertise and training in scientific techniques essential to understand or assess the forensic evidence. They also did not receive detailed information on the tests being undertaken, yet differing interpretations of the test may be crucial to the outcome of the case. In *R v Ward (Judith)* (1993) 96 Cr App Rep 1 the Court of Appeal said that senior government forensic scientists knowingly placed a misleading scientific picture before the jury. The government forensic scientists were also criticised in the May Reports into the convictions arising out of the Guildford and Woolwich bombings, which included the Maguires' case (May, 1990, 1993). Sir John May said that had the jury seen the contents of the scientists' notebooks, their evidence would have been viewed very differently. In this case, traces of nitroglycerine on the defendants' hands were wrongly interpreted as explosives (*R v Maguire and others* (1992) 94 Cr App R 133). In the Birmingham Six case, the work of the scientist Frank Skuse was strongly criticised as the scientific tests used to establish traces of nitroglycerine were not as precise as the jury had been led to believe.

Walker and Stockdale (1995) reviewed the use of forensic evidence in terrorist trials and found problems regarding the accidental contamination by the police or prosecution in collecting evidence of which they may be unaware, misunderstandings over the way forensic evidence and scientific experimentation translate into legal proof and lack of funding for the defence. When the forensic evidence gets to court, the court may not grasp its significance. The more complex forensic evidence becomes, the more the jury may rely on extraneous factors such as the expert's demeanour (Redmayne, 2001). The May Report also criticised the Court of Appeal for its failure to understand that challenging the specificity of forensic tests for nitroglycerine also undermined the prosecution's case against the Maguires (May, 1993).

These cases arose before DNA profiling, improvements in the recording of interviews and the changes to the appeal procedures discussed in chapters 5 and 6, but forensic evidence has continued to cause concern. In some later miscarriages of justice, doubts were raised regarding forensic evidence and the expert witnesses involved. For example, in the case of Sally Clark, accused of murdering her babies, the prosecution did not reveal relevant medical evidence and the prosecution expert witness also miscalculated the likelihood of two children dying from cot-death syndrome (*R v Clark (Sally)* [2003] EWCA Crim 1020).

The advances in forensic science in recent years, notably DNA profiling, might suggest that the interrogation of the suspect and the suspect's testimony are less important than in the past. Forensic science seems to offer a great chance of arriving at the 'truth' compared to relying on witnesses who may lie or be mistaken. Forensic evidence may provide a means for the police to bypass the problems of non-cooperation of suspects. DNA evidence may be used by the prosecution and police to inculpate and eliminate suspects. It may also be of value to the defence in exonerating the accused and DNA has been used retrospectively to clear up older cases and to rectify wrongful convictions in the UK and in the United States, including cases on Death Row. Gary Dotson was the first wrongfully convicted person to be exonerated by DNA evidence in 1989. There have also been cases, including the cases of Stefan Kiszko and the Cardiff Three, where many years after successful appeals, the DNA database has helped to find the perpetrators. Improvements in scientific techniques also make it possible to reopen cold cases many years after the event and the changes to the double jeopardy rules also allow for re-prosecution of the accused in more serious cases. The use of post-conviction DNA testing to exonerate individuals who may have been wrongfully convicted is also examined by Roman *et al.* (2012).

Greater awareness of the problems with false confessions has undermined confidence in the quality of confession evidence, so forensic evidence may make it easier to persuade the jury of the guilt of the accused. Juries may be 'bedazzled' by science and scientific expertise, so may overestimate its probative value. While forensic evidence can establish presence at the crime scene, identity and in some cases the *actus reus* of the offence, it clearly reveals nothing regarding the *mens rea* of the offence, and in crime scenes where large numbers of people are present, the fact of presence may also have little probative value and the time of presence may also be crucial. As we saw in Chapter 6, flawed forensic evidence and dubious scientific claims have figured in many proven wrongful convictions (Little, 2008; Naughton, 2013). Because of the high levels of probability of DNA evidence compared with other forms of forensic evidence, it has constituted a substantial advance, but this also may mean juries will accord it too much probative value in determining the guilt of the accused, when all the DNA evidence does is establish identity and does not address all the elements of the offence. Even where it is crucial to the *actus reus* of the offence, for example, the fact of having sex with the victim in a rape case, it obviously does not address the issue of consent, or in a case of the transmission of a sexually transmitted disease which has serious health consequences does not address the issue of knowledge, intent or recklessness for the purposes of ss 18 and 20 of the Offences Against the Person Act 1861.

But the rapid growth of forensic science in England and Wales, as McCartney notes, 'has taken place almost entirely in a vacuum of socio-legal academic interest with minimal research undertaken on the impacts, and potential implications' (McCartney, 2006: xix). Relatively little attention has been given by criminologists to issues raised by DNA profiling or its links to wider trends of risk management, while the scientific community, she observes, has shown little interest in the legal issues. While the UK has gone further than other European states in terms of who can be sampled and the retention of samples, the civil liberty issues arising from this have received less debate here than in Australia, New Zealand and Canada.

The retention of samples is part of the move towards increasing retention of information and surveillance of populations, also expressed through the use of CCTV and the growth of databases on medical and other aspects of individuals' lives and the surveillance powers of local authorities under the Regulation of Investigatory Powers Act 2000. As such it can be seen as an element of the New Penology, or actuarial justice, acquiring data to manage the risk of crime. The growth of surveillance has accelerated with concerns over insecurity and with the fear of terrorism as we saw in Chapter 7. Further extensions of state surveillance powers were proposed in the controversial and much criticised Draft Communications Data Bill 2012 which proposed to hold records of electronic communications for the whole population.

Forensic evidence is of value to the defence and prosecution, but questions have been asked regarding its regulation, the adequacy of quality assurance procedures, and defence access to it, as well as the retention of biometric data. While the use of DNA profiling has restored, to some extent, the tarnished reputation of forensic science engendered by the revelations of miscarriages of justice in the 1980s and early 1990s, there have still been concerns relating to the use of this evidence.

The provision of forensic science services

The Runciman Commission reviewed the provision of forensic evidence in 1993 and found considerable improvements in the way it was obtained and presented since the 1970s. However, it noted that prosecution counsel were still often poorly prepared on scientific evidence and defence lawyers still lacked the understanding of scientific evidence needed to assess that evidence. The Commission proposed establishing a

Forensic Science Advisory Council which would issue a Code of Practice for forensic scientists, monitor laboratories to ensure high standards were maintained and promote the development of high-quality work in universities and public and private laboratories. The Commission also favoured better defence access to laboratories. Research conducted for the Royal Commission by Roberts and Willmore (1993) found problems with the Forensic Science Service reports, including a tendency to adopt a very adversarial approach, and that they offered very selective reports without discussing possible objections to their findings. There were also problems for the defence in finding experts and getting authorisation from the Legal Aid Board to make use of them. They found that opportunities for the defence to challenge forensic evidence were lost, particularly in relation to medical evidence. This was partly due to the complexity of scientific evidence and lack of expertise on the part of the defence lawyers, but also because of the problems in obtaining authorisation easily or speedily. Steventon's (1993) study of DNA evidence for the RCCJ also highlighted problems in finding experts. In her study expert witnesses were rarely called by the defence, even though two-thirds of the defence lawyers in her sample were contesting the DNA evidence.

During the 1990s the Forensic Science Service was improved with new procedures for monitoring. The FSS was originally an executive agency set up in 1991. It later became a government owned company in 1996 but was closed in 2012 when forensic services were privatised. Prior to its demise it was the principal provider of forensic services. When it closed its staff and work were transferred elsewhere and now private forensic services providers are the major suppliers of forensic services. However, Northern Ireland and Scotland still have publicly funded forensic service providers. The closure of the FSS by the Coalition Government expressed the desire to reduce costs and operating losses, as well as the ideological commitment to privatisation. The closure was criticised at the time by scientists and defence lawyers, as well as by the House of Commons Select Committee, which expressed fears that miscarriages could occur because of the use of outdated technology and that work would be conducted by unaccredited laboratories when contracts were put out to tender. It also criticised the lack of funding for forensic science and concluded that the wider costs of closure had not been fully considered by the government (House of Commons, 2013). Some police laboratories had failed to meet the level needed for accreditation. Although many of the staff transferred to other forensic service providers, some experienced staff left the profession and where staff had been transferred, their skills were not being fully used.

The transition was managed by the National Policing Improvement Agency and the Committee thought the transition had gone relatively smoothly. However, it criticised the lack of transparency regarding police forensic services. There is a system of accreditation and all forensic laboratories must be accredited to ISO 17025 to provide services, but police laboratories can conduct forensic services without such accreditation at present, although the Committee recommended that all police laboratories should achieve and maintain accreditation.

New Codes of Practice for forensic standards were published in December 2011 by the Forensic Science Regulator, but the FSR is not a statutory body and has no powers to enforce compliance with regulatory standards. The Committee therefore recommended that the FSR have statutory powers to do so. The Committee also found that there are still disparities between prosecution and defence. The defence experts only had access to forensic material after the prosecution had looked at it and did not have access to the evidence in its original condition. Defence experts were also less likely to be accredited. The Committee also advocated more support for forensic science research and stressed the need for a wider strategy for forensic science to avoid fragmentation and instability.

The admissibility of DNA evidence

Following its discovery in 1984, DNA profiling soon found acceptance by the courts in the United States and the UK. Since then the Guidelines on the use of DNA evidence in the UK have been updated to reflect scientific changes and legal changes governing the use and retention of this evidence. Parents have also been encouraged by private companies to store samples of children's DNA in case of their abduction and DNA evidence was used to trace missing children of the Disappeared in Argentina.

At the time DNA profiling was first developed, the courts were using the *Frye* test, derived from *United States v Frye* 293 F 1013 (DC Cir. 1923) to determine whether evidence based on new scientific discoveries is admissible in court proceedings. The court at a pre-trial hearing would decide whether the scientific principle or discovery, from which the expert testimony is deduced, had received 'general acceptance in the particular field in which it belongs'. This meant identifying the appropriate field and then determining the degree of acceptance. DNA profiling met this test and was admitted, despite the problems raised over the procedures used in the *Castro* case. However, the Supreme Court later ruled in *Daubert v Merrell Dow Pharmaceutics Inc.* 509 US 579 (1993) that the *Frye* test for admitting expert scientific testimony had been superseded by Federal Rule of Evidence 702 which requires relevance and reliability. Federal Rule 702 states that a witness who is qualified as an expert by knowledge, skill, experience, training or education may testify in the form of an opinion or otherwise if: the expert's scientific, technical, or other specialised knowledge will help the trier of fact to understand the evidence or to determine a fact in issue; the testimony is based upon sufficient facts or data; the testimony is the product of reliable principles and methods and the witness has reliably applied the principles and methods to the facts of the case. Key issues cited by the Supreme Court in *Daubert* included whether the theory or technique has been tested, subjected to peer review and publication, its known or potential error rate, the existence and maintenance of standards controlling its operation and whether it has attracted widespread acceptance within the relevant scientific community. In *Kumho Tire Co. v Carmichael* 526 US 137 (1999) the Supreme Court extended the *Daubert* guidelines to all expert testimony and reasserted the trial judge's discretion regarding how to decide whether a particular expert's testimony is reliable.

Although initially there were several challenges to the use of DNA profiling, it has been assessed against the *Frye* test, reliability test and the *Daubert* test and has met them all. In *US v Bonds* 12 F. 3d 540 (6th Cir.) 1993, the Sixth Circuit affirmed that DNA profiling met the *Daubert* test. To avoid repeated challenges regarding the underlying methodologies, many states have enacted statutes ruling that DNA evidence is admissible and based on reliable scientific techniques. The statutes in turn have been tested in the courts but upheld. Similarly, in the UK, DNA evidence has received a level of scrutiny far in excess of other types of forensic evidence and has emerged largely unscathed.

The United States has now firmly embraced DNA technology and there are statutory provisions authorising collection of DNA from those arrested or convicted under federal and state law. The DNA Fingerprint Act 2005 provides that any adult convicted of a federal crime must provide a DNA sample. Since then 25 states have enacted DNA collection provisions for arrestees and the five states did so prior to the federal law. In addition, all states and the Federal Government require those convicted of certain offences to provide samples for storage in the federal Combined DNA Index System database (CODIS) as well as the state databases. The CODIS unit at the FBI manages CODIS as well as the National DNA Index System (NDIS) which was established in 1998, and contains profiles submitted by federal, state and local laboratories.

In most states there are procedures to have them removed if the person is acquitted, but this must be initiated at the request of the arrestee and it appears that very few requests are made (Samuels *et al.* 2012). Because demand for analysis is so great, laboratories are working through backlogs.

The UK does not have a test exactly comparable to *Frye* or *Daubert* but the court will consider the relevance and reliability of scientific evidence and the judge may rule on questions regarding the admissibility of such evidence at a preparatory hearing. In *R v Gilfoyle (No. 2)* [2001] 2 Cr App R 5, 57, the Court of Appeal did endorse the *Frye* test but by then it had already been superseded in the United States. However, it approved the *Daubert* test in *R v Dallagher* [2002] EWCA Crim 1903. The Law Commission Consultation Paper on Expert Evidence favoured a *Daubert*-style reliability test combined with appropriate training for judiciary and practitioners as the best means of excluding unreliable expert evidence from criminal proceedings (Law Commission, 2009). Its Report on Expert Evidence recommends that expert evidence is admissible only if it is sufficiently reliable to be admitted and incorporates this in a Draft Bill (Law Commission 2011). However, there has been no disagreement on the theoretical basis underpinning DNA fingerprinting, but in the first few years of its application, there were arguments in both the UK and the United States over the guidelines used in interpreting test results, and over problems during the actual process of profiling which may have implications for its probative value.

In *People v Castro* 545 NYS 2d 985 (Sup Ct Bronx County, 1989) questions were raised over the way band sizes were calculated and the number of bands. The judge accepted that DNA profiling could provide reliable evidence, but thought the procedures followed by the testing laboratory in this case were inadequate. Consequently the evidence showing that the blood of the victim matched blood on the defendant was excluded. The judge criticised the laboratory for its unscientific methods, recommended guidelines for future pre-trial hearing procedures and stressed the need for quality assurance procedures and greater accessibility to the types of testing used. Since *Castro* there have been challenges over bandshifting, problems relating to the collection, handling and analysis of samples, as well as with the presentation of likelihood ratios. There have also been Fourth Amendment challenges to their retention although such a challenge was rejected by the US Supreme Court in *Maryland v King* 569 US (2013).

In the UK there have been fewer arguments over the validity of DNA evidence, but there has been suspicion of forensic evidence *per se* because of its role in some of the miscarriages of justice and because of unequal access to scientific evidence. In the UK in recent years the critique has primarily focused on the rights issues relating to the retention of samples.

Since the discovery of DNA profiling, there have been significant advances in the techniques available to amplify DNA through the technique of PCR which can be used on much older samples. PCR-based testing has also been ruled admissible under both the *Frye* and *Daubert* tests. Low Template DNA analysis, also referred to as Low Copy Numbering DNA analysis, allows minute samples to be tested and profiled, even where the crime scene has degraded. It increases the number of PCR cycles, allowing for an amplified sample. There were initially some concerns over Low Template DNA. In *R v Hoey* [2007] NICC 49, a case relating to the Omagh bombing, evidence was excluded because of concerns over the validation of the technique and possible contamination. However, a review commissioned by the Forensic Science Regulator reported favourably on the methods and measures employed to prevent contamination. In *R v Reed and Another; R v Garmson* [2009] EWCA Crim 2698 the Court of Appeal considered that profiles obtained by such means were capable of reliable interpretation. Detailed guidance on how DNA evidence should be presented at trial was also given.

Mitochondrial DNA analysis has also been developed which allows for the extraction of DNA from very small profiles not amenable to PCR analysis, by analysing different parts of the cell. Mitochondrial analysis is particularly useful for familial analysis. There has also been improved detection of male DNA through Y-chromosome analysis. Current research is focusing on the miniaturising of DNA-testing instruments and new technology is being developed to allow samples to be tested at the crime scene and to automate processes of testing to reduce the cost and speed up the process.

Initially questions were raised regarding statistical problems in calculating the odds of a chance occurrence of band matching. The statistical probability of a random match has to be calculated using assessment of the frequency of DNA bands in specific populations. With subpopulations the samples may be small so it may be difficult to identify the number of potential suspects with matching configurations. A suspect's gene may be common in his area of origin, but less rare in a place where he is now living, so calculations of match probability in such cases may be difficult. There has also been controversy over mixed profiles where more than one person is present, or incomplete profiles which, as Naughton and Tan (2011) have warned, should be treated with caution.

The risk of false matches, of contamination of the crime scene and the way samples have been obtained and transferred to the database have been highlighted. Mistakes may potentially arise in the labelling, recording and storing of samples. It is essential to maintain the integrity of the crime scene and there should be a clear chain of custody of the forensic evidence with full documentation of the individuals with physical possession, and obviously the fewer people handling the evidence the better.

Misrepresenting the probative value of DNA evidence has been referred to as the prosecutor's fallacy. It may be committed by expert witnesses, or the judge or prosecuting counsel in summing up, because the issues are not properly understood, or through imprecise use of language. Even if properly directed the jury may make the same mistake. This fallacy is discussed by Balding and Donnelly (1994) by first distinguishing the following questions:

1. What is the probability that the defendant's DNA profile will match the profile from the crime sample, given that he is innocent?
2. What is the probability that the defendant is innocent, given that the DNA profile matches the profile from the crime sample?

The second question is most relevant to the court, but the fallacy is committed by giving the answer to the first question as the answer to the second question. The fallacy here refers to the wrongful equation of the odds against an innocent person having that DNA profile with the odds against the accused with that profile being innocent. In *R v Deen, The Times* (10 January 1994) the court found the prosecutor had confused the two and a retrial was ordered. The fallacy was also referred in *R v Doheny and Adams* (1997) 1 Cr App 369 and *R v Adams (No. 2)* [1998] 1 Cr App R 377.

We also know that DNA evidence has a very significant impact on juries (Brody 2002; Sallavaci 2014). Brody (2002) found that juries were more likely to convict if DNA evidence was admitted. For juries, a statement from an expert witness will carry considerable weight, especially as DNA evidence itself is seen as reliable. The jury is likely to be persuaded by forensic evidence when authoritative experts present it as cut and dried and any methodological problems are unlikely to be routinely considered when a technique becomes well established. As McCartney

(2006) notes, the 'uncritical acceptance of science' may mean that uncertainties or problems may be overlooked and too much weight based on expert evidence as the source of the 'truth'.

Jurors may also not understand the statistical calculations or reasoning behind them and may struggle with them. For this reason the courts have resisted the encroachment of the use of Bayes' Theorem, a formula for calculating conditional probabilities, in the courtroom. In *R v Adams (Denis)* (1996) 2 Cr App R 467 the Court of Appeal said the introduction of the theorem or any comparable method into a criminal trial 'plunges the jury into inappropriate and unnecessary realms and complexity deflecting them from their proper task' (481). There is a danger that expert evidence will be overvalued or its limitations misunderstood. Prior to the hearing there should be a discussion of the expert evidence and the court may direct the experts to prepare statements on the matters on which they agree or disagree. The expert should explain evidence to the jury in a comprehensible way. The expert should help the court by giving objective unbiased opinion on matters within his own expertise (Criminal Procedure Rules, r 33). The role of the expert is to assist the jury in areas of science where they cannot be expected to form a view without expert assistance. But the decision on matters on which he has expressed an opinion is a matter for the jury.

Where statistical evidence is produced to support an expert's conclusion it will be necessary to closely examine any data produced on which the evidence is based and to ensure that conclusion is supported by data and to explain to the jury with a health warning if necessary (Judicial Studies Board, 2010). Judges should be careful in summing up to present expert evidence in terms that will assist the jury to an understanding and also increase the jury's awareness of any limitations, but it may mean that jurors need to familiarise themselves with scientific techniques.

The privilege against self-incrimination

In most jurisdictions there are provisions enabling the state to obtain bodily samples from suspects. Efforts have been made and have sometimes succeeded in excluding forensic evidence on the ground that the accused cannot be coerced into supplying bodily samples where the resulting evidence would connect him with the crime and in arguing that the privilege against self-incrimination should be extended from speech to samples. But the issue of self-incrimination has received less attention in the UK than in the United States where the refusal to speak is protected by the Fifth Amendment. We will consider whether the refusal to provide a bodily sample is different from a refusal to testify and whether the supply of bodily samples can be compared to testimonial communications. In both the United States and the UK efforts to include bodily samples within the scope of the privilege have been resisted.

The relationship between the privilege and samples was considered by Wigmore (1961) who argued against extending the scope of the privilege which, he said, was intended to prevent testimonial compulsion rather than compulsion *per se*. He cites the case of *Block v People* 240 P.2d 512 (Colo. 1951), where the court said the purpose of the privilege is to prevent a man from being compelled to utter words that will incriminate him, and not to obliterate all evidence of physical facts, showing who he is and in what condition he is in. So treating blood samples or bodily features such as tattoos or the imprinting of footprints as comparable to speech is absurd. The accused also would not be permitted to hide his features from the courtroom at trial to avoid identification by witnesses. What is significant about distinguishing physical features, or tracks, fingerprints or tattoos, he argues, is that the accused is not being asked to disclose his knowledge and it would be possible to obtain the evidence without the cooperation if the state had access to his passive body, so these cases therefore lie outside the scope of the privilege.

Knowledge is not being extracted when a suspect is asked to pronounce words, or spell a word, or submit to a medical examination to establish his sanity, or to make a particular stance in court, although cooperation is clearly required. These cases should also be excluded from the scope of the privilege, he argues, as they lack the two elements of testimonial compulsion and knowledge. Wigmore acknowledges that truth serums and lie detectors are on the borderline of the privilege, although normally consent is required. The use of a lie detector, he says, is closer to the situation where the suspect is forced to make an incriminating communication of knowledge, where the accused is protected by the privilege.

In *Schmerber v California* 38 US 757 (1965) the US Supreme Court held that the privilege does not extend to the extraction and use of samples in evidence, which in this case was a blood sample. The sample in question was extracted from the applicant without his consent when he was being treated in hospital following an accident and he was convicted of driving under the influence of alcohol. His claim that taking the blood and admitting the evidence violated the Fifth Amendment was rejected by the court. It made clear that 'the privilege protects an accused only from being compelled to testify against himself, or otherwise provide the State with evidence of a testimonial or communicative nature...the withdrawal of blood and use of the analysis in question in this case did not involve compulsion to those ends' (at 761). The court approved Justice Wendell Holmes's ruling in *Holt v United States* 218 US 245 (1910) that the 'prohibition of compelling a man in a criminal court to be a witness against himself is a prohibition of the use of physical or moral compulsion to extort communications from him, not an exclusion of his body as evidence when it may be material' (252–3).

In *Schmerber* the court said the privilege encompassed testimony and communications, whatever form they took, including the production of the accused's papers. It followed the case of *Boyd v United States* 116 US 616 (1886), where the court had held that compelling production of an individual's papers to be used against him was the equivalent of compelling him to be a witness against himself, but this did not extend to bodily samples. So historically the privilege has been treated as a barrier to compelled communications or testimony, but as Justice Brennan said in *Schmerber*, 'compulsion which makes a suspect or accused the source of "real or physical evidence" does not violate it' (764). The blood test evidence in Schmerber's case was clearly incriminatory and obtained by compulsion but was admissible as it did not relate to testimony or any communicative act. But the court did acknowledge the difficulty of applying the distinction to situations such as lie detector tests.

But not all the justices agreed that a sharp distinction could be drawn between speech and samples. In a dissenting judgement, Justice Black argued that compulsory blood testing does have a testimonial and communicative nature and should be included within the protection of the privilege: 'It is a strange hierarchy of values that allows the State to extract a human being's blood to convict him of a crime because of the blood's content but proscribes compelled production of his lifeless papers' (775). The blood test still communicates the defendant's guilt. He criticised the majority judgement for its narrow liberal interpretation of the privilege and moving away from the broader construction in *Boyd*. The fact of the split judgement in *Schmerber* highlights the problem of maintaining the sharp distinction between speech and bodily samples. Subsequently the court rejected *Boyd* in *Fisher v United States* 425 US 391 (1976) and *United States v Doe* 465 US 605 (1984), where the court held that the state may seize documents in certain circumstances and that the privilege is confined to testimonial aspects of production rather than to the document itself. While this resolved the status of 'lifeless papers', the status of bodily samples remained controversial.

The question of whether admitting a refusal to submit to a blood alcohol test in evidence against the accused constituted a violation of the Fifth Amendment was reserved in *Schmerber*. However, the issue was considered in *South Dakota v Neville* 459 US 533 (1983) where the US Supreme Court, reversing the judgement of the South Dakota Supreme Court, ruled that admitting a refusal to take the test in evidence did not violate the Fifth Amendment. It noted the absence of compulsion as Neville had the choice whether or not to take the test even though refusal meant he would lose his driver's licence.

Although the body has mostly been construed as an item of real, physical evidence, comparable to a knife or murder weapon, we can also find cases where there has been some recognition of the relevance of the privilege to the use of the body as evidence. The history of the courts' treatment of the body as evidence has been inconsistent, as there are some older cases where the courts accepted that using the defendant's body as physical evidence is effectively forcing him to be a witness against himself, so bodily identifications and examinations in these cases have been excluded. For example, the courts refused to allow a suspect to be tested for sexually transmitted infections in *State v Newcomb* 220 Mo 54 (1909), where the compulsory examination of the defendant to obtain evidence to support an accusation of rape was held to violate the privilege. Evidence of childbirth was excluded in *People v McCoy* 45 How Pr 16 NY Sup Ct (1873), while in *Cooper v State* 386 Ala 610, 6 So 110 (1889) the refusal of the defendant to make tracks to compare with those found at the scene of the crime, was deemed inadmissible. The privilege has also been successfully invoked in some cases of self-identification. In *Allen v State* 183 Md 601, 611, 39 A 2d 820 (1944) the court held that compelling an individual to try on a hat in court was wrong where doing so might assist in establishing his guilt. However, in other cases the court has admitted evidence of clothing found in the defendant's washing machine which was not communicative or testimonial evidence. The courts have also allowed the use of compulsion to obtain voiceprints and samples of handwriting. One way to sidestep the privilege is to admit testimony on bodily identifications from a third party, for example, the testimony of prison officers reporting on the bodily scars on the accused, so the accused is not being asked to incriminate himself.

We also find cases prior to *Schmerber* where the privilege has been successfully invoked in bodily sample cases, but neutralised by the doctrine of waiver. The privilege has been deemed to be waived either because the accused entered the witness box or because he consented to the test, so the evidence has been provided voluntarily rather than by compulsion. For example, in *Neely v United States* 2 F 2d 591 (1943) the defendant, who denied he had been shot, was asked to show his arm, on the grounds that he had already waived his privilege by testifying. In *Spitler v State* 221 Ind 107, 46 NE 2d 591 (1943) it was held that a motorist who voluntarily submitted to an intoximeter test had waived his constitutional protection against self-incrimination. But these cases still acknowledge the relevance of the privilege even if a waiver is inferred. These strategies reflect the difficulty in formulating a sustainable distinction between the body and its secretions as an object of evidence on the one hand and communication on the other.

Some states have 'implied consent' statutes where a driver suspected of driving while intoxicated is deemed to have consented to testing, including blood testing, when he applies for a licence. Although refusal may be permitted to avoid a violent confrontation between the police officer and the suspect, refusal is discouraged through penalties such as revocation of the driver's licence for a fixed period and admission of the refusal in evidence against the accused.

Similarly, in the UK drivers may be requested under ss 4–7 of the Road Traffic Act 1988 to provide a sample and may be prosecuted for the offence of refusing to supply a sample. The penalties for refusal to supply a sample in road traffic cases match those for the substantive offences of drink-driving, namely six months' custody, up to a £5,000 fine and a driving ban for one year, although for the substantive offence it can be increased to three years if convicted twice within ten years. The severity of the penalties reflects the fact that it is obviously crucial to obtain the evidence within a limited time as the body will process the alcohol. Drivers may also be tested for drugs under these provisions.

There are similar provisions in Canada where the penalties for failing to provide a sample match those of the driving offence, in s 254 of the Criminal Code. However, apart from the impaired driving context covered by s 254, evidence that a person failed or refused a blood or breath test or that such a sample was not taken is not admissible nor shall such a failure or refusal or the fact that a sample was not taken be the subject of comment by any person in the proceedings (s 258). In *R v Stillman* [1997] I SCR 607 the Canadian Supreme Court ruled that the privilege covered speech and bodily samples obtained by the state.

In most states there is an obligation to supply a bodily sample or to take a test under road traffic law. In France it is compulsory for drivers to carry breathalysers in their cars to be used by the police when required.

In New Zealand a refusal to supply a blood test when requested can lead to custody and a fine. But there is a difference between the road traffic case and the obligation to provide a DNA sample for profiling. In the case of *R v Martin* [1992] 1 NZLR 313, the court ruled that an individual had a right to refuse to give a blood sample for DNA profiling and no adverse inferences could be drawn from such a refusal.

In the UK there are wide powers to obtain physical evidence of intoxication from motorists to prove the *actus reus* of the offence as well as powers to test for drug use with penalties for noncompliance. Blood samples can be taken from drivers in accidents who are unconscious. Similarly, it is well established in European Convention jurisprudence that obtaining blood or saliva samples from a driver to investigate an offence can be justified under Article 8(2) of the Convention, as illustrated by *X v The Netherlands* App. No. 8239/78 (4 December 1978).

In the United States, the Fourth Amendment, which protects against unreasonable searches and seizures of person, might also be seen as relevant to the extraction and retention of bodily samples. In assessing reasonableness the court could consider the balance between individual and state interests, the gravity of the offence, the invasiveness of the test and the importance of the evidence to the prosecution's case (Amar and Lettow 1995). A Fourth Amendment challenge regarding retention of DNA samples was brought in *Maryland v King* 569 US (2013), but the US Supreme Court ruled that obtaining DNA samples from those arrested for serious assaults was reasonable under the Fourth Amendment. King was swabbed for DNA in connection with assault charges in 2009 and it was found that his DNA matched a sample in a cold case of rape from 2003, for which he was later convicted.

In the UK we also find a clear distinction between speech and samples. The Runciman Commission rejected the analogy between speech and samples and concluded that the two cases are quite different (RCCJ, 1993: para 2.27). In the earlier case of *R v Smith* [1985] Crim LR 590 the court had declined to extend the right to silence to bodily samples and distinguished the refusal to speak and to supply samples, although it did not make clear its reasons for doing so. In *Brown v Stott* [2003] 1 AC 681 the Privy Council said that samples and speech were quite distinct.

But is there a fundamental difference between relying on words from the individual or on bodily features or fluids? In both cases the individual is the source of the incriminating evidence whether through a confession or bodily sample, irrespective of whether compulsion or persuasion is used. It is difficult to draw a sharp Cartesian distinction between the body and the mind, despite its influence on tort and criminal law as well as Fifth Amendment jurisprudence. While the mind is usually seen as the source of communication, the body may initiate nonverbal communication, which may betray the person's feelings and attitudes, whether or not the person intends to do so. As we saw in our discussion of interrogation, correctly interpreting gestures and physical signs may be problematic but this may also apply to speech. Both speech and samples can inculpate and exculpate.

The Cartesian distinction between the two and its impact on the privilege has been subjected to criticism. Although the courts have drawn a sharp dichotomy between speech and bodily samples, it may be more appropriate to see them as lying on a continuum (Easton 1995). At one end are communications, statements, admissions and exculpatory as well as inculpatory statements. Close by would be physical gestures intended to communicate, for example, a knife slitting the throat, intended as a threat. Then further along would be nonverbal communications which may not be intended, such as involuntary demonstrations of fear, timidity or deference. Further down would be external bodily signs such as tattoos, scars or distinguishing physical features. This might also include signs of lifestyles, such as athletes' muscles, or the effects of occupational diseases or wounds. Next would be bodily fluids, whether supplied voluntarily or involuntarily, so this could be a blood sample given voluntarily or a hair removed from a coat. At the far end would be the extraction of DNA from a corpse, as in the case of the identification of the remains of Richard III found in a Leicester car park centuries after his death, identified through mitochondrial analysis, using a comparison with a DNA sample taken from a descendant of his sister, Anne of York. The relative position of items of evidence on this continuum may change with scientific and technological progress, as DNA samples may now be extracted without cooperation.

Farahany (2012) draws on insights from neuroscience to challenge the speech-samples dichotomy found in *Schmerber*. She argues that evidence can arise automatically without conscious processing, through memorialized photographs, papers or memories or through responses, uttered silently or aloud. Fox and Stein (2015) draw on psychology and psychiatry, as well as neuroscience, to challenge the dualism that has underpinned Fifth Amendment jurisprudence, as well as the law of tort, where it has been used to justify denial of recovery for mental harm. In criminal law, intentionality has been treated as a function of the defendant's thoughts separate from his bodily movements. In relation to the privilege, Fox and Stein argue that the invasion of the person causes harm whether through compelled physical or testimonial evidence. The focus, they argue, should be on the impact of the compulsion on the suspect rather than whether evidence comes from his mind or his body.

The question of illegally obtained evidence may also apply to the acquisition of bodily samples as well to confession evidence. Evidence of samples obtained improperly may be excluded under s 78 of PACE as in the case of *R v Nathaniel* [1995] 2 Cr App R 565 in relation to illegally obtained evidence. In *R v Weir, The Times* (16 June 2000) the court ruled that the DNA evidence was inadmissible because it was wrongly retained, even though that sample clearly incriminated the defendant.

The Strasbourg Court has also distinguished between the extraction of samples and the compulsion to speak or to furnish pre-existing documents to state officials. In *Funke v France* App. No. 10828/84 (25 February 1993), the court found a breach of Article 6(1) when Funke was fined for refusing to supply bank statements to Customs Officers, so here the provision of documentary evidence was protected by the privilege. In *Saunders' v UK* App. No. 19187/91 (17 December 1996), as we saw in Chapter 4, the Strasbourg Court noted that the privilege against self-incrimination, as commonly understood, does not extend to the use of material that might be obtained from the accused through the use of compulsory powers, but that has an existence independent of the will of the suspect, such as *inter alia*, documents acquired pursuant to a warrant, breath, blood and urine samples, and bodily tissues for the purpose of DNA testing (para 69). However, in Saunders's case the answers to questions provided under compulsion to DTI Inspectors were used in subsequent criminal proceedings against him which was unfair and breached his right not to incriminate himself. In *JB v Switzerland* App. No. 31829/96 (3 May 2001) a similar case to *Funke*, the Strasbourg Court found a breach of Article 6(1), the privilege against self-incrimination. JB had been fined for refusing to provide details of income to tax inspectors and that information could have been used as evidence against him in tax evasion proceedings. The court distinguished JB's situation from a driver asked to provide a blood or urine sample.

The relevance of Article 3 has also been discussed in relation to the methods used to obtain a bodily sample, but now that DNA may be obtained by non-invasive methods this is less relevant. In *Ribitisch v Austria* (1995) 21 EHRR 573 the court said that using a mouth swab would not ground an Article 3 challenge, as the degree of force would need to exceed what is necessary for detention. Inside prisons mandatory drug testing is a key feature of the modern prison regime. The Commission accepted that prisoners may be subjected to drug testing in the interests of prison security in *Peters v the Netherlands* App. No. 21132/93 (6 April

1994). The testing did not fall within Article 3 and while it infringed the prisoner's right to privacy, it was covered by Article 8(2).

But while speech and samples may be distinguished in terms of the communication of knowledge, they both raise similar rights issues, including the right to privacy, which lie at the heart of the Fifth Amendment to the US Constitution and Article 8 of the European Convention, the respect for private life. The right to privacy in the UK has been strengthened by the Human Rights Act. Both samples and speech raise questions of privacy in relation to the use and retention of information. Taking a bodily sample may constitute a greater intrusion of privacy than interrogation. A DNA profile is private and personal data that may have implications for health status and treatment and access to insurance. The provision of genetic information gives the state and also private companies intimate knowledge of personal matters such as paternity and ill health. The acquisition of samples is also intrusive. In English law consent is required under PACE s 62(1) only to the taking of intimate samples, which reflects the desire to protect the police from allegations of assault, rather than a recognition of the suspect's privilege against self-incrimination. Consent has become less important as mouth swabs have been reclassified as non-intimate samples, so while the police are still required to request consent, these samples can be taken without it.

Article 8, the right to respect for private life, has been used to challenge the extraction and retention of samples. However, the courts, while acknowledging the infringement of Article 8, have applied the principle of proportionality and in the majority of cases have deemed extraction and retention necessary to prevent disorder or crime, so falling within the qualifications to Article 8(2), and this approach has been followed in the domestic courts. Yet in *Marper*, as we shall see, the court was critical of the retention of samples for those acquitted or where proceedings were halted. But because of the principle of proportionality, in cases where a sample is taken or retained for a relatively minor offence, the invasion of privacy may not be seen as justified.

One difference between bodily samples and speech is that the body does not lie, whereas pressure on a suspect to speak will not guarantee he speaks the truth. So the futility argument does not apply to bodily samples. The suspect cannot intentionally produce a false negative. The most he can do is to arrange for a bone marrow transplant which would be very difficult, or to ask someone else to take his place when there is a community screening, as in the case of Colin Pitchfork, although this fraud was exposed when his friend admitted he had taken Pitchfork's place. Pitchfork was the first homicide case in the UK where a conviction was achieved through the use of DNA profiling (*R v Pitchfork, The Times* (23 January 1988)). Moreover, anxiety on the part of the suspect, or pressure on the suspect, will not taint the physical evidence, whether DNA or fingerprints, whereas, as we saw in Chapter 6, clumsy police tactics or the suspect's fragile mental state may distort communicative evidence. Very little cooperation is required from the suspect so he is very much a passive object of the process and even when dead may supply the evidence. However, as forensic science becomes more sophisticated and persuasive to juries, offenders are increasingly aware of its incriminatory potential, so in some cases will go to great lengths to eliminate it. For example, embalming a body makes it much harder to extract the DNA and obviously using cremation instead of burial will destroy forensic evidence.

Both samples and speech raise issues regarding privacy and the presumption of innocence, as the suspect is being asked to prove his non-involvement. The sample may give incriminating evidence, which is used to corroborate other evidence against the accused, so the suspect thereby contributes to his own incrimination. So it would seem more coherent to treat samples as falling within the privilege and of course in European Convention jurisprudence, as we have seen, the privilege is not construed as an absolute right, but the focus is on the degree of compulsion. A refusal to supply a sample may be put in evidence just as a refusal to speak may ground an adverse inference. If the sample is provided and links the suspect with the crime scene, then the police may be even less likely to search for independent evidence. In her interviews with officers, McCartney (2006) found this point was raised by several respondents in the sample. As we have seen, tunnel vision has been a key element in past miscarriages of justice as once the focus is on the suspect – whether through physical evidence or testimony – there may be less incentive to consider other possibilities. Usually the fact that the accused's profile is found at the scene means the accused will admit his presence, so the focus will be on his explanation for his presence.

Moreover, the common sense assumption that only the guilty are likely to refuse because they have something to hide may be even stronger with samples than silence, especially as a DNA sample may exonerate the suspect. But of course there may be other reasons for non-cooperation, for example, the suspect may be nervous about how a sample will be taken or whether and how it is retained, have concerns over the accuracy of the result if the science behind it is a mystery, or regarding the testing procedures which may not be properly understood. The use of mouth swabs is frequently seen in crime dramas on TV and at the cinema, so this may have allayed fears regarding extraction, but there may still be anxieties over the procedures for retention of samples and fears of contamination of samples and possible false matches in the future. There may also be fear, anxiety or embarrassment regarding one's presence at a crime scene for reasons unrelated to guilt.

Inferences may also be drawn from a refusal to consent to an intimate sample. So s 62 (10(b)) of PACE allows the 'court or jury, in determining whether that person is guilty of the offence charged to draw such inferences from the refusal as appear proper'. So the focus again is on the defence's response rather than the prosecution's case. In the case of voluntary screenings, there may be a great deal of pressure from the local community to come forward which is hard to resist and an unwillingness to help may be seen by others as very suspicious.

Obtaining and retaining bodily samples

The extraction and use of bodily samples in the UK is governed by PACE 1984 as amended by the Criminal Justice and Public Order Act 1994, the Criminal Justice and Police Act 2001 and the Criminal Justice Act 2003. Under PACE a distinction is drawn between intimate and non-intimate samples. Section 65 of PACE refers to an intimate sample as a sample of blood, semen or any other tissue fluid, urine or pubic hair, a dental impression, a swab taken from a person's genitals or from a body orifice other than the mouth. An intimate search means a physical examination of a person's body orifices other than the mouth. In *R v Hughes, The Times* (12 November 1993), the Court of Appeal held that an intimate body search as defined by PACE requires a physical intrusion into a body orifice and a physical rather than a visual examination. So it did not cover the situation in *Hughes* where an attempt was made to make the suspect spit out a plastic bag containing drugs by holding his jaws open and his nostrils shut.

Intimate samples may be obtained only under specific circumstances set out in ss 55 and 62 of PACE. Authorisation from a police officer of the rank of inspector is now required (s 55(1)) as well as the suspect's consent. Authorisation should not be given unless there are reasonable grounds to believe it cannot be found without the suspect being intimately searched and there are reasonable grounds to suspect involvement of the person in a recordable offence and believing that the sample will tend to confirm or disprove that involvement (s 62(2)).

Force may not be used to obtain intimate samples, but s 62 of PACE provides that where consent is refused without good cause, the court or jury in determining whether the person is guilty of the offence charged may draw such inferences as appear proper (s 62(10)). 'Good cause' here would include the accused's mental or physical condition. Intimate samples other than urine should be taken by a registered medical practitioner or health-care professional and in the case of dental impressions by a qualified dentist (ss 62(9A) and 62(9)).

The Runciman Commission recommended taking hair and mouth swabs without consent and broadening the category of serious arrestable offences for the purpose of taking samples. It advocated reclassifying hair and saliva samples as non-intimate samples to avoid the need for consent (RCCJ 1993: paras 2.28 and 2.29). It also recommended broadening the category of intimate samples to include dental impressions. These recommendations were given effect by s 58 of the CJPOA which amended ss 62 and 63 of PACE.

The provisions on intimate and non-intimate samples in PACE now refer to suspected involvement in a recordable offence, which has replaced the original reference to a serious arrestable offence and this has increased the range of offences for which the taking of samples may be authorised. A recordable offence is defined in s 118 of PACE and covers all offences punishable with imprisonment, as well as many other non-imprisonable offences specified in regulations made under PACE.

An intimate sample may be taken from a person whether or not he is in police detention or custody, if two or more non-intimate samples have been taken in the course of investigation which proved insufficient, if authorised by an officer of at least the rank of an inspector and with the suspect's consent (s 62(1A)). There must be reasonable grounds to suspect that the person is involved in a recordable offence and to believe that the sample will prove or disprove the person's involvement in the offence (s 62(2)). Without consent it would infringe the individual's right not to be assaulted. Before a sample is taken, the suspect should be informed of the reason for taking it, the fact that authorisation has been given and, if the sample is taken at a police station, the fact that it may be the subject of a speculative search (62(5)). Section 62 does not apply to suspects arrested or detained under terrorism provisions, or the taking of specimens under ss 4–11 of the Road Traffic Act 1988 (ss 62(11) and 62(12)).

Non-intimate samples are dealt with by s 63 of PACE. A non-intimate sample means a sample of hair, other than pubic hair, a sample taken from a nail or under a nail, a swab from any part of the body other than a part from which a swab taken would count as an intimate sample, and a skin impression that includes footprints (s 65(1)). Suspects are asked if they consent to giving a non-intimate sample, but they may be taken without consent if the suspect is in detention in consequence of arrest for a recordable offence and he has not previously provided a non-intimate sample or it has proved insufficient (s 63(2A–2C)).

Police powers to obtain samples have increased since PACE was enacted. We also now have a national database of DNA samples which was established in 1995, covering England and Wales, following the recommendations of the Royal Commission on Criminal Justice (RCCJ, 1993). Speculative searches may be made by checking against the database (Home Office Circular 16/95, 58/2004). DNA samples can be taken from every suspect arrested, suspected, cautioned or convicted of recordable offences and DNA profiles taken from crime scenes. The information may be used to check whether the suspect is involved in other unsolved crimes recorded on the National DNA Database (NDNAD), which is now the responsibility of the Home Office. There have been numerous convictions supported by DNA evidence since DNA profiling was discovered in 1985, as well as exonerations of suspects through this evidence.

Samples taken from one investigation may be checked against samples from other investigations held on the database regarding different offences. This has been very useful in rectifying miscarriages of justice as in the cases of Barri White and Keith Hyatt who were wrongfully convicted for, respectively, the murder of Rachel Manning and for perverting the course of justice. Her murderer, Shahidhul Ahmed, was convicted only in 2013, 13 years after her death and was linked to the case when he gave a sample in relation to a sexual assault for which he was convicted in 2010. The retention of information taken from samples has also facilitated the re-investigation of cold cases. The use of familial samples has also broadened the scope of investigations with some success.

Over the past 20 years the class of citizens from whom samples may be taken has broadened and the scope for retention increased. By 2006 the database held over four million samples and by 2009 it held profiles of 7.39 per cent of the UK population. Of this, 8,251 samples were linked to crime scenes including offences of murder, rape and sexual offences. By 2013 it had 6,737,937 profiles from individuals and 428,634 profiles from crime scenes (Home Office, 2013c). The UK has the highest number of profiles per head of population, holding over six million profiles. The development of the database can be seen as part of the move towards actuarial justice discussed earlier.

The material for the DNA profiling may include samples taken from victims and witnesses for elimination purposes. In this case those profiles may not be used for speculative searches or placed on the DNA intelligence database. Samples may be taken for all recordable offences, although initially they were obtained from offenders involved in offences against the person, sexual offences and burglaries.

There are also databases of fingerprints and DNA profiles run by INTERPOL. Its DNA Gateway Database was set up in 2002 and by the end of 2013 it held over 140,000 profiles submitted by 69 states. Other states have developed their own databases, expanding the classes of persons whose samples can be retained. In the United States the FBI operates an extensive national database and the police also have recourse to other databases. Under the Justice for All Act 2004, profiles of persons charged may be stored even if they are not convicted. So samples can be compared with those already held on the database and compared to those taken at the crime scene.

The construction of the database in the UK and its expansion has met with objections from civil libertarians, who argue that if a person is not charged or not convicted then samples should be destroyed. Civil libertarians have been critical of the retention of data in such cases and of the abandonment of the presumption of innocence and the use of a blanket rather than an individualised approach of the kind found in Scotland (Liberty 2009). The large numbers of young black males on the database has also raised concern.

This issue has been subject to considerable controversy which has led to several legislative changes over the past twenty years. PACE was enacted shortly before the discovery of DNA profiling, so it has since been updated to take account of it, with amendments in the Criminal Justice and Public Order Act 1994, the Criminal Justice and Police Act 2001, the Criminal Justice Act 2003, the Serious Organised Crime and Police Act 2005 and the Protection of Freedoms Act 2012.

The CJPOA 1994 broadened the range of offences for which a sample may be taken and increased the power of the police to obtain bodily samples. Saliva was reclassified as a non-intimate sample so it can be taken without consent under conditions set out in s 63 of PACE. The CJPOA permitted DNA samples to be taken from a person charged with, or convicted of, a recordable offence. It also permitted profiles obtained from those samples to be retained and used in speculative searches against other profiles obtained from crime scenes or victims of a crime. If a person was acquitted samples and profiles were required to be destroyed. Section 81 of the Criminal Justice and Police Act 2001 allowed more scope for speculative searches of DNA and ordinary finger-prints. Section 82 of the Act removed the obligation in s 64 of PACE to destroy samples of fingerprints and DNA samples and profiles if the suspect was not prosecuted, or was acquitted of the offence with which he was charged. The Criminal Justice Act 2003 broadened the class from whom the sample may be taken to arrestees for a recordable offence, whether or not they were subsequently charged. The sample and profile derived from it could then be retained indefinitely. In 2005 the National DNA Database held 181,00 profiles from individuals who would have been entitled to have them destroyed prior to the amendments in 2001. The Serious Organised Crime and Police Act 2005 made all offences arrestable, further broadening the scope for taking samples. But the Protection of Freedoms Act 2012 introduced new provisions relating to the retention of biometric data from suspects who are not convicted of any offence and reduced the length of time for which data can be held. Only the data of those convicted of the most serious offences can be kept indefinitely.

The recent changes reflect the litigation over retention, especially the Strasbourg Court's decision in *Marper* in 2008. However, prior to *Marper* the domestic courts had raised the issue of retention and dealt with it on a discretionary basis. In *R v Kelt* [1994] 1 WLR 765 the Court of Appeal ruled that a DNA sample taken lawfully from a suspect in one investigation could be compared with blood found at another crime scene. But samples taken for the purpose of one investigation could not be used in another investigation, if the accused was assured that they would be destroyed if he were acquitted of the crime, and the sample was mistakenly retained and used in a trial relating to a separate incident.

In *R v Nathaniel* [1995] 2 Cr App R 565 the defendant was convicted of rape on the basis of evidence obtained from a DNA sample he gave in relation to an earlier charge of rape from which he had been acquitted and which matched a sample taken from the victim. When he gave the earlier sample he was told that it would be destroyed if he were acquitted. The Court of Appeal held that the evidence should have been excluded from the later trial and its use in the later trial had an adverse effect on the fairness of the proceedings. Here the evidence in question was reliable and there was no evidence of bad faith on the part of the police.

However, in the case of *R v Cooke* [1995] Crim LR 497, the Court of Appeal deemed that the trial judge was right to admit the evidence obtained from a DNA sample as its reliability was not affected by the fact that it was obtained improperly. In *Attorney-General's Reference No. 3 of 1999* HL (14 December 2000), another rape case, the House of Lords ruled that there was an obligation to destroy samples and fingerprints of persons acquitted. But if they were wrongfully retained, they could be used in a later trial unless excluded at the judge's discretion. The decision reflected the fact this was a very serious offence and the need to protect victims.

The concerns over retention were addressed by the Strasbourg Court in *S & Marper v UK* App. Nos. 30562/04 & 30566/04 ECHR 1581 (4 December 2008) where the court found that the UK system of retention and destruction of samples of persons who had been acquitted, or where proceedings had been discontinued, breached their Article 8 right to privacy and could not be justified under Article 8(2). The Court of Appeal and the House of Lords had dismissed the appeal, upholding the necessity of retention for re-analysis to prevent miscarriages of justice and thought that the benefits outweighed the risks. Lord Steyn did not think that the privacy right was infringed, or at most only to a small degree. But the Strasbourg Court accepted that there was a breach of Article 8(1) and then considered whether the retention was proportionate in relation to Article 8(2), the prevention of disorder and crime and the protection of the rights and freedom of others. The court acknowledged that the aim of detection in the future of offenders was a legitimate one and that the DNA Database contributed to the detection and prevention of crime. But it also recognised the concerns of the individuals and noted the need for clear and detailed rules regarding the purpose for which samples were kept and did not think the requirements of Article 8(2) had been satisfied. It noted that the UK was the only member state of the Council of Europe to store fingerprints and DNA material indefinitely for any person suspected of any recordable offence. The court criticised the blanket and indiscriminate nature of the powers of retention, regardless of the age of the suspect or the gravity of the offence and was especially anxious regarding the impact on juveniles. In an earlier Canadian case, *R v RC* [2005] 3 SCR 99, the Canadian Supreme Court had ruled that retention of data from a first-time juvenile offender on the national databank was disproportionate given the aims of the youth justice system and breached the Charter right to informational privacy.

In *Marper* the Strasbourg Court highlighted the implications for the presumption of innocence as the profiles of those acquitted were treated the same as those convicted. While volunteers could have their samples destroyed at their request, the acquitted could not. In view of this the court concluded that:

the blanket and indiscriminate nature of the powers of retention of the fingerprints, cellular samples and DNA profiles of persons suspected but not convicted of offences, as applied in the case of the present applicants, fails to strike a fair balance between the competing public and private interests and that the respondent State has overstepped any acceptable margin of appreciation in this regard. Accordingly, the retention at issue constitutes a disproportionate interference with the applicants' right to respect for private life and cannot be regarded as necessary in a democratic society.

(para 125)

The Strasbourg Court has, however, endorsed the retention of profiles of convicted offenders for a limited period, based on the maximum sentence for the offence in *W v the Netherlands* App. No. 20689/08 (20 January 2009). In response to *Marper* the UK government introduced new legislation in the Crime and Security Act 2010 (ss 14–23) which limited the retention of such samples to six years.

But this was still deemed unsatisfactory by critics including Liberty. So Chapter 1 (ss 1–25) of the Protection of Freedoms Act introduces new provisions for the retention and destruction of DNA samples, fingerprints and footwear impressions, which came into force on 31 October 2013. Under the PFA regime, profiles taken from persons arrested for, or charged with, a minor offence will be destroyed following a decision not to charge or following acquittal. For persons charged with but not convicted of a serious offence, fingerprints and DNA profiles may be retained for three years, but a single two-year extension is available on application by a chief officer of police to a District Judge. The police are also able to apply for permission from the new Independent Commissioner for the Retention and Use of Biometric Material to retain material for the same period (three years plus a two-year extension) where a person has been arrested for a qualifying offence but not charged. There are also new provisions for retention of fingerprints and DNA profiles for persons convicted of an offence or given an extended penalty notice and for extended retention on national security grounds. The Act is based on the Scottish model of extended retention for those convicted or cautioned for serious offences.

Numerous back-up samples have now been destroyed: 592,777 profiles were deleted in 2012–13 (Home Office, 2013c). There are also concerns about the impact this will have on familial testing where it may be necessary to re-examine the original sample. Some offenders who are not themselves on the database have been identified through familial testing which can be very helpful in investigating historic offences. For example, James Lloyd was jailed in 2006 for a murder he committed 20 years earlier. He was not on the database but was identified when his sister was charged with a drink-driving offence. Similarly, Paul Hutchinson, who was not on the database, was convicted of a murder committed 26 years earlier when a match was found with a relative, his younger son who was charged with a driving offence. Also in relation to the Soham murders of Holly Wells and Jessica Chapman in 2002, the perpetrator, Ian Huntley, had prior contact with the police before the murders and if he had supplied a sample, this may well have focused police attention on him earlier in the investigation.

McCartney (2012) has criticised the response of successive governments to the *Marper* judgement for failing to develop a principled approach to the issue of retention, but instead highlighting risk and crime prevention without consideration of rights issues and for the absence of robust supporting evidence for their claims. While both Labour and Coalition Governments have drafted new regimes for retention, she questions whether the issues have been satisfactorily resolved. The Coalition Government accepted a Scottish model for the reforms in the Protection of Freedoms Act, but still failed to give full consideration to human rights issues and focused instead on risk. Liberty, however, has welcomed the rejection of the blanket and indiscriminate retention.

The court also acknowledged in *Marper* that retention of ordinary fingerprints and photographs raise privacy issues. Ordinary fingerprints have been used in the courts since the early twentieth century and are also stored in a national database, the National Fingerprint Identification System (IDENT1). Under s 61 of PACE, ordinary fingerprints can be taken without consent where there are reasonable grounds to suspect involvement in a criminal offence and they will help to ascertain identity or prove or disprove involvement and are authorised by an officer of at least a rank of inspector. Procedures for taking and using ordinary fingerprints are found in the manual issued jointly by ACPO and the National Fingerprint Board. However, there has been disagreement over whether a numerical test should be used, and the number of similar ridge characteristics that is required to indicate a match. From 1953 to 2001 a numerical test requiring a minimum of 16 ridges was used. But in *Buckley* (1999) EWCA Crim 1196, the Court of Appeal said that more than 8 points would be a matter for the judge's discretion, taking into account factors, including the number of ridge characteristics, dissimilarities with the print relied on and the experience and expertise of the witness. If there were fewer than 8 points, the court would be unlikely to admit the evidence as proof of a match. So a non-numerical standard was introduced in 2001. In *R v Smith* [2011] EWCA Crim 1296, the Court of Appeal was very critical of the standards used in dealing with the identification of fingerprints by the Nottinghamshire police whose practice it said fell below the standards expected in modern forensic practice. There have also been challenges to fingerprint identifications in the United States. However, in *US v Byron Mitchell* 365 F. 3d. 215 (2004), a challenge to fingerprint identification failed; the District Court was satisfied fingerprint evidence met the *Daubert* test and upheld the admissibility of fingerprint evidence and this was affirmed on appeal.

Conclusion

If forensic evidence is used to determine guilt then it is essential that the defence have equal access to laboratories and experts to prepare their case and to challenge scientific evidence. If we compare the position of the parties, the police and prosecution have substantial budgets for access to forensic services as well as their own forensic scientists specialising in various forms of evidence such as ballistics, and access to the DNA and other databases. There are few independent private laboratories specialising in defence work. While the defence has access to experts working in universities and hospitals, those experts may lack the resources to undertake large amounts of defence work. There may also be problems in obtaining authorisation for legal aid for expert advice. It may not be given or granting approval may be slow. The defence needs access to high-quality independent forensic laboratories with adequate legal aid. Forensic evidence can be crucial to the defence and the state's failure to make proper provision for defence access has been strongly criticised. Some prisoners have had to undertake their own research on the available scientific evidence and procedures to support their appeals, as in the case of Kevin Callan (1997). There are also problems regarding access to DNA testing by those claiming that they have been wrongfully convicted. Naughton and Tan (2010) cite two cases of alleged wrongful conviction where the Criminal Cases Review Commission failed to make use of DNA testing which could have exonerated the applicants.

Even if the reliability and accuracy of forensic tests may be guaranteed, other goals of the criminal justice process than rectitude need to be addressed, including respect for privacy and fairness to the accused, and the legitimacy of the verdict. From the standpoint of the rationalist model in which the rational determination of guilt and innocence is the prime goal of the criminal trial, DNA evidence has a key contribution to make. It is not subject to the futility objection that pressure to obtain testimony will lead to perjury. The rationalist model operates with a notion of verisimilitude, of moving towards the truth, but legal truths and scientific truths do not always coincide. Legal truth is constructed in the trial process itself and claimed by the successful party. Even within scientific discourse, models that see scientific research as acquiring more accurate knowledge about the external world and progressing towards the truth have been questioned by Kuhn (1962), Feyerabend (1974) and others. There may be disagreements over what counts as conclusive evidence for or against a hypothesis and in the context of the criminal trial, the notion of verisimilitude is harder to sustain.

Nonetheless the rationalist model remains the ideal and miscarriages of justice are condemned precisely because of their failure to arrive at the correct determination of guilt and innocence. But the goal may be constrained by other goals of the law of evidence, including respect for fairness. As Dennis (1989) has argued, truth finding is the means by which the legitimacy of the verdict is achieved, so it has an instrumental role. But the moral authority of the verdict would be undermined if obtained in violation of the fundamental values of the criminal law. Rectitude is part of the integrity of the judgement, but integrity may be undermined by improper tactics even if the correct result is achieved. While access to reliable forensic evidence is to be welcomed, its use in the criminal trial should also take account of other core values of the criminal justice system, including the right to privacy and the presumption of innocence.

9
Conclusion

Introduction

Numerous advances have been made in the treatment of the suspect over the past 20 years, including more support for vulnerable suspects, improvements in the quality of legal advice as well as more effective interviewing methods and police complaints procedures and improved review and appeal procedures to address the safety of convictions. Expert testimony on issues of suggestibility is now permitted in the UK and judges and juries are much more aware of this problem. There have also been advances in the presentation of forensic evidence and the development of new techniques to extract DNA evidence. In addition, we also have a new system of advance disclosure. We have also highlighted the valuable contribution experimental research has made to illuminating the dynamics of interrogation and to jury perceptions and the expansion of work in these areas is to be welcomed.

But, as we have noted, many suspects are still vulnerable during the interrogation process and the risk of false confessions has been reduced but not eliminated despite the efforts made to prevent and remedy miscarriages of justice during this period. The suspect is still seen as the key source of information and the focus on encouraging him to speak has been strengthened by the evidential significance attached to silence. Audio and visual recording, while beneficial to both suspect and the police, does not necessarily guarantee protection against a false confession which is made voluntarily. Given the concerns that false confessions have played in wrongful convictions, many would argue in favour of a corroboration requirement for confessions, so the accused could not be convicted on the basis of confession evidence, unless it is corroborated by independent evidence which points clearly to the guilt of the accused and links the accused with the crime. The requirement for independent corroboration of a confession, for example, by witness testimony or forensic evidence, would also influence the earlier stages of the process, principally the decision to prosecute. Given the considerable advances in forensic science since PACE was enacted, including DNA profiling, there are now other sources of evidence widely available, so the suspect's own admissions may be less significant in many cases.

The benefits for the accused endowed by PACE were used to justify limits on other due process rights, notably the right to silence as well as the stronger duties of disclosure. The balance between the suspect and the state has now changed with the weakening of the right to silence, as well as changes in legal aid provision. If the privilege is intended, in part, to redress the inequality between the state and the citizen, then arguably the imbalance may be even greater today, in some respects, than in the seventeenth century when the privilege developed. While the suspect has many more due process rights than in the earlier period, the prosecution now has access to highly developed forensic techniques, including DNA profiling, an organised and professional police force, highly developed communications systems, the police national computer and much more sophisticated surveillance techniques. More areas of life are subject to scrutiny and surveillance has extended beyond prisons, work and education to housing estates, transport, shopping malls and leisure venues which are increasingly monitored by CCTV (see, Lyon 2006; Crossman 2007; Coleman and McCahill 2010). Movements are also charted through ATM use and Automatic Number Plate Recognition. Surveillance technologies have been increasingly used as a form of crime management on the expectation that crime will not be eliminated, but may be reduced, and resources should be targeted selectively and efficiently to cut costs and manage the risks.

Corroboration of confession evidence

A key protection for suspects would be a legally enforceable rule preventing the prosecution from proceeding on the basis of confession evidence alone, that is, focusing on independent evidence rather than seeing the suspect as the prime source of evidence. Nonetheless, a corroboration requirement was rejected by the Royal Commission on Criminal Justice in favour of a warning. But so far demands for a corroboration requirement for confessions have been resisted. Despite its awareness of the problem of false confessions, the majority of the Runciman Commission rejected such a requirement arguing that it would undermine public confidence in the criminal justice system and would increase the risk of wrongful acquittals (RCCJ 1993). The problems of relying on uncorroborated confession evidence had been highlighted in submissions to the Commission and illustrated by the recent revelations of miscarriages of justice involving false confessions, which formed the background to its work. The experience of the Guildford Four had heightened demands for a supporting or corroborative evidence requirement. But since that case concerns have been raised over the tactics of officers in particular crime squads and further cases have emerged where fabricated evidence has led to wrongful convictions. However, the Commission said that if a confession passes the PACE tests and is credible it should be put to the jury even in the absence of other evidence, although the jury should be warned of the dangers of convicting in the absence of supporting evidence in such a case. By supporting evidence it meant evidence that convinces the jury that the contents of the confession are accurate. But the majority of the Commission argued that there should be no formal requirement for such supporting evidence and a conviction should still be possible in the absence of supporting or independent evidence. A minority favoured a requirement of supporting evidence similar to the *Turnbull* guidelines for identification evidence. Under those guidelines the jury should be warned to treat such evidence with caution where the prosecution's case depends wholly or substantially on such evidence, and where the quality of eyewitness evidence is poor, the judge should withdraw the case from the jury and direct an acquittal unless there is other evidence that supports the correctness of the identification (*R v Turnbull* [1977] QB 224).

But once the focus is on the accused's account, the incentive on the prosecution to search for other independent evidence is weakened. This was stressed in *Miranda v Arizona* 384 US 436 (1966) where the Supreme Court stressed the need for the prosecution to obtain evidence from its independent labours, rather than by the cruel, simple expedient of compelling it from the suspect's own mouth. If the individual is relied on as the source of the prosecution's case against him, this will impair the search for independent evidence and may also encourage impropriety and 'lazy' prosecutions. We noted in Chapter 6 the problem of tunnel vision and confirmation bias, when criminal inquiries may be limited to particular tracks, so that other relevant evidence and suspects are excluded with damaging consequences for the accused.

While Bentham (1843), as we saw earlier, the suspect's own testimony as the most valuable form of evidence, the findings of empirical research into the criminal justice process suggest that the quality of prosecution evidence will be enhanced if the prosecution is obliged to search for independent evidence. In terms of the rationalist goal of evidence, finding the truth should be a key goal, and addressing the above issues will be important in achieving the conviction of the guilty. The framework of evidentiary rules is designed to further this goal, for example, by focusing on relevant evidence to ensure that the probative value exceeds the prejudicial effect of evidence. It also underpins the rules governing the admissibility of bad character and hearsay evidence and the privilege against self-incrimination. While reliability and rectitude of decision-making must be paramount, the other principles we have highlighted, including fairness and the legitimacy of the verdict, do not necessarily conflict with the goal of truth-seeking. Treating vulnerable witnesses fairly may improve the quality of their evidence if the experience of giving evidence is less stressful. So the fair treatment of all parties, including the accused, but also complainants and other witnesses, is essential.

Would a corroboration requirement impose too onerous a burden on the police and prosecution? This depends on how important the suspect's own admission is to obtaining a conviction. McConville's (1993) research for the Commission showed that in the majority of cases in his sample (86.6 per cent) the confession was supported by admissible evidence from an independent source. So this suggests that the requirement would not be too burdensome or the risk of wrongful acquittals too high. The police would have needed to find more evidence to meet such a requirement in only 8 per cent of prosecutions in his sample. In many cases, he says, the additional information is already in the possession of the police, so it would not need much effort to marshal additional evidence. The effect of a corroboration requirement would enhance the evidence-gathering of the police, while without it they may be less inclined to collect or preserve corroborating evidence. He concludes that the assumption that a corroboration requirement results in 'lost convictions' is difficult to sustain. It would actually strengthen the weaker cases which may collapse at trial and 'would additionally lead to the avoidance of some convictions based on dubious foundations' (ibid: 87).

The changes in police interviewing techniques discussed in Chapter 6 have meant a move towards intelligence-based detection and investigation and more proactive policing which provides a more favourable environment for such a change. In most cases evidence can be obtained from independent sources without relying on confession evidence and given the role of false confessions in wrongful convictions, the use of evidence beyond the suspect's admission is desirable. In international criminal trials where due process rights are strongly protected, including the right to silence and right to counsel, convictions have been obtained in some cases without admissions because of the availability of other evidence. Conversely, in many of the most notorious miscarriages of justice, individuals have been convicted on the basis of uncorroborated and false confession evidence.

Despite the best efforts of police and the requirements in PACE and improvements in interviewing techniques, we know that false confessions may still arise and, given this, a major protection against wrongful conviction would be a corroboration requirement, although the consensus seems to be that this is unlikely to be introduced in the foreseeable future. There is no general principle in English law requiring corroboration: the accused can be convicted on the basis of a single item of evidence with exceptions made only for speeding, perjury and treason. Since the 1980s there has also been a move away from requiring mandatory corroboration warnings for evidence from members of a class of 'suspect' witnesses, to focusing instead on the reliability of individual witnesses. The mandatory warnings for child witnesses were removed in the 1988 Criminal Justice Act and for accomplices and complainants of sexual offences in the 1994 Criminal Justice and Public Order Act. Instead, a warning that caution or care is needed before relying on a witness's evidence should be given only where there is evidence to suggest that a particular witness is unreliable and where appropriate the jury should be advised to look for supporting evidence (*R v Makanjuola* [1996] Crim LR 44). So perhaps it is not surprising that neither a corroboration requirement or care or caution warning for confessions has been introduced, although s 77 of PACE, as we have seen, has performed this role in some limited cases.

But the need for a corroboration warning has received support from others. Dennis (1993) has argued that a corroboration warning is the best means of dealing with the problem of false confessions, combined with the use of techniques such as the ESDA test and stylometry, which uses statistical analysis to identify ways in which speech and writing of the individual differs from others, and statement reality analysis, which examines how the recall of real events differs from fictitious recall. Our knowledge of techniques for detecting lies has also been enhanced by the findings of experimental research as we saw in Chapter 6.

The Fisher Report (1977) on the *Confait* case recommended that there should be a supporting evidence requirement for confessions in certain cases, including where the accused has learning disabilities; where a young person has confessed in the absence of an independent adult; where an audio recording is unavailable; and where there has been a breach of the rules governing interrogation. Efforts should be made by the police to obtain further evidence to support or undermine a confession before reaching any firm conclusions. By supporting evidence, the Report meant evidence that would be relevant to the truth of the confession itself, such as special knowledge of the crime scene, as well as independent evidence linking the suspect to the crime.

Would a corroboration requirement necessarily prevent wrongful convictions? In some other jurisdictions, including the United States, corroboration of the reliability of the confession is required as made clear in *Warzower v United States* 312 US 342 (1941) and *Opper v United States* 348 US 84 (1954). However, in practice it may be that facts supplied to the accused in the course of the interrogation may be seen as corroboration, so the actual level of corroboration may be pitched quite low and we still find evidence of miscarriages of justice involving unreliable confessions (Huff and Killias 2013). Closer to home, in Scotland, there has been a long-standing corroboration requirement, so the prosecution has to prove that the crime was committed and the accused was the person who committed the crime, which requires two pieces of independent evidence. No person can be convicted on the basis of one source of evidence or one witness's testimony. But in practice very little has been required to support confessions in Scotland; there has been more use of self-corroborating evidence or 'special knowledge', even where the information in the confession is known by others. So the corroboration requirement there has been eroded and there has been concern that special knowledge could be passed to the suspect by officers conducting the interview.

Nonetheless, the corroboration requirement in Scotland has come under attack. Following the case of *Cadder v HM Advocate* 2011 SC (UKSC) 13, which affirmed the principle that suspects have the right to consult with a lawyer before and during questioning, individuals were given a statutory right to legal assistance in interrogation. One consequence was that many suspects gave no comment interviews based on legal advice and, as adverse inferences cannot be drawn from silence in Scotland, it was argued that many prosecutions were lost because of the corroboration requirement as one source of evidence was now unavailable (White and Ferguson 2012). The Carloway Report (2011), which reviewed Scottish criminal procedure, recommended abolition of the corroboration requirement for all categories of evidence. It described it as an 'archaic rule that has no place in a modern legal system where judges and juries should be free to consider all relevant evidence' (at para 7.2.55). It took the view that it hindered justice by preventing the prosecution of credible and reliable cases while failing to provide an effective protection against miscarriages of justice. Victims' groups had cited the problems of obtaining prosecutions and convictions in rape cases. The Scottish Government has endorsed these changes despite concerns that the abolition of corroboration could result in less diligent police investigation pre-trial and a relaxation of the search for supporting evidence, if they know that corroboration is not required, as well as the increased risk of wrongful convictions based on false confessions (JUSTICE Scotland 2012). Davidson and Ferguson (2014) consider the implications of the corroboration requirement for visual identification evidence and extra-judicial confessions and discuss whether a weighted majority jury verdict would compensate for the absence of a corroboration requirement and conclude that it would not, given the problems with both these forms of evidence. But despite the opposition, the proposals are now in the Criminal Justice (Scotland) Bill being considered in the Scottish Parliament.

Future directions

Of course false confessions are not the only cause of miscarriages of justice. Other important issues have been eyewitness identifications, dubious 'scientific' testimony', and the use of informants, which deserve closer attention. Although the most notorious miscarriages in justice occurred decades ago, as we have seen, wrongful convictions are still coming to light, despite the advances we have noted. The problem is not confined to the UK. A recent examination of wrongful convictions in North America and Europe has highlighted the extent and persistence of the problem (Huff and Killias 2013). Other issues that need to be considered are the provision of legal aid funding for defence access to forensic evidence, especially in a period of unprecedented cuts in the legal aid budget, consistency in the training and provision of appropriate adults for vulnerable adults, and speedy and appropriate compensation for victims of miscarriages of justice.

Much of the debate in recent years has focused on rebalancing the criminal justice system in favour of the law-abiding majority, communities and victims (Home Office 2006). But the problem of wrongful convictions is clearly a more pressing problem than wrongful acquittals. This is acknowledged by Bentham (1825: 197) who rightly saw convicting the innocent as a greater evil than acquitting the guilty and says that the judge should proceed on the presumption of innocence and, in doubtful cases, consider the error that acquits as more justifiable or less injurious to the good of society than the error that condemns.

Bibliography

ACPO (1993) *The Right of Silence Briefing Paper,* London, ACPO.

ACPO (2002) *Investigative Interviewing Strategy,* Wyboston, ACPO.

ACPO (2009) *National Investigative Interviewing Strategy,* Wyboston, NPIA.

ACPO (2012) *Guidance on the Safer Detention and Handling of Persons in Police Custody,* 2nd edn, London, National Policing Improvement Agency.

Amar, A. R. and Lettow, R. B. (1995) 'Fifth Amendment First Principles: The Self-Incrimination Clause', *Michigan Law Review* 93(5): 857–928.

Amnesty International (1978) Northern Ireland: Report of an Amnesty International Mission to Northern Ireland (28 November 1977–6 December 1977), London, Amnesty International.

Anderson, D. (2011) *Report on the Operation in 2010 of the Terrorism Act 2000 and of Part I of the Terrorism Act 2006,* London, The Stationery Office.

Anderson, D. (2013) *The Terrorism Acts: Report of the Independent Reviewer of the Operation of the Terrorism Act 2000 and Terrorism Act 2006 in 2012,* London, The Stationery Office.

Asch, S. E. (1951) 'Effects of Group Pressure upon the Modification and Distortion of Judgments', in H. Guetzkow (ed.) *Groups, Leadership and Men,* New Brunswick, NJ, Rutgers University Press.

Asch, S. E. (1956) 'Studies of Independence and Conformity: A Minority of One against a Unanimous Majority', *Psychological Monographs* 70: 9.

Ashworth, A. J. (1977) 'Excluding Evidence as Protecting Rights', *Criminal Law Review:* 723–35.

Ashworth, A. J. and Blake, M. (1996) 'The Presumption of Innocence in English Criminal Law', *Criminal Law Review:* 306–17.

Bahadur Lamb, J. (2013) 'Preventing Violent Extremism: A Policing Case Study of the West Midlands', *Policing* 7(1): 88–95.

Balding, D. J. and Donnelly, P. (1994) 'The Prosecutor's Fallacy and DNA Evidence', *Criminal Law Review:* 711–21.

Baldwin, J. (1992a) *Video-taping Police Interviews with Suspects – An Evaluation,* Police Research Series Paper, London, Home Office.

Baldwin, J. (1992b) *The Role of Legal Representatives at the Police Station,* RCCJ Research Study No. 3, London, HMSO.

Baldwin, J. (1994) 'Police Interrogation: What Are the Rules of the Game?' in D. Morgan and G. Stephenson (eds), *Suspicion and Silence,* London, Blackstone 66–76.

Baldwin, J. and McConville, M. (1980) 'Confessions in Crown Court Trials', RCCP Research Study No. 5, London, HMSO.

Baldwin, J. and Moloney, T. (1992) *Supervision of Police Investigations in Serious Criminal Cases,* RCCJ Research Study, No. 4, London, HMSO.

Baumgartner, F., De Boef, S. and Boydstun, A. (eds) (2008) *Decline of the Death Penalty and the Discovery of Innocence,* New York, Cambridge University Press.

Bentham, J. (1825) *A Treatise on Judicial Evidence,* ed. E. Dumont, London, Rothman.

Bentham, J. (1843) *The Works of Jeremy Bentham*, Bowring Edition, Edinburgh, William Tait.

Birch, D. (1999) 'Suffering in Silence: A Cost-Benefit Analysis of the Criminal Justice and Public Order Act 1994', *Criminal Law Review*: 769.

Bonner, D. (2014) 'Of Outrage and Misunderstanding: *Ireland v United Kingdom* – Governmental Perspectives on an Inter-State Application under the European Convention on Human Rights', *Legal Studies* 34(1): 47–75.

Bottomley, K., Coleman, C., Dixon, D., Gill, M. and Wall, D. (1991) 'The Detention of Suspects in Police Custody: The Impact of the Police and Criminal Evidence Act 1984', *British Journal of Criminology* 31(4): 347–64.

Bowling, B. and Phillips, C. (2007) 'Disproportionate and Discriminatory: Reviewing the Evidence on Police Stop and Search', *Modern Law Review* 70(6): 936–61.

Brody, M. (2002) 'The effects of DNA evidence on sexual offence cases in court', *Current Issues in Criminal Justice* 14(2) 159–81.

Brown, D. (1989) *Detention at the Police Station under the Criminal Evidence Act 1984*, Home Office Research Study No. 104, London, HMSO.

Brown, D. (1994) 'The Incidence of Right of Silence in Police Interviews: The Research Evidence Reviewed', *Research Bulletin* No. 35, London, Home Office Research and Statistics Department, 57–75.

Brown, D., Ellis, T. and Larcombe, K. (1992) *Changing the Code: Police Detention under the Revised PACE Codes of Practice*, No. 129, London, HMSO.

Bucke, T. and Brown, D. (1997) *In Police Custody: Police Powers and Suspects' Rights under the Revised Codes of Practice*, Home Office Research Study No. 174, London, HMSO.

Bucke, T., Street, R. and Brown, D. (2000) *The Right of Silence: The Impact of the Criminal Justice and Public Order Act 1994*, Home Office Research Study No. 199, London, Home Office.

Callan, K. (1997) *Kevin Callan's Story*, London, Little Brown and Company.

Cape, E. (1997) 'Sidelining Defence Lawyers: Police Station Advice after *Condron*', *International Journal of Evidence and Proof* 1: 386.

Carlisle, Lord (2008) *Report on the Operation in 2007 of the Terrorism Act 2000 and of Part One of the Terrorism Act 2006*, London, Home Office.

Casale, S. (2013) *Report of the Independent External Review of the IPCC Investigation into the Death of Sean Rigg*, London, IPCC.

Chaplin, R., Flatley, J. and Smith, K. (2011) *Crime in England and Wales 2010/11*, London, Home Office.

Choo, A. (2012) ' "Give Us What You Have": Information, Compulsion and the Privilege against Self-Incrimination', in J. Hunter and P. Roberts (eds), *Criminal Evidence and Human Rights: Reimagining Common Law Procedural Traditions*, Oxford, Hart, 239–58.

Choo, A. (2013) '*The Privilege against Self-Incrimination and Criminal Justice*, Oxford, Hart.

Choongh, S. (1997) *Policing as Social Discipline*, Oxford, Clarendon Press.

Choudhury, T. and Fenwick, H. (2011) *The Impact of Counter-Terrorism Measures on Muslim Communities*, EHRC Research Report 72, London: Equality and Human Rights Commission.

Clare, I. and Gudjonsson, G. (1993a) *Devising and Piloting an Experimental Version of the Notion to Detained Persons*, RCCJ Research Study No. 7, London, HMSO.

Clare, I. and Gudjonsson, G. (1993b) 'Interrogative Suggestibility, Confabulation and Acquiescence in People with Mild Learning Disabilities (Mental Handicap): Implications for Reliability during Police Interrogations', *British Journal of Clinical Psychology* 32: 295–301.

Clare, I. and Gudjonsson, G. (1995) 'The Vulnerability of Suspects with Intellectual Abilities during Police Interviews: A Review and Experimental Study of Decision-Making', *Mental Handicap Research* 8: 110–28.

Clarke, C. and Milne, R. (2001) *National Evaluation of the PEACE Investigative Interviewing Course*, London, Home Office.

Clarke, C., Milne, R. and Bull, R. (2011) 'Interviewing Suspects of Crime: The Impact of PEACE Training, Supervision and the Presence of a Legal Advisor', *Journal of Investigative Psychology and Offender Profiling* 8(2): 149–62.

Coleman, R. and McCahill, M. (2010) *Surveillance and Crime*, London, Sage.

Colville, Viscount (1987) *Review of the Operation of the Prevention of Terrorism (Temporary Provisions) Act 1984*, Cmnd 264, London, HMSO.

Commission on a Bill of Rights (2012) *A UK Bill of Rights? The Choice Before Us*, London, Ministry of Justice.

Cooke, D. L. and Philip, L. (1998) 'Comprehending the Silence Caution: Do Offenders Understand Their Right to Remain Silent?' *Legal and Criminal Psychology* 3(1): 13–27.

Cory, P. (2004a) *Collusion Inquiry Report: Patrick Finucane*, London, HMSO.

Cory, P. (2004b) *Collusion Inquiry Report: Rosemary Nelson*, London, HMSO.

Crewe, B. (2009) *The Prisoner Society: Adaptation and Social Life in an English Prison*, Oxford, Oxford University Press.

Criminal Cases Review Commission (July 2013) *Annual Report and Accounts 2012/13*, London, The Stationery Office.

Criminal Law Revision Committee (1972) *Eleventh Report: Evidence*, Cmnd 4991, London, HMSO.

Crossman, G. (2007) *Overlooked: Surveillance and Personal Privacy in Modern Britain*, London, Liberty.

Crown Prosecution Service (2011) *Achieving Best Evidence in Criminal Proceedings*, London, Ministry of Justice.

Cutler, B. (ed.) (2011) *Conviction of the Innocent*, Washington, DC, American Psychological Association Press.

De Silva, Sir D. (2012) *The Pat Finucane Review*, London.

Daly, Y. M. (2013) 'The Right to Silence: Inferences and Interference', *Australian and New Zealand Journal of Criminology*: 1–22.

Davidson, F. and Ferguson, P. (2014) 'The Corroboration Requirement in Scottish Criminal Trials: Should It Be Retained for Some Forms of Problematic Evidence?' *International Journal of Evidence and Proof* 18(1): 1–27.

Dennis, I. (1989) 'Reconstructing the Law of Criminal Evidence', *Current Legal Problems* 42(1): 21–48.

Dennis, I. (1993) 'Miscarriages of Justice and the Law of Confessions: Evidentiary Issues and Solutions', *Public Law*: 291–313.

Dennis, I. (2010) 'The Right to Confront Witnesses: Meanings, Myths and Human Rights', *Criminal Law Review*: 255–74.

Department of Health (2009) *The Bradley Report: Lord Bradley's Review of People with Mental Health Problems or Learning Disabilities in the Criminal Justice System*, London, Department of Health.

DePaulo, B. M., Lindsay, J. L., Malone, B. E., Muhlenbruck, L., Charlton, K., and Cooper, H. (2003) 'Cues to Deception', *Psychological Bulletin* 129: 74–118.

Dershowitz, A. (2002) *Why Terrorism Works: Understanding the Threat and Responding to the Challenge*, New Haven, CT, Yale University Press.

Dershowitz, A. (2004) 'When Torture Is the Least Evil of Terrible Options', *The Times Higher Education Supplement* (June 11), 20.

Dickson, B. (2010) *The European Convention on Human Rights and the Conflict in Northern Ireland*, Oxford, Oxford University Press.

Diplock, L. (1972) *Report of the Commission to Consider Legal Procedures to Deal with Terrorist Activities in Northern Ireland*, Cmnd 5185, London, HMSO.

Docking, M., Grace, K. and Bucke T. (2008) *Police Custody as a "Place of Safety" Explaining the Use of Section 136 of the Police Act 1983*, IPCC Research and Statistics Paper 11, London, IPCC.

Dworkin, R. (2011) *Justice for Hedgehogs*, Cambridge, MA, Harvard University Press.

Easton, S. (1995) 'Bodily Samples and the Privilege Against Self-Incrimination', *Criminal Law Review*: 18–29.

Easton, S. (1998) 'Legal Advice, Common Sense and the Right to Silence', *International Journal of Evidence and Proof* 2: 109–22.

Easton, S. (2000) 'Adverse Inferences and the Right to Silence: *R v Beckles and Montague*', *International Journal of Evidence and Proof* 4(1): 63–8.

Easton, S. (2011) *Prisoners' Rights: Principles and Practice*, London, Routledge.

Eastwood, J. and Snook, B. (2009) 'Comprehending Canadian Police Cautions: Are the Rights to Silence and Legal Counsel Understandable?' *Behavioural Sciences and the Law* 28: 366–77.

Eastwood, J., Snook, B. and Chaulk, S. J. (2010) 'Measuring Reading Complexity and Listening Comprehension of Canadian Police Cautions', *Criminal Justice and Behaviour* 34(4): 453–71.

Ekman, P. (2001) *Telling Lies: Clues to Deceit in the Marketplace, Politics and Marriage*, New York, Norton.

Elks, L. (2008) *Righting Miscarriages of Justice? Ten Years of the Criminal Cases Review Commission*, London, JUSTICE.

Equality and Human Rights Commission (2010) *Stop and Think: A Critical Review of the Use of Stop and Search Powers in England and Wales*, London, EHRC.

Equality and Human Rights Commission (2014) *Stop and Think Again: Towards Race Equality in Police PACE Stop and Search,* London, EHRC.

Evans, R. (1993) *The Conduct of Police Interviews with Juveniles*, RCCJ Research Study No. 8, London, HMSO.

Fairlie, M. (2013) 'Miranda and Its (More Rights-Protective) International Counterparts', *UC Davis Journal of International Law and Policy* 20: 1–45.

Farahany, N. A. (2012) 'Incriminating Thoughts', *Stanford Law Review* 64: 351–408.

Fenner, S., Gudjonsson, G. H. and Clare I. (2002) 'Understanding of the Current Police Caution (England and Wales) among Suspects in Police Detention, *Journal of Community and Applied Social Psychology* 12(2): 83–93.

Feyerabend, P. (1974) *Against Method*, London, New Left Books.

Fisher, H. (1977) *Report of an Inquiry by the Hon. Sir Henry Fisher into the circumstances leading to the trial of three persons on charges arising out of the death of Maxell Confait and the fire at 27 Doggett Road*, London S.E.6, London, HMSO.

Fisher, J. (1996) *Fall Guys: False Confessions and the Politics of Murder*, Carbondale, Southern Illinois University Press.

Foster, J., Newburn, T. and Souhami, A. (2005) *Assessing the Impact of the Stephen Lawrence Enquiry,* London, Home Office.

Fox, D. and Stein, A. (2015) 'Dualism and Doctrine', *Indiana Law Journal* 90.

Friendly, H. (1968) 'The Fifth Amendment Tomorrow: The Case for Constitutional Change,' *University of Cincinnati Law Review* 37: 671.

Gallini, B. P. (2010) 'Police "Science" in the Interrogation Room: Seventy Years of Pseudo-Psychological Methods to Obtain Inadmissible Confessions, *Hastings Law Journal* 61: 529.

Garrett, B. L. (2008) 'Judging innocence', *Columbia Law Review* 108: 55–142.

Garrett, B. L. and Neufeld, P. J. (2009) 'Invalid Forensic Science Testimony and Wrongful Convictions', *Virginia Law Review* 95(1): 1–97.

Gifford, T. (1984) *Supergrasses: The Use of Accomplice Evidence in Northern Ireland,* London, The Cobden Trust.

Goldstein, N. et al. (2003) 'Juvenile Offenders' Miranda Rights Comprehension and Self-Reported Likelihood of False Confessions', *Assessment* 10: 359–69.

Grace, K. (2013) Deaths during or following Police Contact: Statistics for England and Wales 2012/13, Paper 26, IPCC Research and Statistics Series, London, IPCC.

Greer, S. (1994) 'Review of *Suspect Community* by P. Hillyard', *British Journal of Criminology* 34: 501–11.

Greer, S. (1995) *Supergrasses: A Study in Anti-Terrorist Law Enforcement in Northern Ireland*, Oxford, Clarendon Press.

Greer, S. (2010) 'Anti-Terrorist Laws and the United Kingdom's "Suspect Muslim Community": A Reply to Pantazis and Pemberton', *British Journal of Criminology* 50: 1171–90.

Greer, S. and White, A. (1986) *Abolishing the Diplock Courts*, London, The Cobden Trust.

Griffiths J. and Ayres, R. (1967) 'A Postscript to the *Miranda* Project: Interrogation of Draft Protestors', *Yale Law Journal* 77: 305–19.

Grisso, T. (1981) *Juveniles' Waiver of Rights: Legal and Psychological Competence*, New York, Plenum Press.

Grisso, T. *et al.* (2003) 'Juveniles' Competence to Stand Trial: A Comparison of Adolescents' and Adults' Capacities as Trial Defendants', *Law and Human Behaviour* 27, 333–63.

Gudjonsson, G. H. (1992) *The Psychology of Interrogations, Confessions and Testimony*, Chichester, John Wiley.

Gudjonsson, G. H. (1994) 'Psychological Vulnerability: Suspects at Risk', in D. Morgan and G. Stephenson (eds), *Suspicion and Silence*, London, Blackstone, 91–106.

Gudjonsson, G. H. (1997) *The Gudjonsson Suggestibility Scales Manual,* East Sussex, Psychology Press.

Gudjonsson, G. H. (2003) *The Psychology of Interrogations, Confessions and Testimony: A Handbook*, London, Wiley.

Gudjonsson, G. H. and MacKeith, J. A. C. (1982) 'False Confessions: Psychological Effects of Interrogation – A Discussion Paper' in A. Trankell (ed.), *Reconstructing the Past: The Role of Psychologists in Criminal Trials*, Stockholm, Norstedt.

Gudjonsson, G. H., Clare, I. and Cross, P. (1992) 'The Revised PACE "Notice to Detained Persons": How Easy Is It to Understand?' *Journal of Forensic Science Society* 32: 289–99.

Gudjonsson, G. H., Clare, I., Rutter, S. and Pearse, J. (1993) *Persons at Risk during Interviews in Police Custody: The Identification of Vulnerabilities*, RCCJ Research Study, No. 12, London, HMSO.

Gudjonsson, G. H., Sigurdsson, J. F., Asgeirsdottir, B. B. and Sigfusdottir, I. D. (2006) 'Custodial Interrogation, False Confession and Individual Differences: A National Study among Icelandic Youth', *Personality and Individual Differences* 41(1): 49–59.

Gudjonsson, G. H., Sigurdsson, J. F. and Sigfusdottir, I. D. (2009) 'Interrogation and False Confession among Adolescents in Seven European Countries: What Background and Psychological Variables Best Discriminate between False Confessors and Non-false Confessors?' *Psychology, Crime and Law* 15(8): 711–28.

Haldane Society (1992) *Upholding the Law? Northern Ireland: Criminal Justice under the Emergency Powers in the 1990s*, London, Haldane Society.

Hannan, M., Hearnsden, I., Grace K. and Bucke, T. (2010) *Deaths in or following Police Custody: An Examination of the Cases 1998/99 – 2008/09*, IPCC Research Series Paper: 17, London, IPCC.

Hartwig, M., Granhag, P. A., Strömwall, L. A., and Vrij, A. (2005) 'Strategic Use of Evidence during Police Interviews: When Training to Detect Deception Works', *Law and Human Behaviour* 30: 603–19.

Hasel, L. E., and Kassin, S. M. (2009). 'On the Presumption of Evidentiary Independence: Can Confessions Corrupt Eyewitness Identifications?' *Psychological Science* 20: 122–6.

Hillyard, P. (1993) *Suspect Community: People's Experiences of the Prevention of Terrorism Acts in Britain*, London, Pluto Press.

HM Inspectorate of Constabulary, HM Inspectorate of Prisons, the Care Quality Commission and Healthcare Inspectorate Wales (20 June 2013) *A Criminal Use of Police Cells? The Use of Police Custody as a Place of Safety for People with Mental Health Needs*, London, HMIC.

HM Inspectorate of Prisons (2005) *Parallel Worlds: A Thematic Review of Race Relations in Prison*, London HMIP.

HM Inspector of Prisoners (2012) *Remand Prisoners: A Thematic Review*, London, HMIP.

Hogan, G. and Walker, C. (1989) *Political Violence and the Law in Ireland*, Manchester, Manchester University Press.

Holdaway, S. (2009) *Black Police Associations*, Oxford, Oxford University Press.

Home Office (2006) *Rebalancing the Criminal Justice System in Favour of the Law Abiding Majority: Reducing Reoffending and Protecting the Public*, London, Home Office.

Home Office (2009) *Keeping the Right People on the DNA Database: Science and Public Protection*, London, Home Office.

Home Office (2010) *Policing in the 21st Century: Reconnecting Police and the People*, Cmnd 7925, London, The Stationery Office.

Home Office (2011) *Guide for Appropriate Adults*, London, NAAN.

Home Office (2013a) *Government Response to the Report by David Anderson QC on Terrorism Prevention and Investigation Measures in 2012*, Cmnd 8164, London, Stationery Office.

Home Office (2013b) *Terrorism Arrests – Analysis of Charging and Sentencing Outcomes by Religion,* London, Home Office.

Home Office (2013c) *National DNA Database Strategy Board Annual Report 2012–13,* London, Home Office.

Home Office Working Group on the Right of Silence (1989) *Report of the Home Office Working Group on the Right of Silence,* London, HMSO.

Hood, R. (1992) *Race and Sentencing,* Oxford, Clarendon Press.

House of Commons, Communities and Local Government Committee (2010) *Preventing Violent Extremism: Sixth Report of Session 2009–10,* HC 65, London: The Stationery Office.

House of Commons, Home Affairs Committee (2012) *Roots of Violent Radicalisation, Nineteenth Report of Session 2010–12,* vol. 1, London, TSO.

House of Commons, Select Committee on Science and Technology (2013), *Forensic Science, Second Report of 2013–14,* HC 610, London, The Stationery Office.

Huff, C. R. and Killias, M. (eds) (2013*) Wrongful Convictions and Miscarriages of Justice,* London, Routledge.

Hynes, P. and Elkins, M. (2013) 'Suggestions for Reform to the Police Cautioning Procedure', *Criminal Law Review*: 966–77.

Imbert, Sir P. (1989) interview, *The Guardian* (30 November).

Inbau, F. E., Reid J. E., Buckley, J. P, and Jayne, B. C. (2001*) Criminal Interrogation and Confessions* (4th edn), Gaithersburg, MD, Aspen.

Innes, M., Roberts, C,. Innes, H., Lowe, T. and Lakhani, S. (2011) *Assessing the Effects of Prevent Policing: A Report to the Association of Chief Police Officers,* Cardiff, Universities' Police Science Institute, Cardiff University.

IPCC (2014) *Review of the IPCC's Work Investigating Deaths,* London, IPCC.

Irving, B. and McKenzie, I. (1989) *Police Interrogation: The Effects of the Police and Criminal Evidence Act 1984,* London, Police Foundation.

Jackson, J. (1989) 'Recent Developments in Criminal Evidence', *Northern Ireland Legal Quarterly* 105.

Jackson, J. (2009) 'Many Years on in Northern Ireland: The Diplock Legacy', *Northern Ireland Legal Quarterly* 60: 213–29.

Jackson, J. and Doran, S. (1995) *Judge without Jury: Diplock Trials in the Adversary System,* Oxford, Oxford University Press.

Jackson, J. and Summers, S. J. (2012) *The Internationalisation of Criminal Evidence,* Cambridge, Cambridge University Press.

Jackson, J., Wolfe, J.M. and Quinn, K. (2000) *Legislating against Silence: The Northern Ireland Experience,* Belfast, Northern Ireland Office.

Jones, I. (2010) '"A Political Judgment"? Reconciling Hearsay and the Right to Challenge', *International Journal of Evidence and Proof* 14: 232.

Judicial Studies Board (2010) *Crown Court Bench Book: Directing the Jury,* London, JSB.

JUSTICE (1994) *The Right of Silence Debate: The Northern Ireland Experience,* London, JUSTICE.

JUSTICE Scotland (2012) *Reforming Scots Criminal Law and Practice: The Carloway Report: Response to Consultation,* London, JUSTICE.

Kassin, S. M. (2005) 'On the Psychology of Confessions: Does *Innocence* put *Innocents* at Risk?' *American Psychologist* 60: 215–28.

Kassin, S. M. (2008a) 'The Psychology of Confessions', *American Review of Law and Social Sciences* 4: 193–217.

Kassin, S. M. (2008b) 'Confession Evidence: Commonsense Myths and Misconceptions', *Criminal Justice and Behavior* 35: 1309–22.

Kassin, S. M. and Wrightsman, L. S. (1985) 'Confession Evidence', in S. M. Kassin and L. S. Wrightsman (eds), *The Psychology of Evidence and Trial Procedure*, Beverley Hills, CA, Sage, 7–94.

Kassin, S. M. and Kiechel, K. L. (1996) 'The Social Psychology of False Confessions: Compliance, Internalization and Confabulation', *Psychological Science* 7: 125–8.

Kassin, S. M. and Sukel, H. (1997) 'Coerced Confessions and the Jury: An Experimental Test of the "Harmless Error" Rule', *Law and Human Behavior* 21: 27–46.

Kassin, S. M. and Norwick, R. J. (2004) 'Why People Waive Their *Miranda* Rights: The Power of Innocence', *Law and Human Behavior* 28(2): 211–21.

Kassin, S. M., Meissner, C. A. and Norwick R. J. (2005) ' "I'd Know a False Confession if I Saw One": A Comparative Study of College Students and Police Investigators', *Law and Human Behavior* 29: 211–27.

Kassin, S. M., Leo, R. A., Meissner, C. A., Richman, K. D., Colwell, L. H. and Leach, A.-M. (2007) 'Police Interviewing and Interrogation: A Self-Report Survey of Police Practices and Beliefs', *Law and Human Behavior* 31: 381–400.

Keith, B. (2006) *Report of the Zahid Mubarek Inquiry*, HC 1082, London, The Stationery Office.

Kemp, V., Balmer, N. J. and Pleasence, P. (2012) 'Whose Time Is It Anyway? Factors Associated with Duration in Police Custody', *Criminal Law Review*: 736–52.

Kuhn, T. S. (1962) *The Structure of Scientific Revolutions*, Chicago: University of Chicago Press.

Lamer, A. (2006) *The Lamer Commission of Inquiry Pertaining to the Cases of Ronald Dalton, Gregory Parsons, Randy Druken, Report and Annexes*, St. John's, NL, Queen's Printer.

Law Commission (2009) *The Admissibility of Expert Evidence in Criminal Proceedings in England and Wales: A New Approach to the Determination of Evidentiary Reliability*, Consultation Paper No. 190, London, Law Commission.

Law Commission (2011) *Expert Evidence in Criminal Proceedings*, HC 829, London, The Stationery Office.

Law Society (1994) 'Changes in the Law Relating to Silence: Advice to Practitioners from the Criminal Law Committee of the Law Society', *Criminal Practitioners Newsletter* (October).

Law Society (1997) 'Advice to Practitioners', *Criminal Practitioners Newsletter*.

Leng, R. (1993) *The Right to Silence in Police Interrogation* , RCCJ Research Study No. 10, London, HMSO.

Leng, R. (1995) 'Losing Sight of the Defendant: The Government's Proposals on Pre-Trial Disclosure', *Criminal Law Review*: 704.

Leo, R. A. (1992) 'From Coercion to Deception: The Changing Nature of Police Interrogation in America', *Law and Social Change* 18: 35.

Leo, R. A. (1996) 'Inside the Interrogation Room', *Journal of Criminal Law and Criminology*: 661–85.

Leo, R. A. and Drizin, S. A. (2004) 'The Problem of False Confessions in the Post-DNA World', *North Carolina Law Review* 82: 891–1007.

Liberty (2009) *Response to the Home Office's Consultation: Keeping the Right People on the DNA Database: Science and Public Protection*, London, Liberty.

Liberty (2012) *Response to the Home Office's Review of the Operation of Schedule 7*, London, Liberty.

Lilburne, J. (1638) *The Worke of the Beast.*

Little, R. (2008) 'Addressing the Evidentiary Sources of Wrongful Convictions: Categorical Exclusion of Evidence in Capital Statutes', *Southwestern University Law Review* 37: 965.

Lloyd, Lord (1996) *Inquiry into Legislation against Terrorism*, Cm 320, London, HMSO.

Loftus, B. (2009) *Police Culture in a Changing World*, Oxford, Oxford University Press; London, Department of Health.

Lorente-Rovira, E., Santos-Gomez, J. L., Moro, M., Villagan, J. M. and McKenna, P. J. (2010) 'Confabulation in Schizophrenia: A Neuropsychological Study', *Journal of the International Neuropsychological Society* 16: 1018–26.

Loucks, N. (2007) *No One Knows: The Prevalence and Associated Needs of Offenders with Learning Difficulties and Learning Disabilities*, London, Prison Reform Trust.

Luke, T., et al. (2013) 'Interviewing to Elicit Cues to Deception: Improving Strategic Use of Evidence with General-to-Specific Framing of Evidence', *Journal of Police and Criminal Psychology* 28: 54–62.

Lyon, D. (ed.) (2006) *Theorizing Surveillance: The Panopticon and Beyond*, Cullompton, Willan.

Macpherson, W. (1999) *The Stephen Lawrence Inquiry, Report of an Inquiry by Sir William Macpherson of Cluny, Advised by Tom Cook, The Right Revd. John Sentamu and Dr. Richard Stone*, Cmnd 4262–1, London, Home Office.

Maguire, M. (1988) 'The Effects of the PACE Provisions on Detention and Questioning', *British Journal of Criminology*: 19–43.

Maguire, M. and Norris, C. (1993) *The Conduct and Supervision of Criminal Investigations*, RCCJ Research Study No. 5, London, HMSO.

Malleson, K. (1993) *A Review of the Appeal Process*, RCCJ Research Study No. 17, London, HMSO.

Masip, J., Herrero, C., Garrido, E. and Barba, A. (2010) 'Is the Behaviour Analysis Interview Just Common Sense?', *Applied Cognitive Psychology*: 593–604.

May J. (1990) *Inquiry into the Circumstances Surrounding the Convictions Arising out of the Bomb Attacks in Guildford and Woolwich in 1974, Interim Report on the Maguire Case*, HC 556 of 1989–90.

May J. (1993) *Inquiry into the Circumstances Surrounding the Convictions Arising out of the Bomb Attacks in Guildford and Woolwich in 1974, Second Report* HC 296 of 1992—3.

May J. (2013) *The Government Response to the Annual Report on the Operation of the Terrorism Acts in 2012 by the Independent Reviewer of Terrorist Legislation*, Cmnd 8745, London, The Stationery Office.

McCartney, C. (2006) *Forensic Identification and Criminal Justice: Forensic Science, Justice and Risk*, Cullompton, Willan.

McCartney, C. (2012) 'Of Weighty Reasons and Indiscriminate Blankets: The Retention of DNA for Forensic Purposes', *Howard Journal of Criminal Justice* 51(3): 245–60.

McConville, M. (1992) 'Videotaping Interrogations', *Criminal Law Review*, 532.

McConville, M. (1993) *Corroboration and Confessions: the Impact of a Rule Requiring that no Conviction Can Be Sustained on the Basis of Confession Evidence Alone*, RCCJ Research Study No. 13, London, HMSO.

McConville, M. and Hodgson, J. (1993) *Custodial Legal Advice and the Right to Silence*, RCCJ Research Study No. 16, London, HMSO.

McConville, M. and Mirsky, C. L. (2005) *Jury Trials and Plea Bargaining: A True History*, Oxford, Hart.

McConville, M., Sanders, A. and Leng, R. (1991) *The Case for the Prosecution*, London, Routledge.

McConville, M., Hodgson, J., Bridges, L. and Pavlovic, A. (1994) *Standing Accused: The Organisation and Practices of Criminal Defence Lawyers in Britain*, Oxford, Clarendon Press.

McEvoy, K. (2011) 'What Did the Lawyers Do during the "War"? Neutrality, Conflict and the Culture of Quietism', *Modern Law Review* 7(3): 350–84.

McGarry, J. and O'Leary, B. (1999) *Policing Northern Ireland: Proposals for a New Start*, Belfast, Blackstaff Press.

McGrory, B. (1994) 'The Solicitor's Advice to the Accused in the Light of the Criminal Justice and Public Order Act 1994', London, 1994.

McGurk, B., Carr, J. and McGurk, D. (1993) *Investigative Interviewing Courses for Police Officers: An Evaluation, Police Research Series*, No.4 London, Home Office.

Meissner, C. A., Redlich, A. D., Bhatt, S. and Brandon, S. (2012) *Interview and Interrogation Methods and Their Effects on True and False Confessions*, Oslo, The Campbell Collaboration.

Milgram, S. (1963) 'Behavioural Study of Obedience', *Journal of Abnormal and Social Psychology* 67: 371.

Ministry of Justice (2010) *Breaking the Cycle, Effective Punishment, Rehabilitation and Sentencing of Offenders,* London, Ministry of Justice.

Ministry of Justice (2013) *Statistics on Race and the Criminal Justice System 2012*, London, Ministry of Justice.

Mirrlees-Black, C. (2001) *Confidence in the Criminal Justice System: Findings from the 2000 British Crime Survey*, Home Office Research Findings No. 137, London, Home Office.

Mitchell, B. (1983) 'Confessions and Police Interrogation of Suspects', *Criminal Law Review*: 596.

Monaghan, R. (2002) 'The Return of "Captain Moonlight": Informal Justice in Northern Ireland', *Studies in Conflict and Terrorism* 25: 41–56.

Moore, T. E. and Gagnier, K. (2008) ' "You Can Talk if You Want to": Is the Police Caution on the "Right to Silence" Understandable?' *Criminal Reports* 51, C.R. 6th, 233–49.

Moore, T. E. and Fitzsimmons, C. Lindsay (2011) 'Justice Imperilled: False Confessions and the Reid Technique', *Criminal Law Quarterly* 57(4): 509–42.

Moston, S. G. (1993) 'The Incidence, Antecedents and Consequences of the Use of the Right to Silence During Police Questioning', *Criminal Behaviour and Mental Health* 3: 30–47.

Moston, S. G., Stephenson, G. and Williamson, T. (1992) 'The Effects of Case Characteristics on Suspect Behaviour during Questioning' *British Journal of Criminology*, 32, 23–30.

Moston, S. G. and Stephenson, G. (1993) *The Questioning and Interviewing of Suspects outside the Police Station*, RCCJ Research Study No. 22, London, HMSO.

Naughton, M. (2011) 'How the Presumption of Innocence Renders the Innocent Vulnerable to Wrongful Convictions', *Irish Journal of Legal Studies* 2(1): 40–54.

Naughton, M. (2013) *The Innocent and the Criminal Justice System*, London, Palgrave.

Naughton, M. and Tan, G. (2010) 'The Right to Access DNA Testing by Alleged Innocent Victims of Wrongful Conviction', *International Journal of Evidence and Proof* 14: 326–45.

Naughton, M. and Tan, G. (2011) 'The Need for Caution in the Use of DNA Evidence to Avoid Convicting the Innocent', *International Journal of Evidence and Proof* 15: 245–57.

Nobles, R. and Schiff, D. (2000) *Understanding Miscarriages of Justice: Law, the Media and the Inevitability of Crisis*, Oxford: Oxford University Press.

Nobles, R. and Schiff, D. (2005) 'The Criminal Cases Review Commission: Establishing a Workable Relationship with the Court of Appeal', *Criminal Law Review*: 173–89.

Northern Ireland Office (2006) *Replacement Arrangements for the Diplock Court System*, Belfast, Northern Ireland Office.

O'Brian, W. E. O., Jr (2011) 'Confrontation: The Defiance of the English Courts', *International Journal of Evidence and Proof*, 15, 93–116.

Owers, A. (1995) *Putting Wrongs to Right*, London, British Irish Rights Watch.

Pantazis, C. and Pemberton, S. (2009) 'From the "Old" to the "New" Suspect Communities: Examining the Impact of Recent UK Counter-terrorist Legislation', *British Journal of Criminology* 49: 646–66.

Pantazis, C. and Pemberton, S. (2011) 'Restating the Case for the "Suspect Community": A Reply to Greer', *British Journal of Criminology* 51(6): 1054–62.

Patten, C. (1999) *A New Beginning: Policing in Northern Ireland. The Report of the Independent Commission for Policing in Northern Ireland* (Patten Report).

Perks, P. (2010) *Appropriate Adult Provision in England and Wales*, London, National Appropriate Adult Network.

Phillips, C. and Brown, D. (1997) 'Observational Studies in Police Custody Areas: Some Methodological and Ethical Issues Considered', *Policing and Society* 7: 191–205.

Phillips, C. and Brown, D. (1998) *Entry into the Criminal Justice System: A Survey of Police Arrests and their Outcomes*, HORS No. 185, London, Home Office.

Pleasence, P., Kemp, V. and Balmer, N. J. (2011) 'The Justice Lottery? Police Station Advice 25 Years on from PACE', *Criminal Law Review*: 3–18.

Plotnikoff, J. and Woolfson, R. (1993) *Information and Advice for Prisoners About Grounds for Appeal and the Appeal Process*, RCCJ Research Study No. 18, London, HMSO.

Porter, S., England, L., Juodis, M., ten Brinke, L. and Wilson, K. (2008) 'Is the Face the Window to the Soul? Investigation of the Accuracy of Intuitive Judgments of the Trustworthiness of Human Faces', *Canadian Journal of Behavioural Science* 40: 171–7.

Quirk, H. (2006) 'The Significance of Culture in Criminal Procedure Reform: Why the Revised Disclosure Scheme Cannot Work', *International Journal of Evidence and Proof* 10: 42–8.

Quirk, H. (2007) 'Identifying Miscarriages of Justice: Why Innocence in the UK is not the Answer', *Modern Law Review* 70(5): 759–77.

Raphael, M. (1990) 'The Right to Silence and Economic Crime', in S. Greer and R. Morgan (eds), *The Right to Silence Debate*, Bristol, Bristol Centre for Criminal Justice, 60.

Redmayne, M. (2001) *Expert Evidence and Criminal Justice*, Oxford, Oxford University Press.

Redmayne, M. (2004) 'Criminal Justice Act 2003: Disclosure and its Discontents', *Criminal Law Review*: 441.

Redmayne, M. (2007) 'Rethinking the Privilege Against Self-Incrimination', *Oxford Journal of Legal Studies* 27(2): 209–32.

Redmayne, M. (2012) 'Exploring Entrapment', in L. Zedner and J. V. Roberts (eds), *Principles and Values in Criminal Law: Essays in Honour of Andrew Ashworth*, Oxford, Oxford University Press, 157–70.

Reiner, R. (2010) *The Politics of the Police*, 4th edn, Oxford, Oxford University Press.

Roberts, P. and Willmore, C. (1993) *The Role of Forensic Evidence in Criminal Proceedings*, RCCJ Research Study, No. 11, London, HMSO.

Roberts, S. (2003) ' "Unsafe" Convictions: Defining and Compensating Miscarriages of Justice', *Modern Law Review* 66(3): 441–51.

Rogers, R., Harrison, S. and Shuman, D.W. (2007) 'An Analysis of *Miranda* Warnings and Waivers: Comprehension and Coverage', *Law and Human Behavior* 31: 177–92.

Rogers, R., Hazelwood, L. L., Sewell, K. W., Harrison, S. and Shuman, D. W. (2008) 'The Language of *Miranda* Warnings in American Jurisdictions: A Replication and Vocabulary Analysis', *Law and Human Behavior* 32: 124–36.

Roman, J., Walsh, K., Lachman, P. and Yahner, Y. (2012) *Post-Conviction DNA Testing and Wrongful Conviction*, Washington, Urban Institute 2012.

Romano, I. (2011) 'Is *Miranda* on the Verge of Extinction? The Supreme Court Loosens *Miranda*'s Grip in Favor of Law Enforcement', *Nova Law Review* 35: 525.

Royal Commission on Criminal Justice (1993) *Report*, Cmnd 2263, London, HMSO.

Royal Commission on Criminal Procedure (1981) *Report*, Cmnd 8092, London, HMSO.

Russano, M. B., Meissner, C. A., Narchet, F. M., and Kassin, S. M. (2005) 'Investigating True and False Confessions within a Novel Experimental Paradigm', *Psychological Science* 16: 481–6.

Sallavaci, O. (2014) *The Impact of Scientific Evidence on the Criminal Trial: The Case of DNA Evidence*, London, Routledge .

Samuels, J., Davies, E., Pope, D. and Holand, A. (2012) 'Collecting DNA from Arrestees: Implementation Lessons', http://www.nij.gov/nij/journals/270/arrestee-dna.htm, accessed 30 September 2013.

Sanders, A., Bridges, L., Mulvany, A. and Crozier, G. (1989) *Advice and Assistance at Police Stations under the 24 Hour Duty Solicitor Scheme*, London, Lord Chancellor's Department.

Sankey, I. (2013) *Liberty's Briefing on Schedule 7 of the Terrorism Act 2000 in the Anti-social Behaviour, Crime and Policing Bill*, London, Liberty.

Sarat, A. and Scheingold, S. (eds) (2006) *Cause Lawyers and Social Movements*, Palo Alto, CA, Stanford University Press.

Scheck, B., Neufeld, P. and Dwyer, J. (2000) *Actual Innocence*, Garden City, NY, Doubleday.

Seidmann, D. J. and Stein, A. (2000) 'The Right to Silence Helps the Innocent: A Game- Theoretic Analysis of the Fifth Amendment', *Harvard Law Review* 11: 430–510.

Senators of the College of Justice (2012) *Response to the Scottish Government Consultation Paper Reforming Scots Criminal Law and Practice: The Carloway Report*, Edinburgh.

Sigurdsson, J.F. and Gudjonsson, G. H. (1996) 'The psychological study of "false confessors". A study among Icelandic prison inmates and juvenile offenders', *Personality and Individual Differences*, 120:3, 321–29.

Skinns, L. (2009a) 'Let's Get It Over With: Early Findings on the Factors Affecting Detainees' Access to Custodial Legal Advice', *Policing and Society* 19(1): 58–78.

Skinns, L. (2009b) 'I'm a Detainee: Get Me Out of Here: Predictors of Access to Custodial Legal Advice in Public and Privatised Police Custody Areas in England and Wales', *British Journal of Criminology* 49(3): 399–417.

Skinns, L. (2011a) *Police Custody: Governance, Legitimacy and Reform in the Criminal Justice Process*, London, Routledge.

Skinns, L. (2011b) *The Overnight Detention of Children in Police Cells*, London, The Howard League.

Smith, D. J. and Gray, P. (1983) *Police and People in London IV*, London, Policy Studies Institute.

Smith, G. (2009) 'Why Don't More People Complain Against the Police?', *European Journal of Criminology* 6(3): 249–66.

Snook, B., House, J. C., MacDonald, S. and Eastwood, J. (2012) 'Police Witness Interview Training, Supervision and Feedback: A Survey of Canadian Police Officers', *Revue Canadienne de Criminologie et de Justice Pénale*, 363–72.

Softley, P. (1980) *Police Interrogation: An Observational Study in Four Police Stations*, RCCP Research Study No. 4, London, HMSO.

Spalek, B., El Awa, S. and MacDonald, L. (2008) *Police–Muslim Engagements and Partnerships for the Purposes of Counter-terrorism: An Examination*, Summary Report, Birmingham, University of Birmingham.

Stevens, Sir J. (2003) *Stevens Enquiry (Overview and Recommendations)*, Belfast, PSNI.

Steventon, B. (1993) *The Ability to Challenge DNA Evidence*, RCCJ Research Study No. 9, London, HMSO.

Stuntz, W. J. (1988) 'Self-Incrimination and Excuse', *Columbia Law Review* 88: 1227–96.

Stuntz, W. J. (1989) 'The American Exclusionary Rule and Defendants' Changing Rights', *Criminal Law Review*: 117.

Sullivan, T. P. (2004) *Police Experiences with Recording Custodial Interrogations*, Chicago, Center on Wrongful Convictions.

Sussman, D. (2005) 'What's Wrong with Torture?', *Philosophy and Public Affairs* 33: 1–33.

Talbot, J. (2008) *No One Knows. Report and Final Recommendations. Prisoners' Voices: The Experience of the Criminal Justice System by Prisoners with Learning Disabilities and Difficulties*, London, Prison Reform Trust.

Talbot, J. and Riley, C. (2007) 'No One Knows: Offenders with Learning Difficulties and Learning Disabilities', *British Journal of Learning Disabilities* 25(3): 154–61.

Tan, A. K-J. (1997) 'Adverse Inferences and the Right to Silence: Re-examining the Singapore Experience', *Criminal Law Review*: 471–81.

Thomas, C. (2010) *Are Juries Fair?* Ministry of Justice Research Series 1/10, London, Ministry of Justice.

van Zyl Smit, D. and Snacken, S. (2009) *Principles of European Prison Law and Policy*, Oxford, Oxford University Press.

Ventress, M. A., Rix, K. J. B. and Kent, J. H. (2008) 'Keeping PACE: Fitness to Be Interviewed by the Police', *Advances in Psychiatric Treatment* 14: 369–81.

Viljoen, J. L., Zapf, P. A. and Roesch, R. (2007) 'Adjudicative Competence and Comprehension of *Miranda* Rights in Adolescent Defendants: A Comparison of Legal Standards', *Behavioural Sciences and the Law* 25, 1–19.

Vrij, A. (2008) *Detecting Lies and Deceit: Pitfalls and Opportunities*, Chichester, Wiley.

Vrij, A. and Winkel, F. (1991) 'Cultural Patterns in Dutch and Surinam Nonverbal Behavior: An Analysis of Simulated Police/Citizen Encounters', *Journal of Nonverbal Behaviour* 15(3): 169–84.

Vrij, A. and Graham, S. (1997) 'Individual Differences between Liars and the Ability to Detect Lies' *Expert Evidence: The International Digest of Human Behaviour Science and Law* 5: 144–8.

Vrij, A. Granhag, P. A. and Porter, S. (2010) 'Pitfalls and Opportunities in Nonverbal and Verbal Lie-Detection', *Psychological Science in the Public Interest* 11(3): 89–121.

Waddington, P. A. J., Stenson, K. and Donn, D. (2004) 'In Proportion: Race and Police Stop and Search', *British Journal of Criminology* 44: 889–914.

Wade, K. A., Green, S. L. and Nash, R. A. (2010) 'Can Fabricated Evidence Induce False Eyewitness Testimony?', *Applied Cognitive Psychology* 24: 899–908.

Waldron, J. (2010) *Torture, Terror and Trade-Offs: Philosophy for the White House*, Oxford, Oxford University Press.

Walker, C. P. and Stockdale, R. (1995) 'Forensic Evidence and Terrorist Trials in the UK', *Cambridge Law Journal* 54: 69–99.

Walkley, J. (1987) *Police Interrogation: A Handbook for Investigators*, London, The Police Review Publishing Co.

Watson, C., Weiss, K. J. and Pouncey, C. (2010) 'False Confessions, Expert Testimony and Admissibility', *Journal of the American Academy of Psychiatry and the Law* 38(2): 174–86.

White, R. M. and Ferguson, R. (2012) 'Sins of the Father? The "Sons of *Cadder*"', *Criminal Law Review*: 357.

Wigmore, J. H. (1961) *Evidence in Trials at Common Law*, Vol III, McNaughton rev. edn, Boston, Little, Brown & Co.

Williams, G. (1987) 'The Tactic of Silence', *137 New Law Journal*: 1107.

Williamson, T. (1993) 'From Interrogation to Investigative Interviewing: Strategic Trends in Police Questioning', *Journal of Community and Applied Social Psychology* 3: 89–99.

Williamson, T. (1994) 'Reflections on Current Police Practice', in Morgan, D. and Stephenson, G. (eds), *Suspicion and Silence*, London, Blackstone, 107–16.

Williamson, T. (ed.) (2006) *Investigative Interviewing: Rights, Research, Regulation*, Cullompton, Willan.

Williamson, T. and Moston, S. (1990) 'The Extent of Silence in Police Interviews', in Greer, S. and Morgan, R. (eds), *The Right to Silence Debate*, Bristol, Centre for Criminal Justice, 36–43.

Willis, C. et al. (1987) *The Tape Recording of Police Interviews with Suspects*, HORS No. 97, London, HMSO.

Winter, J. (1995) 'Human Rights and the Peace Process' *International Journal of Discrimination and the Law* 1(1): 63–6.

Wolchover, D. and Heaton-Armstrong, A. (1990) 'Last Fence for the PACE Codes', *Counsel*: 15.

Yeo, M. H. (1983) 'Diminishing the Right to Silence: The Singapore Experience', *Criminal Law Review*, 89–901.

Zander, M. and Henderson, P. (1993) *Crown Court Study*, RCCJ Research Study No. 19, London, HMSO.

Index

Printed and bound in Great Britain by
CPI Group (UK) Ltd, Croydon, CR0 4YY